DREAMTREADERS

Other Books by Wayne Thomas Batson

The Door Within Trilogy
The Door Within
The Rise of the Wyrm Lord
The Final Storm

Pirate Adventures
Isle of Swords
Isle of Fire

The Berinfell Prophecies
Curse of the Spider King (with Christopher Hopper)
Venom and Song (with Christopher Hopper)
The Tide of Unmaking (with Christopher Hopper)

The Dark Sea Annals
Sword in the Stars
The Errant King
Mirror of Souls

Imagination Station
#8: *Battle for Cannibal Island*
#11: *Hunt for the Devil's Dragon*

Other Endeavors
Ghost

DREAMTREADERS

WAYNE THOMAS BATSON

THOMAS NELSON
Since 1798

NASHVILLE   DALLAS   MEXICO CITY   RIO DE JANEIRO

Dreamtreaders

© 2014 by Wayne Thomas Batson

Published in Nashville, Tennessee, by Tommy Nelson. Tommy Nelson is a registered trademark of Thomas Nelson.

Tommy Nelson titles may be purchased in bulk for educational, business, fund-raising, or sales promotional use. For information, please e-mail SpecialMarkets@ThomasNelson.com.

Library of Congress Cataloging-in-Publication Data

Batson, Wayne Thomas, 1968-
Dreamtreaders / Wayne Thomas Batson.
pages cm
Summary: After discovering that he is a Dreamtreader, one who can enter and explore his own dreams, fourteen-year-old Archer must protect the waking world from the Nightmare Lord, who wreaks chaos in the Dream World.
ISBN 978-1-4003-2366-1 (softcover)
[1. Dreams--Fiction. 2. Fantasy.] I. Title. II. Title: Dream treaders.
PZ7.B3238Dr 2014
[Fic]--dc23
2013047928

Printed in the United States of America

14 15 16 17 18 19 RRD 6 5 4 3 2 1

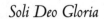

Soli Deo Gloria

CONTENTS

Chapter 1 · Night Terrors   1

Chapter 2 · The Derecho   16

Chapter 3 · Storm Damage   26

Chapter 4 · Master Gabriel's Visit   43

Chapter 5 · The Stalking   55

Chapter 6 · Unleashed   60

Chapter 7 · Bezeal   74

Chapter 8 · Dare to Dream   90

Chapter 9 · Test Flight   101

Chapter 10 · The Lurker's Toys   110

Chapter 11 · Master Gabriel's Second Visit   126

Chapter 12 · A Challenge   133

Chapter 13 · A Near Thing   141

Chapter 14 · There Are Rules   155

CONTENTS

Chapter 15 · Gallows Hall   164

Chapter 16 · Trading in Fate   174

Chapter 17 · The Battle of the Brains   183

Chapter 18 · Scoville Manor   191

Chapter 19 · Master Gabriel's Third Visit   200

Chapter 20 · Patchwork   208

Chapter 21 · Creatures Great and Small   216

Chapter 22 · Beneath the Surface   222

Chapter 23 · The Basement Door   226

Chapter 24 · No Time   233

Chapter 25 · Master Gabriel's Fourth Visit   239

Chapter 26 · Dreamscape War   247

Chapter 27 · Number 6, Rue de la Mort   257

Chapter 28 · The Trees of Life and Death   261

Chapter 29 · Tested Loyalties   267

Chapter 30 · Lure   272

Chapter 31 · The Well   274

Chapter 32 · Dangerous Minds   278

Chapter 33 · Reckoning   282

Epilogue   286

ONE

NIGHT TERRORS

THE HOWLS GREW LOUDER. THE HOUNDS WERE CLOSER, closing in.

"They've got my scent!" Archer Keaton growled as he raced down the moonlit mountain path into a misty dell full of black pines. "Gotta throw them off." But how? Then he knew.

Archer launched himself skyward. He let his feet brush the treetops a moment, and then purposefully let himself crash down through the crisscrossing pine branches.

Creak. "Ouch." *Crunch.* "Oof!" *Crack!* "Oww!"

The fourteen-year-old yelped with each bounce, smack, and breaking branch. He tumbled to the ground in a sticky heap. When he stood up and tried to brush the pine needles from his coat, vest, and pants, the sap kept most of them glued tight. "Good," Archer whispered. "The more sap, the better. Now, gotta go!"

He broke out from beneath the pines and sprinted across the uneven ground. The howls were still there. Deep, throaty, mournful howls. And they were still getting closer.

"No way!" Archer grumbled, searching for any near place to get cover . . . shelter.

Crack!

Something was behind him. In the pines. Something big enough to snap a tree trunk as if it were a twig. Archer knew there were only a few creatures in the area large enough and heavy enough to do that kind of damage, but which beast was it? He had a suspicion but hoped he was wrong. That creature hunted in packs.

Archer spotted the ruins of an old castle, just a half-collapsed keep and a leaning tower, in the crook of a patch of broadleaf trees and more pines. He drove his legs like pistons and dove into the trees. The teenager's sudden arrival startled some blackbirds from their roosts among the branches. They cawed, croaked, and cried their harshly voiced displeasure, but Archer paid them little mind. He careened around the trunks, stumbled to a knee, but drove on.

"Breathe, Keaton," he commanded himself. Archer ducked under an archway in the old ruin and flattened his back to the stone wall inside. "Just breathe."

"What's the matter with you?" a high, nasal voice asked.

Archer jumped. Heart thrumming, he looked down and found his hands no longer empty. He'd summoned a pair of hand grenades.

"Ohhhhhh," the voice said, right next to Archer's ear. "You're a Dreamtreader, aren't you?"

Archer spun left and right but saw nothing. "Where are you?" he gasped.

"Right here."

Archer craned his neck around. The voice really was close. It sounded a little like Razz. No, it was a little huskier and had an odd warble to it. Besides, Razz wanted nothing to do with Archer's mission on this night.

"I still can't see you," he said.

"Of course you can't," the voice said. "I'm stuck here inside your coat!"

Archer willed the grenades to vanish and groped inside his long leather duster. There was nothing there—wait. He felt something prickly, and his left hand came back with a sticky pinecone.

"See, here I am," the voice said, and Archer felt a faint vibration in his palm.

"You're a pinecone?" he asked.

"No, you doofus," the voice said. "I'm a pine coon. There's a big difference!"

Just then, four little clawed feet popped out. A fluffy, black-and-gray tail uncurled as well. And, as Archer stared, he discovered two brown eyes glistening and blinking from a dark mask of fuzz at the cone's point.

"A pine coon?" Archer echoed. Then he shrugged. Why not? Anything was possible here.

The little creature's dark nose twitched. It flicked its head side to side and squeaked, "Uh-oh!" Instantly, its eyes, nose, limbs, and tail disappeared into its pinecone torso.

"What?" Archer blurted. "What's wrong?"

The howl that came next was so loud that Archer felt the sound as much as he heard it.

"Chuck me into a tree!" the pine coon whispered urgently.

There were noises outside the ruin. First, a violent snuffling; then, the scrape of claw on stone; and finally, a very low growl.

"Please! Chuck me, chuck me, chuck me!"

"Just one second," Archer whispered back. "Where can I go?"

"High place," the pine coon said. "Tower?"

Archer had to cross the open courtyard to get to its stairwell, but the creature was right: the tower was the only real shelter.

Another howl. Archer leaped away from the wall and bounded across the stone-strewn courtyard. Just before the Dreamtreader ducked into the stairwell, he tossed the pine coon over the wall and into the waiting branches of a tree bushy with needles.

Up the curling stairs he went. After a long climb, Archer found himself in the highest chamber of the turret. He knelt by the window and dared a look out into the night.

The trees surrounding the ruins were swaying, but there was no wind. Archer saw something dark moving among them. It was a ridge of black fur . . . the spiky spine of a creature, and it was at least twelve feet off the ground. Here and there, the moonlight caught a glisten of red or yellow eyes.

Hounds.

Archer had heard the hounds many times. He'd seen their silhouettes from a distance. But he'd never seen one up close. *That's because I've never been stupid enough to get this close to Shadowkeep,* he thought. *Until now.*

Archer sensed something. He dropped down beneath the windowsill and held his breath. A growl rumbled just outside. Archer cringed. At the same time, he summoned up every bit of will and concentration he could muster. He wasn't certain what he would do, what he would summon to defend himself, but he had to be ready.

The growl trailed off, and the snuffling began again. The turret chamber grew darker. Archer sank down even lower. When he looked up at the window, a leathery black snout hovered there. It twitched and throbbed as it sniffed, filling the air with humidity and a musky scent.

A sword? Archer thought. *Stab it right in the nose. Maybe a stick of dynamite? No, two sticks . . . one for each nostril. Or maybe a chain saw?*

The snout rose high and angled at the window. There was a sharp sniff followed by an angry snarl. Then, the hound's snout withdrew. A howl rose in the distance, while an answering howl echoed just outside the window. With a growling bark and the snap of limbs, the creature thundered away from the tower.

Archer sprang up just in time to watch a dark mass disappear into the trees and mist. The hounds had other business to attend to.

"Thank God," Archer whispered.

But a deep, sonorous chime drowned out his words.

"Old Jack," the Dreamtreader hissed. Archer ran to the other side of the chamber and stepped out on its small balcony. There in the distance, hovering like a phantom, stood the ancient clock tower known as Old Jack.

The strokes of hours rang out, one after the other, and Archer looked to the great clock's massive black hands.

"Eleven?" Archer muttered. "No, no, no. Not enough time."

The Dreamtreader felt the certainty like a cold hunk of lead in the pit of his stomach. He'd taken too long repairing breaches. One hour would never be enough time to break into Shadowkeep and do what he had come to do. Still, he'd already come this far. He'd taken terrible risks. He meant to see it through.

Archer leaped down from the balcony and dashed to the hills in the east. As he ran, he wondered about the rumors he'd heard from kingdoms near his last breach repair. An uprising, they'd said. Hundreds of villagers from Warhaven and Tirbury were gathering weapons and preparing an assault on Shadowkeep. If it were true, it might provide the distraction Archer needed. But it would be costly. The villagers, as brave and resourceful as they were, could not possibly overcome what they were up against. They would fail . . . as they always did. That was precisely why Archer had to succeed.

And yet, time stood as another lethal enemy. Old Jack now showed quarter past the hour—forty-five short minutes before Archer's Personal Midnight—and he still had serious ground to cover. He blazed through the outer borders of Tirbury, cutting across moon-lit farms and shadowy yards. Then, into Warhaven he went, leaping over the foxholes and barbed-wire fences that crisscrossed the landscape. Finally, the Dreamtreader passed under the sprawling canopy and twisted boughs of the Drimmrwood. Leaping thick roots, ducking low branches, and bouncing from trunk to trunk, Archer felt a bit like a pinball. But somehow he managed to avoid knocking himself senseless.

When Archer emerged from the trees at last, his eyes were drawn to the two moons: Shiver and Sliver. The face of the larger moon seemed anguished, frozen forever in a soundless scream. Gouged with craters and dead seas, it and the second moon—a razor-sharp sickle on this night—bled eerie silver beams upon a steep, slithering road.

Rue de la Mort. The Street of Death. Or, as Archer called it, *Zombie Avenue.*

"This might be a mistake," Archer muttered, sprinting away from the protection of the Drimmrwood. He dashed up the hill and skidded to a stop at the very bottom of the infamous street. Someone was coming—many someones.

Villagers armed with crude weapons and torches strode by him and marched up the road like a scene from *Frankenstein.* Here, at least, the villagers had just cause. The monsters on this street were evil. Especially he who sat on the throne of Number 6, Rue de la Mort, the Shadowkeep. That legendary fortress was a house of horrors, a castle mansion from which the Nightmare Lord himself ruled with a jagged iron fist.

And a flaming whip.

Archer winced at the thought. Nothing frightened him more than Vorcaust, Tongue of Fire.

Screams and shouts pulled Archer's attention back to the villagers. So, the rumors had been true after all. They were again attempting a revolt. Archer shook his head. Those unfortunate, desperate souls would never even get to the Nightmare Lord. Shadowkeep's pale, blank-eyed guards—with their bone-breaking hammers and razor-sharp scythes—would sweep the villagers off both sides of the road, down into the yawning deeps below.

It had already begun. He heard their screams. He saw the fight. But where they fell, Archer would not. He had taken a vow. He had a job to do, and he would not, could not fail.

"Razz!" Archer whispered urgently. His Dreamtreading companion still would not appear nor answer. *Impulsive as ever. Figures. Always ducking the tough things.*

The tiny hairs on Archer's neck stood up suddenly. An invisible tingling pulse struck him in the lower back. He stumbled forward a step and grumbled. "Sloppy. I let that one sneak through."

It had been an Intrusion, a wave of dream matter, and a strong one too. Archer knew how powerful and destructive Intrusions could be if they were not kept at bay by his will. The experience reminded Archer of the most important of the Dreamtreaders' Nine Laws: *Anchor first; anchor deep.*

Trying not to watch as villagers fell by the dozen, Archer reached over his shoulder and retrieved an anchor from his backpack. Moonlight glistened down the entire shaft, from the flat striking plate to the sharp stake at the end. The Dreamtreader yanked the rendering mallet from his belt and began to hammer the anchor into the ground. The burnt topsoil didn't provide much support, though. Archer slammed the mallet down harder and harder until the air rang with the sound. Finally, the anchor bit into the char, the bone-hard stone about a foot beneath the soil. The anchor now steady, Archer holstered his mallet and bowed his head to the striking plate.

In order for the anchor to function, it had to be personalized . . .

marked with a symbol of significance to its Dreamtreader. Archer closed his eyes and thought of the well in his backyard at home. It was an old artesian spring that had apparently been on the Keatons' property over a hundred years before it became Keaton property. No one knew who drilled it or built the cobblestone turret that capped it now, but it still had a special importance to the family.

Archer's mother, in particular, had been fascinated by it. She'd called it a wishing well, and Archer believed her. She'd drawn and painted pictures of it. She'd photographed it. She'd drunk out of it every day. It had been Archer's special chore, when he was little, to run down the hill in the backyard to "fetch the water" for his mom to use in her famous summer limeade. She'd always made Archer feel so helpful, so brave for simply filling a pail of water and carrying it up the hill and into the kitchen. He'd felt heroic.

But I couldn't save her, could I? Archer thought, pressing his forehead painfully into the striking plate. The cancer had taken his mother when he was seven, but right to the end she'd sworn that the well water had given her the two extra years of life that had so astounded the doctors. And since she'd believed it, Archer had also.

Now, that old well became his anchor. The Dreamtreader had anchored as close to Shadowkeep as he dared. But with time running short, Archer would need it close. It was his lifeline, his only way home. Even if all the Nightmare Lord's hounds were on his tail, it would only take Archer one touch upon the well to go home.

Archer opened his eyes and stood up straight. The well was there now among the trees: smooth stone, ancient hardened wood, wrought iron, rope, and pail. This was his anchor, and it went *very* deep.

The Dreamtreader turned back to Rue de la Mort and stared up at the crooked fortress high on the mount. There was red light in its upper windows, and the moons lit every angle of its crooked rooftops in eerie yellow. This was the stronghold of the one who caused all the misery.

Archer knew what he wanted. No machine gun or high explosive that might draw out too much of his remaining Dreamtreader energy. No, Archer would use his favorite. He reached once more over his shoulder, and released a little of his will to create something out of pure Dream. This time, his hand came back with a sword: a sleek and silver-gray blade with a ribbed grip and a cross guard that stretched protectively from the haft like eagle's wings to cover the knuckles of Archer's right hand.

Archer held the blade aloft as if in defiance of the moons, in defiance of Shadowkeep and the dark tyrant who sat on its throne. A spark kindled upon the cross guard. Bluish-white flames whirled up the blade. He was ready.

Archer let out a growl that sounded more suited to a werewolf than a teenager. He ran up Rue de la Mort, tapping into a speed that Olympic athletes only dreamed about. He weaved in and out of the sea of villagers. Their forms flashed by in a blur, as did Shadowkeep's shambling guards who nearly fell over themselves trying to catch up to the speedy intruder. It was no use. They could no more catch Archer than a sloth could leap up and grab a soaring hawk.

One of the vacant-eyed guards swung a curved blade at Archer but missed wildly, hacking into another Shadowkeep soldier instead. Archer wrenched his fiery sword around and took out both guards at the knees. The Dreamtreader dove, rolled under another warrior's sweeping stroke, and vaulted to plant both feet hard into the chest of a guard charging from the side of the bridge. The force of impact sent the guard staggering backward. With a moaning yelp, the thing toppled over the edge of the road.

Back on his feet, Archer pulled away from the scuffling guards and charged on. His legs churned but never missed a step. Only a great clang caused Archer to pull up short. He half-skidded, half-stumbled to a stop. The forty-foot iron gate guarding Shadowkeep's yawning mouth began to rise. In the hooded blackness of the opening, fierce eyes shone forth like lanterns.

There came from that dark gate an echoing blast of horse speech. Not some tame neigh or whinny, but rather a fierce and angry scream. A massive black steed with flashing red eyes emerged. Its rider was clothed in night and shadow as if shreds of darkness could be woven together into a garment or hammered into plate armor. Cruel spikes and other wicked shapes jutted out from the metal and even pierced the rings of chain mail beneath.

It was a fierce appearance, even more because of his eyes. The Nightmare Lord's eyes were empty pockets of sickly, whitish-green fire, bubbling like cauldrons of rage within his ram's-horned helm. If indeed eyes are the mirror of the soul, then this warlord possessed a soul like a tomb full of things dead and rotting.

"Gabriel sending boys now, is he?" The Nightmare Lord's voice was raspy, full of thickened syllables, and mingling somehow with the buzzing of frenzied hornets or carrion-mad flies. "The Dreamtreaders must be desperate indeed."

Archer took an involuntary step backward, shook his head, and chastised himself for even a moment's cowardice. In the face of a rabid dog, you could not show fear. In the presence of the Nightmare Lord, fear—any fear at all—was a death sentence. One slip, one tiny gesture of dread revealed to him, would be the beginning of a cruel end. The Nightmare Lord would seize that thread and pull, unraveling a man into nothingness . . . or something far worse.

"I do not fear you!" Archer cried out. He'd practiced these words over and over again prior to this night. His voice rang like church bells, full of hope and promising centuries of faith and resolve.

At Archer's resounding declaration, the Shadowkeep guards caught up to Archer at last, coming to an awkward halt several yards behind him. But the dark rider showed no change. There he sat, unmoving, a black puncture in the fabric of dream. But then, his massive shoulders shifted. The spikes on his elbow and along his forearm glimmered. From an unseen loop or sheath, he drew out a long weapon: Scorghuul.

The axe was a dreadful, dangerous thing, vast and curved, wickedly sharp and shaped like the fang of a venomous snake. It looked immense and heavy, with a curved handle meant for two hands, yet the dark figure held the weapon in a single fist.

"I do not fear you!" Archer cried out again. This time, his voice failed him, and his words fell like shards of glass. The Dreamtreader looked at his sword and tried to will the fire to burn more fiercely . . . brighter. But now it was barely a lick of blue flame.

Archer swallowed deeply, turned toward his enemy, and charged.

The rotting eyes of the Nightmare Lord flashed. His movement was swift and sudden. He swept Scorghuul aloft and pointed it at Archer. His dark steed responded, charging. The thick muscle of the creature's flanks sent the beast and its rider thundering across the drawbridge and down the mountain path. The horse shrieked. Its hoofbeats thundered. The blade loomed.

Archer's own speed almost got away from him. He stumbled, righted himself at the last second, and leaped. But to call it a simple leap was far short of the feat Archer performed. His deed was something just a bit below actual flight. He rose fourteen feet into the air, somersaulted over the Nightmare Lord, and cranked his sword around for the dark king's head.

The blade flared up with white fire once more, but the dark rider lifted his weapon in defense. The collision was that of shadow and light, darkness and hope ablaze. Archer's sword glanced off the crown of the axe. He'd intended to take the Nightmare Lord's head . . . and failed. He had, however, done something that would be remembered in Dreamtreader legends for years to come.

The ram's horn Archer had carved from the Nightmare Lord's helm clattered to the road. Never in all the timeless moments that passed in the realm of Dream had anyone had the audacity and skill to inflict damage upon him who rules the nightmare realm.

Archer finished his acrobatics with a sturdy landing and turned back to face his foe. The Nightmare Lord pulled hard on the reins. The tyrant's mount came to a scraping, gravel-blasting halt. The violence of the steed's turn seemed impossible, as if the creature had reversed, inside out, and now came marching back toward Archer. The Nightmare Lord slowed his mount. The incline became deathly quiet. Indeed, only the hollow clatter of the horse's massive hooves rang upon the stone.

The beast came to a stop just a dozen paces from Archer and snorted. When it raised and shook its head, the chain links of its harness jangled dully. Archer shuddered and then cringed inwardly.

He knew his mistake. Worse still, he knew the Nightmare Lord had seen it.

Instantly, the meager flame upon Archer's sword vanished altogether.

Archer tried to will it to rekindle, but it was no use. This close to Shadowkeep and in the presence of its master, Archer could not produce even a lick of fire. What's more, the grip of the blade grew painfully cold. He could feel the numbing chill spread from his fingers, down his wrist, and all the way to his elbow. He could barely hold on to the sword.

A bit of motion caught Archer's eye. He looked up as the Nightmare Lord holstered his fearful axe.

What is he doing? Archer wondered. "You won't have me!" he cried out.

That's when Old Jack began to toll. The strokes came, and Archer knew. It was twelve, the Stroke of Reckoning, his Personal Midnight.

My anchor, he thought desperately. *I have to get back to my anchor!* But between him and his anchor stood the Nightmare Lord and more than a hundred Shadowkeep guards.

"Your time has run out!" the Nightmare Lord declared, the hornet-buzzing sound louder and more agitated than before.

Archer swallowed and made a slow of slashing his sword. "So has yours!" he yelled. "I won't miss this time!" He made as if to charge but found his legs would not obey. He felt rooted to the road.

The Nightmare Lord leaned forward in his saddle and began to laugh. It was an eerie sound, mirthless and harder than flint. It struck Archer like a physical blow. The Dreamtreader staggered back but kept his eyes trained on his foe. Something was happening to the Nightmare Lord. Archer shook his head and rubbed his eyes, but couldn't change what he was seeing.

"No," Archer whispered, but he knew his hope was in vain. Vorcaust.

The flaming whip flickered out like the lick of a dragon's tongue. The Nightmare Lord cracked it in the air, and thunder crashed in the roiling clouds. The tyrant began to whirl the lash around his head, then his body. The outline of the dark warrior upon his steed seemed to tremble. And yet the movement had purpose. Things began to rise up out from the ribbons of hungry fire and gloom that danced around the Nightmare King. Forms and shapes emerged: shadows of ravens, spiders, and serpents; gnarled, grasping trees and skeletal hands.

Archer could barely force himself to watch as the enemy's storm of horrors continued to grow. Shapes emerged and foundered. There were faces too. Scowling, snarling, vacant-eyed faces.

With sudden shouts of rage, a band of the villagers raced past the guards and dared to lift their pitchforks and crude blades before the Nightmare Lord's pale eyes. Wreathed in red flame, black smoke, and a myriad of misty horrors, the Nightmare Lord scarcely looked down at his subjects. Vorcaust flickered out, and a man went down, writhing in a nest of serpents. The whip cracked again. Another villager screamed, suddenly enveloped in a giant shadow shaped like raven's wings. The other villagers turned to flee. The Nightmare Lord spurred his stallion, and Scorghuul came free. The dark blade swept a downward arc, leaving the villagers maimed in its wake.

Archer couldn't help himself. He turned and ran. He paid no heed to the fact that he was running toward the Shadowkeep, but churned his legs faster and faster. Hoofbeats thundered behind him, gaining. Archer heard the Nightmare Lord's laughter, stumbled, and fell. He tasted blood in his mouth, tried to get up, but failed.

The last thing passing through Archer's muddled and failing mind was a young woman's voice: "I warned you not to attempt this yet," she whispered. "He is above your kind."

"Why?" Archer demanded. "How do you know this? And . . . who are you anyway?"

The Nightmare Lord's black mount shrieked. There was thin, cruel laughter. He was close. Very close.

"There is no time," the maiden's voice replied. "I can deliver you to your anchor. Do you wish this?"

Archer swallowed, tasted blood, and whispered, "Yes."

He blinked, or rather, the world around him blinked. There was a final lash of fire streaking out at him, a flash, and then . . . Archer was kneeling by the well. His anchor. His way home. Archer thrust his hand to its stone and gasped.

TWO

THE DERECHO

FIRE. BLOOD. PALE EYES.

Archer Keaton gasped awake, his top sheet and blankets tangling around him as if they were living things, serpents bent on strangling the life out of him while he slept. Everything was drenched in sweat, especially near his back. And it stung. Archer half-reached over his shoulder, probing for the source of pain. A new line of fire streaked up his back, making him flinch. *What in the world?*

He squirmed a bit on the edge of the bed and shrugged his shoulders slowly. A lash of flame sliced through his thoughts. He shook the image away, but the memory seemed nearer than ever before.

"Hold it!" Archer blurted out. He snatched up at his windowsill and came back with the compact UV light he always kept close to his bed. His breath held captive, his heartbeat seeming to pause, he flicked on the light. *Legs clear,* he thought. *Torso, arms too.* He slid out of bed to stand before the mirror. A few more sweeps of the UV light . . . and Archer exhaled.

"No tendrils," he whispered, switching off the power. "Not still in the Dream." He exhaled a long, relieved breath and flopped back into bed. Dreamtreading was full of dangers, but tendrils were among the worst. Leech-like parasites, about six inches long, but invisible to the naked eye, tendrils infected their hosts with a kind of psychological toxin. Not only did this mental poison hinder the Dreamtreader's ability to wake up, but it hit the imagination and senses, making it nearly impossible to tell dream from reality.

A siren wailed somewhere, maybe just a few streets away from Archer's home. He shuddered involuntarily. As Archer would put it, sirens weirded him out. It wasn't just the sound—unsettling, shrill, and mournful—but more the potential behind the sound. The potential for tragedy.

Archer shivered again, and again felt the sting on his back. "I really need to see what that is," he whispered. But just then, the wind kicked up. Not some little breeze to stir the wind chimes—this was a fist of buffeting, hammering air. It struck the side of Archer's house causing the shutters and siding to rattle like a machine gun. And it kept coming.

A *derecho*.

Archer had never heard the term before science class the day before. Dr. Pallazzo had described the rare atmospheric condition: a line of powerful thunderstorms stretching hundreds of miles up and down the East Coast, the derecho was fueled by a volatile sudden mass of cold air surging down from Canada and sweeping into a cauldron of hot, moist air.

This violent collision often caused thunderstorms and sometimes spawned tornados, but there were exceptional occasions when these conditions would unleash a derecho. Dr. Pallazzo had said that all the weather models pointed to the likelihood that a derecho would form, probably deep into the night.

Archer glanced at the red digital display of his bedside clock.

17

Three in the morning. The wind continued to howl. "Man, Dr. P was right," Archer muttered. He listened to the pounding wind. "I hope—"

Flash. *Bang!*

The thunderclap slammed before the lightning flash faded.

"Snot buckets!" Archer exclaimed, blinking and trying to catch his breath. *As if I need anything else to accelerate my heartbeat.*

The lightning had pierced his curtains and lit the room in ghostly white, leaving a visual phantom of pale eyes.

Those eyes. The memories returned. Defeat. The Nightmare Lord's laughter.

The storm roared outside, gathering strength. Hard rain pelted his bedroom window. Lightning flashes and thunder blasts competed against each other, trying to give Archer a heart attack. He closed his eyes and silently prayed for safety, for him and his family.

An odd musical trill floated across his room.

"What—is—that?" Archer wondered aloud as the tune carried on. It sounded vaguely familiar. Annoying, but familiar.

Wait, he thought. *Is that . . . is that the Bob the Builder theme song? Oh, no. Not again.*

Archer sat up, sending a strip of searing pain blazing up his back. He groaned. The image flickered into his mind again: Vorcaust, the flaming whip. But he wasn't still in the dream. "Why do I still feel it?" Archer whispered. He arched his back and rolled his shoulders.

The music tinkled again. Archer spotted his cell phone on the charger atop his desk. His back still smarting, he managed to pad across the room and snatch up the phone.

"Dang it, Kaylie," he mumbled. He knew good and well what had happened. His little sister had changed his ring tone again. And again, she'd changed it to the most annoying ring tone imaginable. Sure, he'd tried to lock her out of the phone. But when it came to technology, he was no match for Kaylie. Few people were.

At just seven, Kaylie had tested off the charts in every school subject. She'd skipped three grades and had to get county-sponsored private tutoring because the regular Gifted and Talented curriculum wasn't challenging enough. Kaylie wasn't just smart. She was scary. She sent other prodigies running home to their mamas.

And no matter what Archer did to protect his computer, iPod, game systems, and phone, Kaylie always managed to hack in. It was never malicious, but it was almost always an eleven on the Pesty Scale.

Another clap of thunder made Archer jump. He shook his head, exhaled, and looked down at the messages: two, both from his best friend, Kara Windchil. Archer again noted the time. *Way late for texting,* he thought. But that didn't stop him from checking the messages anyway.

Scary storm. Save me.

This wind is crazy. Jk about the save me part. Lol.

Archer snorted a laugh. He detached the phone from the charger and ambled back to bed. Kara had been his best friend ever since they were in day care together before starting kindergarten. They'd climbed trees together. They'd caught fireflies and built snowmen. They'd fetched crates full of little milk cartons together in elementary school and done morning announcements on camera in middle school.

Now, many years later, they went to the same high school and shared numerous classes. Kara was a little different in high school, more worried about being cute and popular. But, in the neighborhood, she was always the same old friendly Kara.

The middle-of-the-night text was unexpected though.

Archer texted back:

Storms still spook you, Kara? What are we, still in kindergarten?

Always the funny guy, right? Except not funny. My house is shaking.

Archer laughed, but it was painful laughter. *My back, again,* he thought, still at a loss for an explanation that made any sense.

He texted:

Storm shouldn't last too much longer. Dr. P said derechos move fast.

A few seconds pause and Kara texted:

Hope so. Creeping me out.

Archer sent back:

Everything else okay?

"Dude, what are you doin' on your phone?" came a voice from the doorway.

Archer's eyes bounced up. "Buster, get back in bed."

"Why?" Buster asked, cocking his head sideways. "This storm is righteous."

Archer shook his head. "Righteous? I don't get it," he said. "Our family has lived in Maryland for all of your life. In fact, we Keatons have been in Maryland, well . . . ever since our ancestors came over on the boat. And you talk like you're a surfer raised on the breakers in California." Buster ignored him.

"Look, Brosef, if I can't bang on my games this late, you can't be messin' around on your phone."

Brosef? Archer rolled his eyes. But it wasn't a put-on or an imitation. It was just the way Buster spoke. And, in spite of the dominant red-hair, fair-skin Keaton genes, ten-year-old Buster had somehow managed to get blond hair and the ability to tan like a beach bum.

The trilling text message music sounded again.

"Dude, tell me that is not the Barney theme," Buster said.

"Kaylie did it," Archer muttered. "She—" A sudden flash. Sharp, crackling thunder followed.

"Cool," Buster said.

Yeah, thought Archer. *Way cool.* "Okay, little bro," he said. "Back to your room."

"Better not let Dad catch you with your cell," Buster warned.

"It's no big deal," Archer explained. "Someone just texted me, that's all."

"Who?"

"Don't worry about it."

"Who?" Buster asked again.

"None of your business."

"I'll tell."

Archer glowered at his little brother. "It's just Kara," he muttered.

"Ewww," Buster said. "Kara's a girl."

"Uh . . . yes," Archer replied. "Pretty much."

"Grody," Buster said, and he scampered back down the hall making very little a sound.

The storm continued to rage on, but another siren pierced the night. Archer cringed as he lay down on his side. He glanced at his phone. The little envelope icon was blinking.

Kara's most recent reply:

Well, on top of this freak storm, I just had a really bad dream.

It felt like an ice-cold needle ran up Archer's spine. He texted Kara:

What kind of bad dream?

A few rumbles of thunder later, the Barney tune announced Kara's reply:

You'll think I'm a nut. It was just a dream. No big deal.

Come on. Tell me.

After several heart-racing moments, Kara texted:

There was this scary guy with white eyes. He had someone tied down to a table. I'm not sure who it was, but somehow, I knew it was someone I cared about. The white-eyed guy he stared at me. And he had . . .

Archer clicked on the text twice, but that was all there was. It just cut off. Then came another Barney text chime.

. . . a knife.

Archer caught another chill as a new text came in.

I thought he was going to murder the person on the table. But, Archer, he handed me the knife. And I did it . . .

Did what? Archer wanted to scream at the phone.

The text came at last:

I killed someone. I can't believe it, Archer! Why would I do that?

Kara's dream flooded Archer's mind. He wasn't afraid. He was angry. And he was making it personal. He texted Kara back:

That's so messed up, but listen: it's just a dream okay? Not real.

But it seemed so real.

Listen, I know you. You would NEVER do something like that.

The wind whistled and howled outside. Kara's next text seemed to take forever. Sheets of rain slapped at the house, and there was one final stone-shattering crack of thunder. Then all went quiet.

Kara's text finally came:

K. Thanks. I needed to hear that. Night.

And that fast, the surging anger came back. Archer popped up out of bed, strode down the hall, vanished into the blue bathroom, and shut and locked the door. He flipped on the light and took off his shirt. Keeping his head turned so that he could still see in the mirror, he rotated his shoulders . . . and then hissed.

A stinging, pencil-thin welt striped his back. "How did you do that?" Archer whispered. He began searching his memory, the years he'd spent Dreamtreading. He'd been injured a hundred times while on missions, but it had never turned into something real.

"I have got to finish this," Archer muttered. The Nightmare Lord had begun pushing the envelope. He'd gone too far. Kara's dream and the burning wound on his back had made that clear. Something had to be done. Something drastic . . . and soon.

Back in his room, Archer started for his closet but stopped at a bright flash of lightning. It had startled him again, but that wasn't why he stopped. In the flickering light, he'd seen something on his bed. Now, even in shadow, among the rumpled sheets and covers, alien shapes stood out. "What?" he whispered, flipping a corner of a sheet. He grabbed up his cell and aimed its waking light to see better.

Two dead leaves. A black feather. A segment of cold, iron chain. Archer blinked away a memory of ravens, swirling darkness, and fire. Then, he whispered, "I've never brought anything back before."

His cell phone held high, spraying the bed with light, Archer reached for the chain. He jerked his hand away once, involuntarily reacting. But when his fingertips brushed up against the metal, there was no shock. It was just cold. So was the feather. The leaves too. It was as if these things had been outside in the night. He placed the items on his bedside table . . . carefully.

With a shudder, Archer went to his closet, moved the boxes heavy with sports cards and trophies, and found a particular metal suitcase. Archer turned the three combination wheels in turn. The container opened like something inside was taking a deep breath. Pale blue light shone through the crack as the lid lifted. Archer reached inside and removed a book covered in worn, dark leather and bound with silvery thread. The lettering of the title, *The Dreamtreader's Creed*, still glowed faintly.

"This is what I need," Archer whispered. "I can always get answers here." He removed the book. The cover was well worn from all the time he'd spent studying. Right from the beginning, the Creeds had helped him understand things.

Archer had known he was different all along. He dreamed differently than other people. He could do things in the dreams, control things, make things happen. The Creeds had explained all that. He'd been born a Dreamtreader, one of three people on earth given unique gifts to be used within the Dream to protect—well, everyone. Turned out, dreams weren't the harmless things most people thought they were. They could be dangerous. And there was a lethal enemy in the Dream.

"And I am way behind in my reading," Archer whispered. He took the book in one hand and closed the case. He hadn't taken three steps back to his bed when he heard sniffling.

And there was Kaylie standing in his bedroom doorway. Her strawberry blond pigtails seemed to droop, and her puffy, cream-white face was as sad as melted ice cream. She clutched her quilted pink blanket and Patches, her scarecrow dolly, as if someone might try to steal them away. Tears ran down her cheeks, her tiny button-sized bottom lip stuck out, and her chin trembled.

Whatever anger Archer had felt toward her from the cell phone incident ebbed away at the sight of her. "Awww, Kaylie," he said, glancing from his little sister to his book and back. "What's wrong? Is it the storm?"

Her head bobbed. "The quasi-linear convective system produced a series of microbursts and straight-line winds near hurricane intensity . . . and it scared me."

In spite of her genius-level mischief, Archer couldn't help himself. He put the Creeds back in the closet, went to Kaylie, and scooped her up. "I think the storm's pretty much over," he said, hugging her close.

"I know," she said, sniffling. "But I'm still scared. Can I sleep on the floor in here?"

"Uhhh . . ." Archer sighed inwardly. He needed to get back to *The Dreamtreader's Creed*. He desperately needed to train his mind, needed to get stronger . . . but . . .

"P-please," Kaylie mumbled, a sob threatening to break out.

"Oh," Archer said, putting her down. "Okay, but you'll have to keep quiet. I have to read—"

"Tell me a story," Kaylie said, her blue eyes glistening, huge, and hopeful.

Archer sighed. "Okay. *One* story coming up."

Kaylie's tears seemed to vanish, replaced by a luminous smile. She ducked out of the room and returned in a flash with two blankets and several pillows. She snuggled into the whole pile right beside Archer's bed.

"Okay," he said, staring thoughtfully at Kaylie upon the pillow bed. "Ah, yes. I have it now. I am going to tell you a story about a princess who lived in the clouds. But first, here." He handed Kaylie his cell phone. "I need you to fix this. No more Barney."

"Have any candy?" she asked.

THREE

STORM DAMAGE

"*WHOA!*"

A collective gasp went up from the students on the bus. Even the driver, Miss Farber, seemed impacted by the sight. She slowed the bus to a crawl.

Archer had never seen so many downed trees. The corner of Laurel Lane and Route 14 looked as though a giant had karate-chopped through the forest. What had been tall white pines or scraggly pitch pines were now just trunks knocked down like dominoes, some uprooted entirely and others snapped at the trunk base.

"See, I told ya!" Jay Stephago said, poking Archer. "A tornado rolled through here. Look a' those trees. See."

"It wasn't a tornado, Bunk," Archer replied using Jay's nickname. "It was a derecho. The wind didn't swirl; it came straight on. That's why the trees all fell the same direction."

"How you know?" Bunk asked, his mop of brown hair swaying in front of his tiny, restless eyes.

Archer was silent a few ticks. He sighed and then muttered, "Kaylie told me."

"Oh," Bunk said. "Guess it's probably true then."

Archer shook his head. "Thanks, Bunk."

"I still think it was a tornado," Bunk said. "I saw this show on cable where these tornado chaser guys . . ."

The bus started rolling again, the grinding of gears overpowering conversation. Archer stared past Bunk to the front of the bus where Kara Windchil sat with Emy Crawford, Bree Lassiter, and a pack of other Dresden High glamour girls.

She used to always sit with me, Archer reflected, the thought leaving a bitter aftertaste. Halfway through ninth grade, Kara had changed her hair, letting it grow out till it flowed like a cape of black silk around her head. Then, a whole new set of friends discovered her, and . . . she just changed.

He watched her for a few seconds more, wondering if maybe she'd turn and wave or wink . . . or something. He turned back to the window and sighed. And waited. And hoped.

A thump on the seat startled him. He jumped.

"Sheesh, who's the scaredy cat now?" It was Kara.

"I guess, I am," Archer said, laughing. He lowered his voice to a conspiratorial whisper. "Get any sleep last night?"

"Not much," she said. "But . . . it was better, after we talked. Thanks for saying, you know, what you said."

Archer shrugged. "Dreams can get pretty bad, but if you know yourself well enough, they won't hurt you."

"Yeah," Kara said. "And I guess, coming from an expert like you, I should probably be able to trust that advice." She got up abruptly and went back to sit with Bree and the other girls.

What had set her off this time? One minute, she seemed to show genuine gratitude. The next, she was really mad. *Just like that,* Archer thought. *Man, I just can't figure her out. Not anymore.*

Archer's father had once told him never to try to understand women, but Kara? Kara had been different. He trusted her. She was the one person who knew him well enough to suspect he had something secret going on. In the end, she was the only one he ever told about Dreamtreading. He couldn't help it. She'd cornered him one day, a little more than a year back.

He'd been reading *The Dreamtreader's Creed* in the family basement that summer afternoon. He was in so deep that he didn't pay any attention to the doorbell when it rang. Archer's father had let Kara in and sent her to the basement to find Archer. He hadn't even seen her standing there. He had no idea how long or what she'd heard. Archer remembered the awkward conversation word for word.

"Archer, what's the matter with you?" Kara had asked.

"What?"

"Archer, what book is that?"

"Book, oh, uh . . . this?" Archer had closed the Creeds and thrown a blanket over it. "It's nothing, just an old book of stories. You know, like fables and legends, that kind of thing."

"That's not like any book I've ever seen," Kara said, stepping closer and peeling back the blanket. She gasped. "I was right. The title *is* glowing."

"Kara," he said. "This is kind of private."

"What are you into, some kind of cult?"

"What? No!"

"Well, what is it then? You were chanting or something."

"That was forms."

"What?"

"Kind of like karate," he said. "You know how you run through a series of movements with your body, blocks and strikes? It's like that, only with your mind."

Kara peeled back the blanket even more. "That sounds strange," she said. "But then again, you always were a little weird."

"Thanks."

"*The Dreamtreader's Creed?*" she mumbled. "Okay, Archer, start from the beginning. I want to know everything."

"You won't believe me," Archer argued. It was the last card he could play.

Kara said, "Try me."

There had been no dissuading her. She'd interrogated him all summer long, and he'd told her everything. When school began that fall, Archer was afraid she'd tell someone. But she hadn't. Not a soul.

Even when conflicts strained their friendship, Kara had kept his secret.

Kara and Archer had sat on a little bench not far from the well in his backyard. "What's going on, Kara?" he asked. "This feels serious."

"It is," she said, smiling sweetly. The hint of green that tinged her blue eyes seemed more prominent somehow. In fact, her eyes danced with eagerness. "I need to ask you a favor. A big one."

"Oh, is that it? You had me worried." He laughed.

She didn't. "You know that thing you do?" she asked, her tone cautious, her features tense now. "Dreamtreading?"

Archer felt the bottom drop out of his gut. He checked over his shoulder to make sure no one else was in the backyard. "Look, Kara, I already told you everything I can."

"But you left out something pretty big."

"Such as?"

"Such as how to do it, Archer? I want in. I want to be a Dreamtreader." She had seemed eager before. Now, there was a feverish intensity about her. Archer could feel her expectations weighing on him.

He wanted to hide under a rock. No, he wanted to dig a trench under the rock, come out on the other side of the planet, and then hide under the Great Wall of China. Ever since the summer, Archer had been afraid of this moment.

At last, he said, "You can't be a Dreamtreader."

Kara's expression hardened. She leaned back against the bench and swiped the hair out of her eyes. "Why not?" she demanded.

"It's something you're born with," Archer said. "Like a talent. Like being able to draw. Some people can, and some can't."

"But everyone can learn to draw, a little," Kara said. She turned to him and took his hands in hers. "If you have a good enough teacher, right? You could teach me, Archer. Will you? Please."

"It's not like that," Archer said. He wished more than anything that he could help her, that he could teach her. "I asked."

"What do you mean?" Kara dropped Archer's hands and crossed her arms.

"Remember, I told you there's a lead Dreamtreader, the highest ranking one? After we talked this summer, I asked him if you could be a Dreamtreader too. He said no. And he didn't leave any room for argument. There are always three and only three Dreamtreaders at a time. Something about mirroring the Perfect Three, whatever that means. I'm sorry."

Kara stood up. "Sorry?" She laughed, but it was more out of anger than mirth. "Sure you are. So what makes you so special anyway? My grades are just as good. I'm very creative. I could be a Dreamtreader."

"I wish you could, Kara," Archer said. "I begged Master Gabriel, but he . . . well, he's set in his ways."

"Fine, Archer," Kara said. "Keep your secrets."

"Keep my—Aren't you listening to me?" Archer watched her walk away.

Is she still stuck on that? Archer wondered. It wasn't his fault.

Archer saw a ripple of slender fingers appear five seats ahead. A pair of bespectacled, owlish green eyes glimmered amiably above both the seat back and an open book. The fingers rippled again.

Hi, Amy, Archer thought, giving her a half-wave, half-salute back. The Salute-Wave—one part friendly, two parts cool.

Amy rolled her eyes and laughed. Archer laughed in spite of himself. He'd known Amy Pitsitakas for almost as long as he'd known Kara. Since grade school, it seemed like they'd always been on the same bus, but Amy's bus stop was several miles from his own.

Flashing lights distracted Archer from his thoughts. The storm had knocked down some power lines just up ahead. Emergency vehicles and men dressed like bumblebees surrounded the area and slowed traffic even further. Archer stared intently at the downed trees and houses with torn-up siding. As the bus crept through the damaged neighborhood, Archer muttered, "Please, please, please . . ."

Dresden Senior High School was the oldest high school in the town of Gatlinburg. It was the oldest school in Washington County. In fact, it was the third-oldest school in the state of Maryland. So it was almost a given that Dresden High would have storm damage from the derecho, possibly extensive damage. *Obviously not enough to hurt anybody or close school,* Archer thought, *but maybe enough to scramble regular classes.*

A couple of hours in study hall or in the gym would be just enough time for Archer to put in the Dreamtreader training session he so needed. He patted the bulky backpack in his lap and hoped for the best.

Dresden High School had been miraculously spared by the storm. Except for the Internet.

A lightning strike had fried the school's server, so it would be a week or two before the students could use online resources. Mrs. Sullivan, Archer's first-block American Literature teacher, had reported the damage sum total with a gleam in her eye . . . right before she assigned the essay topic.

That's it? Archer silently grumbled. *The thunderstorm of the decade, and the only damage to the school is lost Internet?* Feeling pangs of disappointment, Archer glanced down at his backpack. *The Dreamtreader's Creed* would have to wait, as Mrs. Sullivan had made it abundantly clear that the essay would not wait for the Internet.

Fifteen minutes into the essay, a door closed sharply. Archer blinked to find he'd been doodling strange, twisting vines in the margin of his rough draft on Hawthorne's short story "Rappaccini's Daughter." There was also a rather awkwardly placed spot of drool.

Archer discreetly slid his elbow across the offensive dripping. Then he heard hushed voices and looked up. His eyes widened. Mrs. Mears, the principal, was there, dressed as always in an expertly tailored business suit. She looked like she should be CEO of a tech company rather than Shepherd-in-Chief for a bunch of teenagers. She and Mrs. Sullivan were deep in conversation . . . apparently over the tall young man who stood by the door.

Archer leaned over to his nearest classmate, Jake Spindler, and whispered, "Who's this guy?"

Jake shrugged. "I dunno," he said. "Guest speaker?"

Archer shook his head. The kid had to be a student the way he was dressed: cargo shorts and a blazing green tank top that read, "I'm going crazy. Want to come along?" But he couldn't be a sophomore. Not that tall. Not with all that facial hair. The guy had sideburns like Wolverine. In fact, he looked like a teenage version of the superhero. Square, rugged face; driftwood-brown hair that lay atop his head in a stylish flop; large, intense brown eyes; and a kind of sideways cool smirk that seemed to say to the world, *Why yes, actually, I am smarter and cooler than the rest of you.*

Archer glanced over at Kara and found her staring at the new-comer as well. Even Amy was staring.

"Sheesh, Amy." Archer leaned across to her chair and whispered, "I think you fogged up your glasses with steam."

"What?" she asked. Her cheeks went red.

"Umm, class," Mrs. Sullivan said, using her formal announce-ment voice. "We have a new addition to our little society of brilliance."

"This late in the year?" blurted Payton Kersh. "That's dumb."

Mrs. Sullivan shot Payton a withering glare. He pursed his lips and seemed to shrivel.

"I'd like you to meet Rigby Thames," Mrs. Sullivan said, nodding to Mrs. Mears as the principal departed the classroom. "He comes to us from the Glennwood Institute. Please make him welcome."

Glennwood Institute? Archer thought. The Glennwood Institute of Technology, or GIFT, as it was called, was a big deal. And it likely meant two things were true of Rigby: (1) he was rich and (2) he really was smarter than most everyone else. Tuition at Glennwood was higher than some Ivy League colleges, and they were extremely selective about the kids they accepted into their challenging program. Archer's father had once looked into the school for Kaylie. She had all the intellect needed. But the Keatons didn't have the money. GIFT was simply out of reach for regular folk. For crying out loud, the president's daughter attended Glennwood!

Archer shrugged and went back to his essay. He was still a little mad at himself for dozing. Thankfully, it hadn't been a deep enough sleep to trigger a Dreamtreading session. That could have been awkward.

Still, he'd cost himself time on his essay. He might have missed instructions too. As a Dreamtreader, he knew the critical important of intelligence. Every chance he got to build his personal knowledge, every opportunity to stretch his mind creatively, he seized it and never looked back.

I may not have been born a genius like Kaylie, he thought. *But I will outwork anyone.*

As he crafted his arguments and support from the text, Archer couldn't help but be aware of Mrs. Sullivan trying to get the new kid up to speed. She seated him in the empty desk by the window, one desk to Kara's left. Archer pressed the pencil a little harder to the paper.

"We're drafting explanatory essays on a Nathaniel Hawthorne short story," Mrs. Sullivan explained.

"Which one?" Rigby asked.

The way he said *one*, Archer thought. Something odd. Was it an accent?

"'Rappaccini's Daughter,'" Mrs. Sullivan replied. "But you don't have to worry about this essay, we're too far along—"

"I've read it," Rigby replied. "Right brilliant piece. Poison garden and all. Essay, is it? I'll give it a go."

An English accent, Archer thought miserably. Rich, smart, and an English accent. Archer scanned the room. Every single girl in the room was staring at Rigby. Archer rolled his eyes and whispered, "Oh, brother."

Lunch at Dresden High School came in three shifts. Archer's shift, the one for freshmen and sophomores, was the first of the day. When he stepped into the cavernous cafeteria, Archer realized there was actually a little more storm damage after all. The chairs in the lunch courtyard outside had been blown all over the place, some lodged in the limbs of the courtyard's trees. Others had apparently crashed into the lunchroom's wall of windows. The glass had all been cleaned up, and cardboard panels had been taped in place, making the wall of windows look a little like a crossword puzzle.

The lunch line was unusually short. That suited Archer just fine. If Archer had a passion other than Dreamtreading, it was food, even school food. He took up his tray and considered his lunch choices with the seriousness of a chess grand master. Mystery meatloaf? *No, I don't think so.* Mushroom and sausage pizza? *Maybe.*

Then he saw the Little Chiks—his all-time school lunch favorite. Small, square chicken sandwiches with a blot of spicy mayo and a pickle slice. Archer loved them, but they were so small.

When Archer finally came to the cashier, his tray had eleven Little Chik sandwiches, a mountain of mashed potatoes, and a large cup of brown gravy.

"Going light today?" Grandma Cho asked. The blue-haired woman had reportedly worked the cafeteria of Dresden High for more than twenty years. There had never been a gentler, kinder soul. She was everyone's grandma. "Eleven? You sure that's all ya need?"

Archer laughed. "It's actually twelve," he said, handing her his paid lunch card. "I ate one on the way through the line."

"Son," she said, "enjoy this metabolism while it lasts. It'll catch up to ya one day, and *bang!* Every muffin and french fry goes right to the old hips."

"I wish," Archer said. "I'm trying to put on some muscle, but no matter what I eat, I seem to burn it off."

Grandma Cho shook her head. "Have a cookie, Archer."

"Nah, I've already spent too much of my card."

"It's on me," she said. "I baked them myself."

"Thanks, Grandma Cho!" He reached back to the cookie tray and selected a thick, lumpy chocolate chip cookie. It weighed heavily in his hand and smelled of paradise.

Archer ate the cookie first. Absurdly delicious, as advertised. Halfway through his chicken sandwiches, dunking each one in gravy, he noticed that his lunch table too was unusually empty. *Short lunch lines and a half-deserted table,* he thought, chewing absently. *Hmph.*

After a few more sandwiches, curiosity finally got the better of Archer. He scanned the lunchroom and figured it to be at about 50 percent. Was some meeting being held somewhere, but he'd missed the announcement? Or maybe yearbooks had *finally* gone on sale.

No. Something else. Archer jammed home the last couple of sandwiches, vacuumed down the rest of the mashed potatoes, and slurped his third chocolate milk empty. After returning his tray, Archer walked the lunchroom perimeter and found no answers . . .

until he passed by the courtyard windows closely enough to see outside.

"There they are," Archer whispered.

Outside, seated in thrown-together rows of chairs, at least sixty or seventy students surrounded someone. That kind of attention usually meant a fight in progress. But students didn't bring chairs to a fight.

One of the courtyard's trees kept Archer from seeing who had captured the attention of so many. He checked the cafeteria clock. Five more minutes left for lunch. Not much, but Archer had to know.

The sun was warm, perhaps fueling up the atmosphere for another round of evening thunderstorms. Laughter and buzzy conversation filled the yard. Archer drew closer to the others and finally saw the center of attention: the new kid, Rigby Thames.

A fresh round of laughs apparently signaled the end of a joke. Kevin Zoll said, "Nah, man, really . . . why'd you leave GIFT?"

"They 'ave standards," Rigby said wryly. "You've got to 'ave a certain level of intellect to do well there."

"So you flunked?" Kevin asked.

"No," Rigby said. "As I told you, you got to be smart to get in. As it turns out, I'm too smart."

Another laughter explosion.

"Did you meet the president's daughter?" Ellen Stewart asked. "Did you know her?"

"Know 'er?" Rigby replied. "I dated 'er."

"You did not!" Bree Lassiter said. "I read all the magazines."

"Do you really think the Secret Service allows magazines to print everything?" Rigby asked. "We didn't date long, really. I got tired of the agents prying into everything I do. Seriously, you 'ave no idea."

Archer found himself joining in the laughter and then chastised himself. After all, Kara was all too interested in this cool new "bloke" from England.

Raghib Muhammed asked, "So how long have you lived in America?"

"Four years," Rigby replied. "When my uncle died, he left us 'is house. My family, well, we weren't doin' too well in Birmingham, so we came over. Big place now, full of secrets."

"Wait," Kara blurted out. "I think I know who you are now. You're the kid who moved into the inventor's mansion, the old Scoville house!"

"Enchanted," Rigby said with a gallant bow. "That's my Uncle Ebenezer, Dr. Ebenezer Scoville—off-the-charts genius . . . and lunatic."

"Was he really crazy?" Bunk asked.

Rigby never answered. The bell rang. Like a pulsing amoeba, the entire group of kids in the courtyard slowly ambled back to the cafeteria and the hallways beyond.

It wasn't over, though. Archer fell in just behind Rigby and saw the entire scene unfold in front of him.

David "Guzzy" Gorvalec emerged from the moving crowd. He was sickly pale but moved with an easy grace that was somehow serpentine and cool at the same time. He was strong too, white muscle contrasting sharply with his cut-off sleeve, black T-shirt. Strong and dangerous, feared by most students for any number of valid reasons. He'd repeated ninth grade and been suspended half a dozen times, more than once for carrying a weapon.

So when Guzzy slid over to Rigby, Archer knew that Rigby was in for a less than pleasant welcome.

Guzzy flipped the fence of black hair out of his eyes and whispered hoarsely, "Man, I know you got money, right?"

Rigby half turned but kept walking.

"Nah, man," Guzzy went on, grinning so that the silver cap gleamed out from the rest of his yellowed teeth. "Nah, nah, don't do me like that. I know you've got money, living in that great big old house."

"So?" Rigby replied, his voice void of emotion and absolutely no change in his long stride.

"I'm the guy around here," Guzzy said. "You need something, you come see me. If I don't have it, I can get it. Know what I mean? Concert tickets, tablet computers . . ." He paused. "Test answers for any class."

Archer cringed, slowing his pace a little. Rumors about Guzzy abounded in Dresden High's hallways. More than once, Archer had seen something change hands between Guzzy and other students, but it had always been at a distance. Now, here it was right in front of him. How would the new kid respond?

"If I were the needy type," Rigby said, his voice hardening, "I'd come running straightaway. But I don't need your junk. I 'ave something much better."

"Oh, is that how it is?" Guzzy asked. He exhaled a laugh. And just like that, his face went from Mister-Friendly, I'm-the-do-you-a-favor-guy to Cross-me-and-I'll-ruin-your-world. "Don't think you're gonna sell in my territory. Don't think you're gonna step on my toes and get—"

Rigby kept walking, but he turned his head and cast such a hate-filled glare that Guzzy almost tripped over his own feet. Rigby's voice became a simmering snarl. "Do not speak to me again."

Guzzy laughed, but anger flashed in his eyes. "Best take that attitude back to England! I'll—"

Rigby's hand moved in a blur.

Had he made a fist or done some kind of thrust or karate chop?

Archer couldn't tell, but he watched Guzzy stagger backward. His smooth, cool expression had turned to wide-eyed terror. He clutched his throat with both hands. Then he fell to his knees and gagged.

The crowd kept moving. If any of the teachers on lunch duty had seen a thing, they didn't show it. They hadn't made a move to intervene. Clumps of students filed right on by the still-coughing Guzzy.

Archer didn't want anything to do with a kid like Guzzy, but he couldn't stand to see him suffering and no one helping. Archer took a few tentative steps back toward him. "Hey, are you okay?" Archer asked. "You want me to get the nurse?"

Guzzy looked away, angrily swiping his forearm across his eyes. "Be fine," Guzzy said, coughing out his breaths. "But that new kid . . . he just messed up. I'm gonna hurt him. I'm gonna hurt him bad. Now, back up, Keaton!"

Archer hastened from the courtyard, feeling Guzzy's stare hard on his back. *Nothing good will come of this,* Archer thought. *Nothing good at all.*

DREAMTREADER CREED, CONCEPTUS 1

The Waking Mind is a powerful thing in the Temporal world, but it has limitations. While awake, the Waking Mind is active, of course, but the Sleeping Mind is dormant. When you fall asleep, the Waking Mind slumbers, and the Sleeping Mind comes alive and with it come abilities, sensations, and thoughts unlike anything the Waking Mind could ever consider in . . . well, in its wildest dreams.

The Dreamtreader is master of the Sleeping Mind. Unlike the usual dreamer, you will be lucid and much more. Manipulate the Dream world around you, but build your strength slowly, a little at a time. Do not attempt a tree if you have not first created a single leaf. Dare not attempt a storm if you have not first created a single cloud. Create what you know and build from it. Err on the side of caution when you create.

But create you shall: anything and everything your mission requires. To face the minions of the Nightmare Lord himself, summon fire and sword. Run like the wind itself. Call down lightning.

In time, with practice, it will all be within your grasp. Remember this: a Dreamtreader must know his limits. Create too much, too soon, and you will falter. Flying is especially taxing. So many variables for your mind to manipulate. Even the seasoned Dreamtreader will use flight sparingly, for it is quite draining. To fall out of the sky due to exhaustion is not the chief danger as it might seem. Rather, it is the utter depletion of your mental resources, causing deep sleep.

You will slumber within the Dream and be vulnerable to all manner of dangers. Death might be the kindest of things that could happen to one asleep in the Dream.

And so, the Dreamtreader will live by this, the foremost of the Nine Laws: Anchor first. Anchor deep.

When you enter the Dream, resist any temptation that might distract you from anchoring. Your anchor is your tether to life. Lose it at your peril. Stray not far from it. For when you have the need, it is the only real safe place in the Dream. By it, you may return to the Temporal world. Anchor first. Anchor deep.

Be wary of Sixtolls.

Your Personal Midnight is the limit of a Dreamtreader's stay within the Dream. Spend eleven hours in brave completion of your Dreamtreading goals, but note that there is no natural sixth stroke on your clock. The Nightmare Lord has stolen that. It has become his number now. Once every day and night, he overpowers even the ancient might of Old Jack and strikes Sixtolls. His time waxes then. For that hour, chaos reigns.

The hounds roam free.

FOUR

MASTER GABRIEL'S VISIT

ARCHER PUT *THE DREAMTREADER'S CREED* BACK INTO ITS protective case and surrounded it on the closet shelf with all of his trophies and shoeboxes. Armed with Dreamtreader lore and its powerful techniques, Archer flopped into bed and turned out the bedside light.

Turkey sandwich, check. Glass of milk, check. Ten cheesesticks, check. Archer had eaten his "lights out" meal an hour earlier. *L-tryptophan should be powering up right about now,* Archer thought, closing his eyes to the dark room and reveling in a deep yawn. All the unexpected events at school surrounding the arrival of Rigby Thames, the after-school chores, and several hours of Dreamtreader reading all made for an exhausting day. Archer was ready for sleep . . . and ready to report for duty.

But Archer's thoughts came in a swarm, preventing him from drifting away. Kara certainly seemed interested in Rigby. *She hasn't sent me a text all day,* Archer thought, absently clutching the edge of his pillow. *How is that fair? Rigby's from England, with the coolest accent known to mankind. He's rich and lives in a mansion. He's mysterious, the nephew of Mad*

Doc Scoville. He's ridiculously smart. Oh, and he looked the school's muscle-bound junior criminal in the eye and neutralized him with one punch . . . well, with one something.

Archer let out a slow sigh, loosened his grip, and felt his muscles relax. He began to think about his essay topic, about "Rappaccini's Daughter," how sad it was. The young Giovanni's obsessive love for a poisonous Beatrice: tragic in so many ways. For her too. Beatrice was a victim of her father's horrible, heartless experiments.

Thoughts of gardens led Archer's mind to wander into the tomato plants growing in his dad's garden in the backyard. *Dad's summer salsa,* he thought. Summer. The annual trip to North Carolina's Outer Banks. *This year, I'll make it. I'll run to the boardwalk and all the way back to the beach house.* That idea led to a flashlight tag manhunt with his cousins. And that thought led to . . .

"Oh, no you don't!"

The voice, like thunder, snapped Archer from his presleep ramblings. But Archer didn't leap from his bed and sprint for his door. He didn't cry out for help or cower in fear. He recognized the voice.

"No sleep for you," the voice continued. "Not yet. Not until I am through with you."

Master Gabriel, Archer thought. *A nice surprise.*

Archer rubbed the sleep out of his eyes and sat up in bed. His bedroom door was shut tight and bordered by ethereal wisps of bluish light—as usual when Gabriel came to visit. Those who came to Archer's door and knocked would immediately forget why they had come, turn, and leave Archer—and Gabriel—undisturbed.

Archer looked away from the door and toward the brighter glow of his visitor. Archer's mouth fell open.

"What?" Gabriel said. The word, spoken in his regal voice, sounded awkward.

"Umm," Archer muttered. He knew better than to speak off-the-cuff to Master Gabriel. In the three realms, Archer's master was the Nightmare Lord's opposite. He was the founder and leader of all Dreamtreaders. He was wise, powerful, and kind of sagely, but saying Gabriel was subtle and quick to anger was like referring to a bolt of lightning as a spark. Archer organized his thoughts and said, "I apologize for my . . . reaction to your appear . . . your presence. What happened to your incredible armor?"

"I am permitted two garbs," Gabriel replied, a frown deepening the creases on his weathered face. "The Incandescent Armor you have seen so often, and the style of the day."

"Style of the day?" Archer winced as he took in his visitor's outfit. Gabriel wore khaki cargo shorts; a bright green, blue, orange, and yellow Hawaiian print shirt; a seashell necklace; dark sunglasses; and a floppy gray fisherman's hat. He looked like a tourist who'd just spent a fortune in a beach souvenir shop. Well, except that most tourists didn't have ghost-white skin that glowed with its own golden aura.

"Confound it, Archer!" Gabriel thundered. "You are always telling me to moderate my appearance. You said the armor made me frightening."

"Not as frightening as that outfit," Archer mumbled.

"Tell me, then," Gabriel said, "what is the problem with this? Is it not the garb of your day?"

Archer held in the laughter that was begging to come out and said, "Master Gabriel, you have always demanded honesty, so I will tell you now that what you are wearing is *not* the garb of my day. You look like you just walked in from a cruise ship. Honestly, I was getting used to the armor."

Master Gabriel crossed his muscular arms and scowled. Then, without a word, he raised one of his gray-and-black striped eyebrows.

Instantly, the tacky beachcomber outfit dissolved, revealing his mighty armor. Except for the shades. Those remained.

"I like the sunglasses," Gabriel said. "I think I shall keep them."

"Okay, that's kind of cool," Archer said.

In truth, the Dreamtreader thought the Incandescent Armor was absolutely ten-plus levels above cool. From chestplate to greaves, the armor was a pale, etched gray that looked as if it had been painstakingly hewn from rich stone rather than forged from metal. And each piece was built out of layers, cunningly articulated so that Gabriel could move his body as freely as he might without the encumbrance of heavy armor. Archer especially liked the shoulder plates: massive cannonball-shaped guards terraced with blade-like ridges and thorny prongs. They made Master Gabriel look like he could play linebacker for a football team full of medieval juggernauts.

Designs and symbols, images and rune-like language had been carved into the armor. It was from these intricate markings that the radiant light came, as if each groove had its own private reservoir of liquid white fire. Light pulsed, faded, glistened, and ran over every inch of the armor, becoming more active and brighter whenever Master Gabriel moved.

The armor kindled brightly when Gabriel said, "I have come to bear you grave tidings."

Archer sat up a little straighter. "What's going on?"

Master Gabriel shifted his stance, seemingly tensed for battle. The hilt of his sword, the legendary Murkbane, the Nightcleaver, came into view. "More breaches, I am afraid," Gabriel explained. "In greater numbers than ever before. The Nightmare Lord has been marking new territories and trespassing far beyond his borders."

"So that's my mission tonight?" Archer asked. "Patch up the holes again?"

Master Gabriel's frown was so deep that his mustache and beard sagged. The same scraggly striped eyebrow arched and bristled above the rim of his sunglasses. Gabriel exhaled a mingling of impatience and anger, slowly ran a hand from his widow's peak all the way back along the length of his long, steel-gray hair, and said, "You tread lightly enough on disaster. Your mastery of Dreamtreading has made you bold . . . and foolish."

Foolish? I may be a lot of things, but not foolish. Archer blinked. *What did I say?* "Forgive me, Master Gabriel," he said. "I meant no disre—"

"Need I explain what will occur if the breaches begin to fray and connect? Need I paint the picture of what will become of this world, should a mighty rift be opened at last?"

Archer swallowed. "No, Master Gabriel," he said. "I didn't guard my thoughts before I spoke them. I think I've fallen behind in my training. I've been trying to squeeze in extra study time, but it's never enough."

Master Gabriel crossed his arms. One corner of his mustache twitched upward. "Humility," he harrumphed. "There may be a grain of hope in that vast sea of shifting sand after all. There is so much more for you to learn beyond the Nine Laws. For now, know this: if enough breaches fray and a rift tears through, your world will devolve."

"Devolve?" Archer squinted. "I don't know what that—"

"It means the breakdown of reality, Archer," Gabriel explained. "Imagine a world where no one can tell the difference between dream and awake. Do you see?"

So many terrible images flooded Archer's mind that he thought he might pop. "People would lose their minds; they'd kill each other."

"It would be the end of humanity," Gabriel said. "And my Superior will not have that."

Archer took a deep breath. "Okay, got it. I won't underestimate the breaches. I'll get to work right away."

Gabriel's arms fell. One hand went to the hilt of his sword; the other rested at his hip, thumb tucked into his belt. "Your mission is threefold," he said. "Dreamweave the breaches. Bind them up tight, mind! Then, if time permits, ask around about your fellows, Duncan and Mesmeera. They have not checked in . . . in some time. Go to the usual sources, but be discreet. Take Razz with you. She will help."

"That's if she shows up," Archer muttered.

"What do you mean by that?"

"She's cool and all," Archer said, tiptoeing through the realm of criticism. After all, Razz had been a gift from Gabriel. "But she doesn't always show up when I need her. The last time . . . well, never mind."

"Never mind, eh?" Gabriel's armor flared once. His eyebrow seemed to corkscrew above the frame of the sunglasses this time.

"Sir?" Archer asked, changing the subject quickly. "You want me to ask about the other two Dreamtreaders? Sometimes, missions run long. We don't always have time to check in. What's the big deal?"

Gabriel's eyes darted to the side as if he'd heard something worrisome outside Archer's window. "Just mention their names casually as if seeking an entertainment or rumor. Oh, and be extraordinarily shrewd and cautious if you should speak with Bezeal. That rhyming weasel can be an excellent source of information, but he often manages to pry more news from the questioner than he reveals himself. I am not entirely sure where his loyalties lie."

"I've dealt with Bezeal before," Archer said. "He has a weakness. I'll use it against him."

"Good, good," Gabriel said. "But be mindful of your own weaknesses. You can be certain that Bezeal will."

"Right," Archer said. "Got it." He waited a few thick seconds and then asked, "Has something changed?"

"What do you mean?" Gabriel asked, pushing the sunglasses up the bridge of his nose so that his eyes were completely hidden.

"Well," Archer began, his thoughts racing. *Yes, what do I mean?* "I guess it's several things, really. For one thing, it's May third. You don't usually show up unless it's the seventh day of the month or . . . unless it's something urgent. You've got Murkbane with you is another thing. And last, well . . . you seem, uh, nervous."

"Nervous?" Gabriel said the word as if he had tasted something spoiled. "Nerves, lad, are for mortals. But I am *concerned* about a great many things. The Lord of Nightmares has ever been ambitious and cunning. His plans . . . blunt and destructive. But he and his kind have failed through the centuries due to the valor of the Dreamtreaders and one . . . other . . . thing.

"The world, you see, has always had a critical measure of discernment, knowing wrong from right, dream from reality. When the Nightmare Lord came calling, trying desperately to tear the dream fabric asunder, people knew better. They rejected his sorcery for what it was: an illusion of fear echoing from a dream. He was never able to gain the traction needed to open a rift."

"But now?" Archer asked.

"But now, who in your world can be certain? Of anything?" Gabriel's lips curled in a snarl. "The people of your world are forgetting their foundations. Discernment erodes and muddies all waters, no matter how pure. Your world is losing its anchors, Archer."

"Anchors?" he echoed. "But anchors are for Dreamtreaders."

Master Gabriel's armor flared like a flash of lightning. "You really are far behind in your studies," he muttered. "Anchors are of critical use for Dreamtreaders, yes. But we all need anchors, Archer, in every area of our lives. If not, we drift far from the truths that matter . . . and the meaning of it all."

Archer could think of a hundred questions. But he dared not ask one for fear of looking even dumber than he felt. Still, it was as if Master Gabriel had just laid a map at his feet, a map to an ultimate treasure. Archer had a feeling Master Gabriel's words would echo in his mind for some time to come, but for now, it would have to wait. Archer went back to the business at hand. "Are you saying the Nightmare Lord is winning?"

"The Nightmare Lord's advances now are very methodical . . . precise, even," he said. "But no, he is not winning. I am beginning to suspect that he knows how close he is to a rift. My chief concern for now is that he will soon open enough breaches to allow things to pass through the dream fabric into the Temporal."

Archer felt as if frost had flash frozen on his spine. He shrugged his shoulders against the discomfort and felt the sting of his wound. "Master Gabriel, what do you mean by allowing things to pass through?"

Gabriel took off his sunglasses, which promptly disintegrated in his hand. His large, deep-set eyes looked weary, each dark pupil nearly vanishing in its iris, a kaleidoscopic ocean of blue and silver. He exhaled. "It would be the beginning of the end, Archer. When inhabitants of the Dream enter your world and those of your world become lost in Dream; when dreamers bring back tokens from the dream, and nightmares take from your world; when your people will awaken only to find that they can no longer tell whether they are awake or dreaming . . . that is what I mean."

Archer threw off his blanket and slid from the bed. "Something like that happened to me," he said. "Last night."

Master Gabriel gripped his sword pommel so tightly that his knuckles crackled. "Do not tell me you forgot to check for tendrils?"

"No, not that. I'm pretty careful about that. Well, just look." He lifted the back of his nightshirt and turned.

Gabriel looked at the long, angry red welt. "You mean to say that you tossed and turned in your dream . . . so much so that you wounded yourself?"

"No," Archer whispered.

"It will heal soon enough," Gabriel said. "I fail to see what—" His words failed. The master Dreamtreader's pupils grew so huge that his eyes appeared black and haunted. "You suffered this wound in your dream?"

Archer let his shirt fall back and nodded.

"This is dire news," Master Gabriel said. He turned hurriedly to Archer's closet as if he might burst through it to depart.

"There's more."

Master Gabriel spun on his heel. "What do you mean, more?"

Archer led the way to his bedside table and gestured. "After the Dream," he said, "the same dream where I was wounded, I found these. I—"

The expression on Gabriel's face was so sudden and so severe that Archer's mouth shut with a snap.

"Dead leaves twain," the old master muttered, "raven's fletching, and wrought-iron chain."

Archer swallowed. "You know these?"

"They are the Tokens of Doom," Gabriel said, his expression far away.

"Tokens of Doom?" Archer echoed. "I've never heard of those before."

"Of course you have not," Gabriel shot back. "You are, as you say, behind in your studies. They are legendary omens of disaster for a Dreamtreader. How did you come by these?"

Archer hesitated. "I . . . well, I'd finished repairing the breaches . . . so I—"

"Archer Percival Keaton." Master Gabriel ground out each word through his teeth. "Do you mean to say that you . . . approached Shadowkeep—alone—after all of my warnings? That you *dared* face the Nightmare Lord this early in your studies? For it is only *he* who can bestow the Tokens of Doom."

Archer stared at the floor. "I . . . I still had time." Archer said. "Old Jack was—"

"Your available time is not the issue. We are talking about the Nightmare Lord! There will come a day when his reign will end at the collective hands of the Dreamtreaders, but now? Now, Archer, you are overmatched."

Overmatched. That word stung. Archer knew Master Gabriel was right. Of course he was. He knew everything there was to know. But still . . .

"If I'm so overmatched," he found himself saying, "how'd I sheer off one of the horns of his war helm?"

Master Gabriel's head cocked backward. He started to speak three times before words actually came. "Are . . . are you completely mad, Archer? The Nightmare Lord could pick his teeth with your— You cut a horn from his helm?"

Archer nodded. "I somersaulted over him, went to take off his head, but he deflected the blow with his axe."

That brought Master Gabriel up short. "Well, that is something of a feat," he said. "Few have been brazen—or stupid—enough to attempt such a thing. Congratulations."

"Thank you," Archer said, feeling the red surge into his cheeks. "It was—"

"Congratulations for making yourself and everyone you love

targets of the Nightmare Lord's most focused vengeance! You realize that he can trace your entrance vortex. He probably already has."

Archer thought about Kara, the night of the derecho . . . the terrifying dream. She'd said there was a hideous pale-eyed man. *My fault.* He didn't want those words in his mind, but there they were.

"You have no idea how relieved I am that you survived relatively unharmed," Master Gabriel said, his voice mercifully gentle. "But it was not worth the risk. Not yet."

"But the villagers . . . they were storming Shadowkeep. They couldn't get through the guards. They were being slaughtered."

"Dispatched, you mean," Master Gabriel muttered. "They should not be in any mortal danger, not really. When will you understand that?"

Archer continued to stare down.

"At worst, one of your kind might awaken with a bloody nose," Master Gabriel went on. "He might be haunted by irrational fears or even develop a severe sleep disorder. No, those people who became villagers in the Dream would not likely die. The fabric keeps them safe enough physically. But this layer of protection does not exist for you. Oh, no. Not for the Dreamtreader. You might have been killed . . . or worse. Noble intent, Archer, but foolish actions."

"I'm sorry," Archer muttered.

"Sorry does not remove the scar on your back," Gabriel replied. "How on earth did you survive?"

Archer thought about the mysterious maiden's voice, but something warned him not to mention it to Gabriel. "I . . . well, I got to my anchor before he could do any real damage."

"That scar is real damage," Gabriel said, his words hissing like steam. "The Tokens of Doom are worse still."

"What are they?" Archer asked. "What do they mean?"

"Too much to tell," he said. "Go to the Creeds, for what I know is contained within them."

"Well, are they dangerous?" Archer asked, pacing in front of the small table. "I touched them!"

Master Gabriel reached out for Archer's shoulder and held him still for a moment. "You are in no danger from them," he said. "In and of themselves, they can do no harm. But, they bear an ancient and ominous significance, warning of deadly peril, especially for the Dreamtreaders. Now, Archer, I must go and go quickly. There are many decisions to be weighed and preparations to be made."

"Master Gabriel," Archer said. "You told me there were three parts to my mission. You only explained two of them."

"The last part of the mission, Archer," he said, "the most important part now, is to stay alive. Anchor first."

"Anchor deep," Archer said.

He watched Master Gabriel dissipate into a twinkling of stars, and then . . . nothing. Archer's bedroom was dark. It seemed darker than it ever had before.

FIVE

The Stalking

What brings you to Main Street in Gatlinburg? KARA WON-
dered. She'd followed him, expecting him to swing a right onto
Hemlock Avenue, his street. But Rigby hadn't. He'd kept walking
straight on Sweetbriar Lane, and now they were just a stone's throw
from the quaint shops on Main Street.

"Going shopping, are you?" Kara muttered. She watched him
slow at the intersection and then, as expected, he disappeared around
the corner to the right. She felt certain Rigby hadn't seen her and
didn't want to blunder into him, so she bided her time before turning
the corner herself. A breathless twenty count later, she slipped onto
Main Street.

Kara hung back and pretended to look at the colorful jewelry on
a sidewalk display in front of Diamond in the Rough. Truth be told,
she couldn't care less about the cheap trinkets sold in that little bou-
tique. She had her sights set on bigger treasures. Much bigger.

She glanced sideways. He still seemed consumed by his cell phone.
Even while walking, he waved his arm around, apparently making an
animated point to someone about something. She let him get a little

more ahead of her. Then, she stealthily followed. Rigby passed by Replay Sporting Goods, paused at Garner's Electronics, and seemed interested in something in the storefront window. No, Kara realized. Rigby was just checking his hair in the reflection.

After mussing his flop of wavy brown hair, he continued on. And on. Kara thought he was going to bypass all the stores until finally, he disappeared into The Creamery. *Why not?* Kara thought. *It's plenty hot enough for ice cream.* She approached cautiously, and that saved her from immediate detection when Rigby emerged from the shop a lot quicker than she'd anticipated he would. She stumbled through the picket fence gate of Lacey's Smoothies and found a seat at a little table behind a potted juniper tree.

She watched Rigby carry a colossal hot fudge sundae to his table. He was still on that phone call, but managed to take heaping spoonfuls of his ice cream.

"Look," Rigby said, jamming his spoon into the sundae, "I didn't invent the Cerebral Countdown, but I did perfect it. No, not like that at all." He paused, ate some ice cream, and said, "That was a part of the original theory. That never worked, and it was bloody dangerous."

Kara couldn't believe her good fortune. It wasn't hard to piece together the subject of Rigby's conversation, and it was precisely what Kara wanted to hear.

Rigby's voice grew tight with agitation, quieter but somehow still very easy to hear. "If you think I'll just tell you—over the phone— you're more of a nutter than my uncle. Right, and that goes for Anchor Theory too. That's why we call this a negotiation, mate. Now, call me back when you're serious."

Rigby exhaled loudly, set the phone down on the table, and took another bite of ice cream. Then, he said, "What's this, then, Kara? Are you stalking me?"

"I . . . What?" Kara blurted. "Rigby, oh, hey . . . what are you doing here?"

Rigby didn't turn or look up. He ran his index finger side to side across his phone screen. "You've been following me since the bus," he said.

"Following you?" Kara scoffed. "As if. I just came here for . . . a smoothie."

"A bit of advice, Kara Windchil," he said. "If you're going to sneak around, try not to be so beautiful."

Kara felt the blush burn in her cheeks. She willed it away. Rigby's charm was disarming, but she wouldn't let it go to her head. Not much, anyway. "So maybe I was following you a bit," she said. "What now?"

"I was thinking you'd join me for some ice cream," he said. "We 'ave a few things to discuss."

Kara's embarrassment fought a losing battle with curiosity for a moment, but she found herself getting up, skirting the picket fence, and sitting at Rigby's little table. She looked at him expectantly, projecting as much self-assurance as she could muster. Sure, he'd caught her stalking him, but she wasn't going to give him the satisfaction of watching her squirm.

He held up his index finger. "Where are my manners?" he asked. "One minute."

He was gone and back in less than a minute. "That's for you," he said, sliding a tall cup toward Kara.

"I didn't ask you for a shake."

"Well, no," he said. "But it seemed rather rude to wolf down a hot fudge sundae in front of you. Besides, what 'ave you got against chocolate?"

Kara relented and drank a sip of the milkshake. The Creamery was, in fact, her favorite ice cream shop on the planet. And chocolate was her favorite. *Lucky guess.*

Rigby rubbed the back of his hand down his long sideburn and asked, "So, why does an intelligent young lady like yourself follow the new kid? I suspect it's not because I dated the president's daughter and I'm ruggedly handsome."

"You're right," she said, her voice bright with laughter. "Your time at GIFT, while entertaining, isn't of interest to me. And I'm not looking for a boyfriend. Not really."

"Why then?" Rigby asked.

Kara sipped at her shake. "I wanted to find out if you're legit."

Rigby's eyes became amber slits. He tapped the edge of his spoon on the tabletop. Then he sighed. "Yes, I really did go to GIFT. Yes, I really am quite smart. I do have quite a bit of money, and I do live in a very big house."

"That's not what I mean," she said. "I want to know if you really are Dr. Ebeneezer Scoville's nephew."

"Well, barring a genetic test," he said, "you'll just 'ave to take my word for it. The Scovilles are on my mother's side of the family."

"Did he really go insane?"

"That's kind of personal, isn't it?"

"Well, did he?"

Rigby pushed his unfinished sundae to the side and folded his hands. His expression was an odd combination of grief and fury. He teared up just a bit, but his brow lowered fiercely. "Was he really insane?" Rigby asked. "Well, I suppose it all depends on your definition. Would you call chasing family members with an axe insane?"

"Absolutely," Kara said. "But, uh, he wasn't always insane. He did brilliant scientific work . . . in some fields, right?"

"That's right," Rigby said. He sat back in his chair and nodded once. "Oh, so that's what you wanted. Funny, that. Not too many know about Uncle Scovy's particular niche. Dream science is quite obscure, really."

"I love dreams," she said, lowering her guard but not caring. "I want to know everything there is to know about them. I thought you might, well, that is, I hoped you might, y'know, have learned something from your uncle."

Rigby smiled and leaned forward with an almost predatory gleam in his eyes. "Kara Windchil, what would you say if I told you that I could make your wildest dreams come true?"

SIX

UNLEASHED

"Tokens of Doom," Archer whispered. He thought of Master Gabriel's stern warnings from the night before. *They bear an ancient and ominous significance, warning of deadly peril, especially for the Dreamtreaders.* "They don't seem so scary." He picked up one of the dead leaves. It was shaped like a roughly hewn teardrop and looked like it might have come from a redbud tree or an ivy bush. Whatever it had been, it was completely dried out now. It felt brittle to the touch and its edges looked singed. Archer let it fall back to the tabletop and picked up the second leaf. He'd never seen a tree or shrub with foliage like this one. Though long dead and somewhat singed like the other, this leaf's shape was like that of a bat's wing. Its ribbed stem formed a kind of L, and a thin, scalloped membrane stretched between its two ends. It was weightless but gave off a faint odor, something Archer couldn't quite place, but it was not a good smell.

He put down the leaf and let his eyes wander over the feather and then to the short length of chain. These were no hardware-store-bought links. These were old metal, rigid and severe like something you might find in an ancient dungeon. Archer picked up the chain, and it clinked dully. It was still cold to the touch, but there was something different. It was lighter, maybe. Or the texture of the metal was grainier . . . perhaps due to advancing corrosion.

He dropped the chain links and looked again at the clock. It showed 11:55, and still, sleep would not come. He turned on his side again. But before his next breath, there came an anguished, wailing scream. It was his father.

Archer bounded out of bed. He'd only heard his father scream like that once before: the night Archer's mom at last succumbed to her cancer. Archer charged around the doorjamb, took three pounding steps, and pushed through his father's bedroom door. He flicked on the light, raced to his father's bedside, and froze. Archer's father lay there on the bed. His eyes were wide open. His mouth was open too, locked now in a desperate scream . . . but there was no voice. His arms were raised, bent as if trying to fend off some unseen thing. His whole body trembled.

"Dad, Dad, wake up!" Archer exclaimed. "Dad, please! You're having a nightmare!"

But Archer wasn't certain that it was a nightmare. His father turned his head slightly in Archer's direction but seemed to look right through him. His mouth worked, but there were still no words.

Archer heard movement in the hallway. He was terrified that Kaylie and Buster might see their father in this state, but he didn't know what to do. "Dad, you're having a dream!" he said. "A bad dream! That's all. It's not real!" He took hold of his father's hand.

That did something. His father let out a groan. "I tried, Em, I really tried!" His voice was a wet whisper, but Archer heard each word. "No! No, don't say that, Em! You don't mean it! Please, Em!"

Archer's father was sobbing now, the tears pouring over his cheeks and dripping from his chin. Archer embraced his father. "It's okay,

Dad," he said. "We're at home. We're in the house. You're safe now. You've got to wake up."

"Daddy?" Kaylie said from the door.

"Dad, what's goin' on?" Buster asked. He stood just behind his sister.

Mr. Keaton blinked, pulled away from Archer, and said, "Archer . . . you're here."

"Yeah, Dad," he said. "We all are."

He pulled away from Archer and craned his neck. "Kaylie, Buster . . . but where's Emily?"

"Dad," Archer whispered gently. "Mom's gone. She's been gone for years now."

Archer lay in his bed now and fumed. *First Kara, now Dad,* he thought bitterly. The Nightmare Lord needed to pay for these attacks. "I'll take you down," Archer whispered. "You'll see. If I have to pick apart Shadowkeep brick by brick, I'm going to take you down." He tossed and turned, trying to simply will himself to sleep. He wanted to charge right into the Dream, wanted to destroy each and every one of the enemy's plans, wanted to make him pay.

"Trying to destroy my anchor too, aren't you," Archer whispered. "Not going to happen. I remember the well because my mom loved it. And she loved me."

He sighed and focused on his breathing . . . and his thinking. "It all begins with the mind," Archer whispered, quoting the Creeds. "That is the real battlefield you must master. The stronger the mind, the longer and stronger you Tread."

He closed his eyes and began with *forms.* These were mental projections of his physical self, his breathing, his heartbeat, his movements. He felt the elongation and contraction of his muscles, choreographing their rippling through a series of mental exercises. He was very still in his bed, but mentally, a version of himself ran through an arduous chain of martial arts movements: lunges, sweeps, thrusts, kicks, blocks, throws, turns, and holds. After enough time, Archer switched to *patterns*. Spinning stars slid and wove themselves into place on a tapestry of ever-shifting shapes and colors. Seams unzipped and symbols danced, but Archer managed to lasso them all. One by one, he assigned them places until a brilliant mosaic was born.

Archer was about to move into *verse* when he felt the telltale heaviness on his eyelids, like feather-soft fingers were lightly pressing upon his brow. Each new breath was a release of tension and an infusion of relaxation. He felt weightless, weightless and drifting. Sleep had finally come.

Falling. That's exactly what it feels like, Archer thought. Falling though the deepest, darkest, windless night until you hit the canopy, a dense layer of dream fabric. Archer had never thought to ask Gabriel if that was its name, but canopy sure seemed right.

Oof! Floof! Archer plowed into a cushion of air. Fuzzy, swirling air. At last there was a dim gray light. Archer felt the rotation begin to take him in. He'd broken through the canopy, and a sleeve of dream fabric began to whirl around him. *Tornado slide!* Archer thought as he reclined, arms behind his head. This was his favorite part. *Booyaaaah!*

The light increased, bathing him in a constantly spiraling swirl of turbulent indigo, electrically charged amethyst, and dark steel gray. Through the translucent funnel, Archer saw a dark, mountainous landscape. In the distance, more funnels dropped down. Many more, dragging slowly across the panorama like the tentacles of a giant deep-sea jellyfish.

A bell clanged. The low, echoing tone lingered a moment and then faded. Another chime, and another. Archer twisted in the funnel and saw it. Obscured by scarlet and lavender clouds rose the steeple and face of Old Jack, the great timekeeper of the Dream. Sometimes a looming giant, other times just a faint watermark near the horizon, Old Jack was almost always visible from any location within the Dream. Its measure of moments was absolute, and Archer knew to pay close attention to its chimes. Six o'clock and the next twelve—those were the ones to beware of. *For now,* he thought. *Time to begin.*

At last, the vortex released Archer. He fell to the ground, dropping to one knee. When he rose again, he was more than Archer.

Dark shades, cooler than Gabriel's. Black vest and combat pants with armor plates sewn in. Black leather Australian bush hat and duster. Commando, cowboy, ninja, knight, warrior: 100 percent US Grade-A, absolute Dreamtreader.

Archer reached over his shoulder for his sword and anchor. He pulled the hat down tightly on his scalp and sprang away toward a Y-shaped tree. *Anchor first. Anchor deep.*

There, between the dark tree's gnarled roots, Archer pounded his anchor. Once more, the well appeared. Archer ran his fingers over its stone. *We all need anchors, Archer,* Master Gabriel had said, *in every area of our lives. If not, we drift far from the truths that matter . . . and the meaning of it all.*

"Right," Archer said aloud. "The anchor's good. Time to Dreamweave some breaches!"

Archer looked out over the vast landscape. If Gabriel was correct, and he usually was, there were far more breaches than normal out there. It was difficult to tell with the Dreamscape in its rudimentary state, like an endless misty moor at twilight, a writhing sea of fog stretching to infinity. Here and there, craggy mountains poked up out of the gloom. There were structures too, indefinite castle-like buildings, begging to be explored. And, of course, there was Old Jack. Yet no breaches showed themselves, not at this level of detail, and time was ticking.

Archer took a deep breath. This was going to take a lot out of him, he knew. But it was unavoidable. He stomped his booted foot, and it sent a shock wave through the mists. The ripple surged forward through the Intrusions and began to change everything.

From the tip of his boot, patches of wind-waving grass rolled forth. Rich forests sprouted up. Meadows bloomed and spread. Mountains became mantled with snow. The sparse castle structures became grand fortresses, each one with a walled-in township to guard, and all vastly different from one another.

Archer wiped a trickle of sweat from his brow. "Much better." It had taxed him dearly, but not as dearly as it might have to reveal this world for the first time. This was the world of the Dream, uncloaked. Archer's Dreamtreading experience and a fair supply of sheer might had washed away the interfering Intrusions to reveal, once again, the realm he'd been chosen to protect. He'd been Dreamtreading for years, and had completed the revealing process many times. Still, any exertion of will this large left Archer winded.

Winded. Archer barked out a laugh. It was all mental, really. Dreamtreading was an ability locked away in the areas of the brain that most people never got to use, except for tiny spurts while asleep. *Taxed* was definitely a better word, Archer thought. But he knew his limits. As a Dreamtreader, he had to know. To overwork the mind in a dream could mean any number of unpleasant outcomes in the real world: coma and death chief among those.

Archer shrugged away those dark thoughts. Besides, he had plenty left in the tank. He lifted the dampening he'd just spread over the landscape and felt the ripples of Intrusions surge in. More than ripples. Waves.

"Sweet," Archer said. He stomped his foot. The air shimmered, and a nine-foot surfboard, a longboard, materialized at his side. Archer released his concentration somewhat, allowing the Intrusions to have much greater impact. He grabbed the board, raced about ten yards, and leaped. He came down flat on the board and felt the current beneath him. It was rising fast; Archer rose to a knee, did the split-step to get to his feet, and then steered into the curl. "Man, if Buster could see me now!" he yelled. "Wooo!"

With a quick shift of his weight, Archer leaned down the length of the wave. Whole kingdoms raced by in a blur. The wing of dark red hair that usually half covered his eyes blew back.

"Yaaa!" Archer shouted, pumping his fist and exulting in the new speed.

Intrusions weren't made of water. Like everything else in the Dream, they were made of dreams . . . the dreams of hundreds of millions of people within Archer's Dreamscape district. In contrast to the coherent features of the Dream like Old Jack, castles, and mountains, the Intrusions were built of chaos. Every dreamer knew them, if not by name, by experience. Sudden, relentlessly changing random ideas and images blend seamlessly into one another. One minute, you're in a classroom but your teacher has a watermelon in place of his head. The next minute, a Ferrari crashes through the chalkboard bringing a forest in its wake, and then you're somehow camping with your cousin from Nebraska. Waking up from a flood of Intrusions was enough to make anyone give up eating spicy food before bed.

Not for Archer. For him, Intrusions were things of beauty, rising up in magnificent swells that propelled him anywhere he wished to go.

"Bavanda first," he muttered, leaning back and to his right. His board dropped off the dying ebb of one wave and onto the curl of a monster jammer, as he called them, shifting his heading forty-five degrees. The wave was a violent thing, surging beneath the board as if it had a mind to throw Archer up into the sky. The Dreamtreader let the wave roll itself out right at the boundary of the kingdom of Bavanda.

Archer hopped off his board and let it vanish behind him. "Razz?" he called out. "You coming on this one?"

"Right away, boss!" a high-pitched voice answered from, well, nowhere. There was a purple puff of smoke, and suddenly, a flying squirrel hovered just in front of Archer's nose: Razz. Razzlestia Celeste Moonsonnet was her full name, but Archer had given that one up long ago.

"Good to see you, Razz," Archer said. "Ready for some breaches?"

"Am I ever," she said, pulling out a barbed needle and a tiny spool of ether silk. She spun three revolutions so that her two fuzzy tails flapped together. It was Razz's way of clapping. "Uhm . . . but where are we?"

"Bavanda, for starters," Archer said. "Now perch, would ya? You're making me dizzy with all the spins."

"Oop! Sorry!" she squeaked. She curled once more and then lighted on Archer's shoulder. He shook his head. Razz couldn't be any cuter. A swirl of brown, gray, and white fur covered every inch of her. She had huge dark eyes, tiny angled ears, and a tapered face. Her nose, feet, and hands were all the same pink flesh tone, and the little black line of her mouth always seemed curled in a smile.

She had a dark, amber-colored stripe that flowed from her wrists down the length of the skin folds that served as her gliding wings. "Racing stripes," Razz called them, and she meant it. For Razz, speed was the meaning of life. Unlike flying squirrels in the Temporal,

Razz propelled herself. Archer wasn't sure how. She flapped her arms a little, but seemed to get most of her speed in the air. Maybe she used Intrusions too, Archer thought. Aside from two tails and powered flight, there was one other feature that made Razz different from her earthly counterparts: she loved high fashion.

Razz bounced on Archer's shoulder. "Well," she said, batting her eyelashes. "What do you think?"

She wore a black acorn hat like a French beret, a bright red rose scarf, and a stylish pocketed vest that seemed cut from some dark blue glossy leaf. In the sun's orange light, the vest looked very much like leather. She wore dark blue pantaloons that caught the air like sails as she posed on Archer's shoulder.

Archer wasn't sure what to say.

"I'll take your speechlessness as a compliment," she said, flicking the scarf over her shoulder.

Archer shrugged. He strode up to the vine-strewn gate of the walled city. "Hail, Bavandan Gatekeepers!" he called out to the pair of dream soldiers patrolling the perimeter.

"Hail, young Archer," the portly guard called back.

"Hail and welcome!" his thinner companion added.

"I'm looking for breaches, as usual," Archer explained. "And news."

"We have both," the first guard replied, his tunic-straining stomach jiggling. "Isn't that right, Harp?"

"That's full right, Jovi. Three breaches in Trellis Square. And you'll get more news than a man can bear from Lady Kasia."

"More than you can bear, Harp," Jovi said. "You've got the patience of an itchy toddler."

"That's enough to beat you in chess any day," Harp replied.

The bell chimed: Old Jack announcing two o'clock. The guards hadn't changed expression, not the tiniest bit. They hadn't heard it. Only Archer had.

"Thank you, gentlemen," Archer said, leaving the guards to bicker in peace at the gate. *Breaches in Trellis Square,* Archer thought turning behind the main wall. *Gabriel knew what he was talking about.*

The kingdom teemed with villagers, light, and greenery. A gentleman and his ladylove rode by on their giant oblong bicycle. It looked like it had been built from junkyard materials. But what they lacked in material riches, they made up for with a wealth of kindness and courtesy. The man saluted Archer, and the lady blew him a neighborly kiss.

Candles burned in every window, on every rail and balcony. It was like touring an open cathedral the size of a football stadium. Archer loved the warm glow of so many flickering lights. He loved everything about the city. The folk of Bavanda took great pride in growing things: trees, shrubs, flowers, vegetables, and vines. Especially vines.

Trellis Square was a grand courtyard, a hundred yards across, and fully scaffolded in every direction by white trellises. There were vines with crimson thorns and blooms of purple and white that exploded to the hand-width overhead. There were dark green cables with elephant-ear leaves and plum-colored, low-hanging fruit. And there were web-like threads of white lace weaving among the other vines. The air was filled with their "wishes": small, feathery floating seeds that glowed a faintly luminous blue.

"I'll be right back," Razz said. Before Archer could object, she catapulted herself into the air. The squirrel disappeared for a moment in the foliage, only to burst out in another place. She resumed her station on Archer's shoulder and wore one of the giant dark purple petals as a kind of cape.

"Accessorizing," she said. "It's what separates us from the beasts."

Archer couldn't help the laugh that crashed through his nose in a monstrous snort. Bavandan villagers stopped and stared, giggled, and continued on their way.

"See what you made me do," Archer grumbled, but he wasn't angry. The whole incident had lifted his spirits. Yet as Archer delved deeper into the square, any levity vanished. The vast beauty of Bavanda gave way to heartache as only the corruption of beauty can. Cobbled stone, intricate wooden lattice, and lush trailing vines fell away to a shredding kind of rot. This corner of Trellis Square looked as if it had been punctured. Dream matter surged in and out of gaps torn right into the air. There were indeed three breaches and what looked like the start of a fourth. Villagers formed small circles at safe distances and spoke in hushed voices. Many stared. A few pointed. Some wept.

"He's here!" a woman gasped.

A multitude of faces turned to Archer.

"She must mean, 'They're here,'" Razz whispered. "We are a team."

"Hush," he said. "Not now."

"Please, sir!" a wide-eyed boy said. "Please close them up."

The Dreamtreader came within ten feet of the breaches. He smelled the rot. He felt the heated air, the eerie tingling gravity. "I will," Archer said, projecting as much confidence as he could. "I'll stitch them up tight."

The crowd cheered. But Archer felt uneasy. These breaches were larger than usual, larger and far too close together for comfort. Neglect them for too long, and Archer knew what could happen. puncturing breaches in the midst of a kingdom? It was the Nightmare Lord's most brazen act to date. Brazen and deeply troubling.

Glowing with dark blue and bloody red vapors, the particle dream matter streamed in and out of each hole. Archer knelt within reach of the first blazing wound. He patted his side, and when his hand came away, he had a coil of glistening ether silk and a barbed needle. He went to work at once, plunging the seven-inch needle into the fraying borders of one breach, looping the silk through the chaotic particle matter, and then driving it down into the other border. Again and again, he stitched until he had an intricate set of laces. Finally, he pulled them tight, shutting off the pulsing flow of matter. Razz leaped down from his shoulder and went to work to patch up the tiny places where even a hint of matter flow still existed.

Archer heard cheers as he jumped to the next breach. And the next. His needle and thread moved with practiced perfection, and the Dreamtreader's pace increased. He pulled hard on the thread, closing up breach number three.

The fourth site, not yet a full breach, was more of a challenge because the breach-eating culprits were still there. A dozen scurions, the Nightmare Lord's parasitic workers, squirmed in and out of the Dream fabric. They looked somewhat like beetle grubs: pale, milky white, several pairs of caterpillar-like forelegs and back legs, and a dark globe of shell over its eyes. But scurions were not small. These were eight to ten inches long, and each one had three sets of jaws capable of tearing out scraps of reality or, if any Dream being were stupid enough to get close to them, tearing flesh from bone.

"Ooh, I hate these things!" Razz exclaimed.

Archer loosed his rendering mallet, held it with a two-handed grip high over his head, and stood over the teeming scurions. "You folks might want to stand back a bit," Archer called to the villagers.

They listened and fell away quickly, but whether they hid by the trelliswork or behind walls of foliage, they kept watch. Archer slammed the mallet down on the nearest scurion. One blow cracked its segmented shell and certainly got the creature's attention, but wasn't enough to kill it. The thing screeched and lunged for Archer's lower leg, but he'd been expecting it. The Dreamtreader slammed the mallet down once more. This time, the creature exploded, sending steaming spurts of yellowish-white gore spattering in all directions.

"I really—really—dislike this part," Archer muttered. But he continued slamming down the hammer until the scurions were duly splattered. Razz surprised Archer by grabbing up a five-inch scurion he'd missed. She took the squirming thing so high into the air that Archer lost sight of her. A moment later, several pieces of scurion fell back to the ground, followed quickly by Razz, whose grin was quite triumphant.

"What did you do to it?" Archer asked.

"Wasn't it obvious?" Razz asked. "I told you I hate scurions."

It dawned on Archer why Razz so passionately hated the crawlies. She was made of the same dream fabric as the world around them now. Just as they'd eaten away at the Dream to create breaches, scurions could consume her as well.

"Don't worry, Razz," Archer said, "I won't let them get you. Ever."

Razz chirruped, landed on Archer's shoulder, and nuzzled under his chin.

"Hey, that tickles!" Archer said, laughing and snorting. "Cut it out."

Archer reddened at the laughter from the villagers. He knew they meant no harm, but still. *It's just the way I laugh,* he grumbled mentally. *They can't help but laugh at all my snorting.*

"Where to now?" Razz asked, tapping a foot on Archer's shoulder.

"The castle," he said. "Lady Kasia might have information we need."

The words had scarcely left his mouth when the bell of Old Jack rang out five echoing chimes.

"Five?" Archer mumbled. Razz shrugged.

I lost track of time, Archer thought. He wasn't sure how. It might have been while weaving up the breaches, or maybe finishing off the scurions. It didn't matter how or when. Losing track of time in the Dream was dangerous. For a Dreamtreader, it could be deadly.

SEVEN

BEZEAL

AFTER SEVERAL GRAVITY-DEFYING LEAPS, ARCHER LANDED
at the castle gate. The Bavandan guards admitted him right away.

"Her Ladyship is in the dome," one said.

After walking up a ten-story stone spiral staircase, Archer and
Razz found themselves in a spectacular enclosed botanical garden. It
was hot and humid, the glass dome above making it feel like a tropi-
cal jungle.

"Up here!" came a voice like wind chimes brushed by a breeze.

Archer saw a flash of bright red dancing among the shrubs and
bushes high on a hill. He and Razz followed a winding path through
the greenery with bees, dragonflies, and all manner of flying insects
buzzing about. Archer turned the corner and almost ran directly into
Lady Kasia.

"My . . ." She exhaled deeply. "But you do know how to make an
entrance."

Archer bowed. "I am *so* sorry, your Ladyship," he said. "I should
have been more observant."

Lady Kasia held out her slender right arm and shook the

Dreamtreader's hand exactly once. A wide, ornamental fan spread between her delicate white fingers.

Razz landed on Archer's shoulder and tugged at his earlobe. Archer cleared his throat. "Lady Kasia," he said, "I wonder if you might have time for a few questions."

"For you," she said, "I have quite a bit of time. Join me for tea, won't you?" She snapped the fingers of her left hand. A small round table covered in a pristine white cloth appeared, along with a rose-colored tea set.

Razz squeezed Archer's earlobe even tighter. "Ow," he said. "Cut that out."

"What was that?" Lady Kasia asked, her expression darkening.

"Nothing," he said. "I didn't say that to you. It's my *friend* here."

"Oh, how sweet," Lady Kasia cooed. "Will she be joining us for tea?"

"No, thank you," Razz squealed. She leaped up into the air, spun in a tight twin-tail-circle, and vanished.

"She's not much into tea," Archer said. "And honestly, I'm on an urgent errand to repair the new breaches, so I really can't—"

"Stay for long," Lady Kasia said, completing his sentence. "I understand, but even a Dreamtreader needs refreshment now and again." She held out a chair for Archer and, with a twirl of her red sundress, sat on her own. "What questions do you have for me, lad Archer?"

Archer figured getting to the point swiftly would be in everyone's best interests. "I'm wondering about my Dreamtreading associates. Have you seen them recently?"

"Mesmeera and Duncan?" she replied thoughtfully. "Not in two moons. Why?"

Archer hadn't planned out an answer. "Well . . . honestly, we've been out of touch, and I'd like to find them."

"Dreamtreaders out of touch with each other?" she asked, pursing her very red lips. "That does not sound good. As I said, I haven't seen them recently, but when they were last here, they seemed very serious. Not at all as jovial as they usually are."

"How do you mean?"

"Well," she said. "Duncan didn't smile once, not even when I tugged on his curly red beard. And he seemed fidgety, like he had ants in his pants, so to speak."

Archer cleared his throat. "And Mesmeera?"

"She was more tense than Duncan," she said. "In fact, she didn't even seem interested in my closet this time."

Archer sat up straighter in his chair. Duncan was the most fun-loving being Archer had ever met. And Mesmeera? Dreamtreading was a job for her, but clothes were her passion. To hear that she passed up a free pass to explore Lady Kasia's famous wardrobe? That was profoundly out of character for her.

"Is there anything else you can tell me?" Archer asked.

"Sadly, no," Lady Kasia replied, sipping at her tea.

Archer started to get up. "Thank you for the information," he said. "The news worries me, but it feels important. I wish I could stay longer—"

"But you haven't even touched your tea."

"It's really kind of you but—"

"Well, there is one eensy weensy bit of news," she said. "Something that might be worth your lingering."

Archer found himself sitting again. He looked up at her expectantly. She said nothing. Kasia was beautiful. Beautiful in a way that Kara Windchil could never touch. None of the glamour girls of Dresden High School could ever aspire to this level of beauty. Lady Kasia of

Bavanda had the beauty of dreams. Mysterious, intriguing, and perfect. It was the kind of beauty reserved for royalty and the imagination.

But Archer knew better. Lady Kasia was an illusion. Someone, somewhere on earth had dreamt her into being. And Lady Kasia was dangerous. Pale skin, dark hair and brows, luminous blue eyes, and red lips. Very dangerous. Especially to a Dreamtreader. Kasia had been known to charm Dreamtreaders into letting their guard down so she could accomplish her personal agendas.

"Your tea," she said, sipping at her own.

Archer picked up his cup and sniffed the warm tea vapors. It smelled fine. In fact, it smelled fantastic. The Dreamtreader wouldn't have put it past Kasia to try to trick him into consuming gort or any other poison. But, beside the slight greenish tint, the tea was clear. Still, his knee bounced under the table, an involuntary trembling, as he sipped.

Peach, a hint of raspberry, and something that had an odd bite. He swallowed and hoped he didn't look as nervous as he felt.

"There now," she said. "You see? Refreshing."

Archer nodded, relieved that he wasn't blacking out or choking. "The other . . . bit of news?" he prompted.

She smirked and set down her teacup. "Oh, that," she said with a sigh. "All business today, are we? Well, I suppose it cannot be helped. You Dreamtreaders are rather narrowly focused."

"The news?"

"Yes, yes," she said, flicking out her fan again. But this time, the motion was anything but delicate and feminine. It was as if Lady Kasia were shooing away a wasp. Her expression changed. The fan vanished, and she leaned forward, elbows upon the table. "Well, you might just find this very much of interest, being what you are," she said. "Aside from you, there are only two other Dreamtreaders at a time, yes?"

Archer nodded. "Never more than three of us at one time," he said. "Master Gabriel always says three is the perfect number." Archer paused, thinking. "Or was it in the Creeds?"

"That is what I thought," Lady Kasia said, glancing left and right conspiratorially before continuing. "But there are rumors of others . . . others who can do what you can do."

The hair on the back of Archer's neck prickled. "Others?"

"There is a maiden," she said. "I have not seen her myself, but my guards have. She moves furtively from place to place. She travels alone in a cloak of gray most times, but always hooded and veiled. Others say she wears all white and dances among the clouds. A certain tradesman told me she dwelt in Garnet Province for a time, studying and asking questions."

"Garnet?" Archer echoed. "The libraries?"

Kasia nodded. "And the Sages," she said. "So many secrets."

"But not the Inner Sanctum," Archer said. "They wouldn't admit . . . a stranger."

"I should hope not. But one wonders about Bezeal."

"Bezeal? What does he have to do with it?"

"Who can say? But he was rumored to be in Garnet at the same time as the veiled maiden. He would sell his grandmother's soul for the right price, and he has sway with the Sages."

Archer mentally filed these things away, especially concerning Bezeal. Archer would need to see about that soon. "You mentioned others?"

"Only rumors," she said. "But since you ask . . . there has been word of an old magician and his apprentice, but they are not of the Dream. They have been seen doing wonders in the mountains of Kurdan. The strangest tales always come from Kurdan. That is, alas, all I know."

"If you hear anything else," Archer said as he stood, "you'll send word?"

"I may," she said. "Or I may summon you to my garden once more. I often find it so very lonesome."

"Have you considered a pine coon?" Archer asked. "They're cute and very resourceful. I have to go now. Many kingdoms to visit, breaches to weave up—Dreamtreading duties, you understand."

"I understand very well, lad Archer," she said. "Pine coon, indeed."

By the time Old Jack sounded its ninth bell, Archer had closed up forty-two breaches: a new personal record for one night, though Razz had helped. Together, they had also visited nineteen of the twenty-one kingdoms in Archer's district. Aside from Lady Kasia's news, Archer had learned precious little about Duncan and Mesmeera. The sum total of information was this: the last time anyone had seen them was two moons ago, two weeks in Dream time; when they had last been seen, they had seemed humorless and pensive; and no one knew where they had gone.

As Archer surfed across the Dreamscape, he wondered aloud, "What could possibly be keeping those two out of the Dream?"

"I'm frightened for them," Razz buzzed from her perch on his shoulder. "They are so kind and friendly."

"And powerful. What about their breaches?" Archer continued. "Who's weaving them if they haven't been? I need to tell Gabriel."

"Are you going to return soon, then? It's getting late."

Archer gazed up at the distant facade of Old Jack. For him, it read just after tenth toll. He'd heard it only moments before. "No," he said. "I have a little cushion of time left."

"A very little cushion."

"Yes, yes," he said. "I remember the last time. But there's one more stop on our journey tonight."

"Where?"

"Kurdan," he said. "I need to talk to Bezeal."

"Bezeal?" Razz chirruped, huge eyes blinking. "That low-down, no good, swindling, cheat-faced—"

"Temper, temper, Razz. You're just angry because he got the better of you dealing for that crate of walnut shells."

"G-got the better of me?" she spluttered. "He practically ripped my heart out! Six golds for walnut shells? I never should have agreed to that!"

"Then why did you?"

Razz avoided his glance. "They were pretty."

"See there? You may have paid a little extra, but you got quality goods."

"I know," she said. "I keep telling myself that, but, Archer, you can't trust Bezeal. Even when he speaks smoothly and kindly, he's up to no good."

"Especially when he speaks smoothly and kindly."

The Dream region known as Kurdan was a peculiar and forbidding land. The mountains were unlike any other ranges Archer had seen. They were like a tempestuous sea that had been turned to stone. Each peak and valley wore its trees and vegetation like a disguise, covering up more numerous nooks and crannies than one could explore in a lifetime. More characteristic of Kurdan than any other detail was its peculiar soil. It was a fine soil, not sand, but soft like peat moss, and

it was dark red, the color of a sunset the night before a hurricane . . .
the color of an overripe strawberry . . .

The color of clotting blood.

The soil began and ended at Kurdan's boundaries with a distinct
line between it and its neighboring realms: Varta, Wightsdown, and
Celosia. It could not have been a cleaner line if it had been drawn on
a map. *Things are weird like that in the Dream,* Archer reminded himself as
he surfed over the border. The Dreamtreader dismissed the longboard
and took to the foothills with great leaping strides. If he was to find
Bezeal before Old Jack struck his Personal Midnight, Archer would
have to go to the famous marketplace of Kurdan City.

The market was more empty than usual, after peak hours in
the Dream. Most of the shops, stands, and stalls were closed up for
the night. That didn't mean Bezeal wouldn't still be there. The real
wheelers and dealers would all still be very busy.

Archer steered toward into the Avenue of Precious Metals,
rounded past the Vault of Gemstones, and entered the Reliquary,
home of very rare inventions and keepsakes. He found two tall men
talking in whispers near a broken-out window. *Men?* Archer thought.
They might *be men.* In the Dream, one never knew.

Archer strode up to them and deepened his voice to address them.
"I seek Bezeal."

"Do you?" one of the tall beings said. He turned, revealing a
feline face with reptilian eyes. He bumped the brim of his wide hat
with the iron hook that replaced his hand. "Then you are in a hurry
to lose your shirt."

"He's fresh meat, ain't he?" the other man replied. His face was
just a bag of mottled flesh pocked with little black vacuums where his
eyes, nose, and mouth should have been. There was something familiar about this being. What it could possibly be, Archer had no earthly

idea. With his thatch of spiky yellow hair, he looked like a scarecrow come to life. Last time Archer checked, he didn't know any talking scarecrows. Well, except for the one in *The Wizard of Oz*.

The scarecrow being shifted his stance, haughtily placing a paw-like hand on the hilt of a small axe holstered at his side. "Bet'ee won't even have skin on his bones when ole Bezeal's done with him."

Archer took a deep breath. He'd been working on holding his temper. But Razz was under no such illusions. She leaped off Archer's shoulder, spun two tight circles in front of the men.

"Listen here, ya know-nothing goobers!" she squeaked, shaking her paw like a shaming finger. "When a Dreamtreader asks you for information, ya speak up, and no guff!"

"Dreamtreader, is it?" Snake Eye asked. "And I'm a great pink dragon!"

"Heh, heh, yeah, prove it," Scarecrow mocked. *There it is again*, Archer thought. There was something in this being's mannerisms that struck him as familiar. The arrogant stance, the tone, maybe? He still wasn't sure.

Razz put a paw up to her open mouth. "Uh-oh," she said before vanishing, the purplish smoke making Scarecrow cough.

"Gentlemen," Archer said. "You might want to look down."

The reptilian eyes became shrewd slits as if he might be trying to process what sort of misdirection Archer was playing.

"No, really," Archer said. "You asked for proof that I am a Dreamtreader. Look down."

Scarecrow looked down first. "Sheejey!" he gasped. "Look!"

Snake Eyes at last lowered his eyes. He grabbed Scarecrow in a desperate embrace. And well he might have. The ground was gone. A chasm had opened beneath them and fell to jagged shards of stone far below.

"That . . . that's not real!" Snake Eyes hissed.

Archer nodded, and the two men fell. They fell, kicking and scrabbling and screaming. Archer stopped them after about fifty feet and then brought them back to a hover at eye level. It was a ridiculous strain, holding those two up by force of will. A greater drain on his mental resources even than flying. Archer just hoped they didn't see him sweating. "Proof enough?"

They nodded furiously.

Archer said, "Now, about Bezeal?"

Both men pointed urgently toward a dark corner where a dim red light burned.

"Thank you, gentlemen," Archer said, and he turned to walk away.

"Wait!" Snake Eyes exclaimed.

"What eebout . . . uh . . . well . . . us?" Scarecrow mumbled.

"Oh, oh . . . sorry," Archer said. He waved his hand, and the ground was there as it had always been.

As he neared the far end of the market, he found himself yawning. "Going to have to watch that," he muttered. The chasm had been impressive, but it had taken its toll. Archer was close to exhaustion. Exhaustion that might lead to sleep. And falling asleep in the Dream meant a disaster worse than not getting answers from Bezeal. Far worse.

Archer made his way toward the red light but stepped aside so that a small group of cloaked beings could pass. Any one of them might have been Bezeal, but Archer had an inexplicable feeling that the renowned merchant still lurked ahead.

He did.

"A Dreamtreader is here," came a voice from the stand where the red light burned. "Good fortune draws near. Come. Have no fear."

Archer blinked the sleep out of his eyes and mustered all his remaining will. He needed his mind sharp for this.

"Long time no see, Bezeal," Archer said. "And, uh . . . still, no see. Where are you?"

"Look again for my kind," the voice said. "Seek and you will find unless, of course, you are most willingly blind."

Archer did look again, and a layer of shadow seemed to unfurl itself into a short, hooded figure with gleaming yellow sparks for eyes. His small, four-fingered hands were sea green and worked deftly to wrap a small mechanical device in a tawny cloth. A wide, wide smile of brilliant, broad white teeth appeared for just a moment.

"I need some information, Bezeal," Archer said.

Bezeal's smile vanished. Only his gleaming eyes remained. "To hear that you are in grave need is music to the ears of greed. Tell me, tell me, so that I might feed."

Mistake number one, Archer thought. "What can you tell me about Duncan and Mesmeera? They seem to have disappeared."

Bezeal put the bundled device into a small chest. "To search for the Dreamtreaders twain will lead thee in time to pain . . . and in the end, all in vain."

The game had begun. "I have brought you something," Archer said. He turned over his right hand, and in his palm sat a small brownish block.

"Is that . . . chocolate?" Bezeal asked.

Ha! Archer thought. He'd thrown Bezeal off. He hadn't spoken a rhyming triplet. "It is chocolate," Archer said. "And it's yours if you'll tell me what I want to know."

Bezeal's eyes flashed white. "Chocolate, chocolate," he muttered, "glorious and real, sneaky play on Bezeal, but . . . we have . . . a deal."

Archer handed over the chocolate. A green hand took it, and the chocolate disappeared into Bezeal's hood.

"Ohhhh, oh yes!" Bezeal said. "Better even than I dared to guess. Creamy and sweet, I do confess."

"There now," Archer said. "Tell me about Duncan and Mesmeera."

"Where they've gone now I cannot say, but they departed two moons ago at the break of day, in search of a relic rare and fey. This antiquity, it lingers in a dangerous place, and the Dreamtreaders twain have given chase. But alas, they are gone without a trace."

"What is the relic you speak of? Where did Mesmeera and Duncan go to find it?"

"It is a puzzle box of clever make. That is what they sought to take, leaving only mystery in their wake. To find them and it, seek the rotten core, the home of evil out on the moor. Knock not once but twice on the Lurker's door."

"The Lurker," Archer whispered, hoping he'd misheard. But Bezeal nodded. "This just keeps getting better." Duncan had once told him about the wandering madman out on the moors in the province called Archaia. No one seemed to know how the Lurker got there, but he wasn't like other beings in the Dream. He wasn't awed or cowed by Dreamtreading power. He had such power himself, but he used it to dark ends.

What was so special about the relic that Duncan and Mesmeera would risk tangling with the Lurker? Archer felt certain that Bezeal knew. But getting him to reveal what he knew would require more . . .

Wait, what would it require? Archer shook his head. He'd nearly drifted off. *More drained than I thought.* Still, he needed a bargaining chip. A chocolate bargaining chip. He breathed deeply, concentrated, and opened his palm once more. The block of chocolate was small and probably hollow, but it was the best he could do for now.

"Here," he said. "Will you take this in exchange for telling me why Duncan and Mesmeera went after this . . . this relic . . . thing?"

Bezeal snatched away the chocolate. "No," he said. "I cannot tell why they sought this thing. But for this, a new deal I'll sing. You find the relic for me to bring."

"You want me to get the relic?" Archer blurted. "You want me to go out on the moors of Archaia, knock on the Lurker's door, and ask for it . . . just so that you can have it? You're crazier than I thought."

Bezeal's eyes flashed red once and the gleaming Cheshire grin appeared again. "Find the relic, find your friends, and something more. When I have it, I'll tell you something you cannot ignore. I know the secret to cast down . . . the Nightmare Lord."

"Cast down?" Archer echoed. "You mean, as in defeat?"

Bezeal nodded.

"You mean gone . . . forever?"

Bezeal nodded again.

Archer's heart hammered against his rib cage. *If I could be the one to destroy the Nightmare Lord, I could help so many people. I could change things.* He didn't give words to the next thought, but he felt in his heart that doing such a mighty deed would somehow make his mother proud.

"I can't find the relic," Archer said, "if I don't know more about it."

"A puzzle box of silver, ornately engraved, with levers and switches for those who are brave. Take it and who knows whose lives you'll save?"

The deep-toned bell of Old Jack tolled once. Bezeal looked up suddenly, and Archer didn't know why the little merchant would hear—

The bell tolled again, ringing out before the lingering sound of the first vanished. The few stragglers still in the marketplace began to scatter. The bell struck four more times.

No, Archer thought. *Not now. Ring again. Ring again.*

But it didn't ring again. This was not his personal time. It was

Dream realm time, and it was the stroke of six: Sixtolls, the height of
the Nightmare Lord's power and a time of utter anarchy in the Dream.

Deep, mournful howls sounded in the distance. "No, not now,"
Archer growled. "I've got more questions. Too many." Archer knew
he'd run out of time, but even if he hadn't, he'd definitely run out of
bargaining chips.

"I've got to go," Archer said. "I've got to go now."

"Wait, wait! First, you must seal . . . the deal . . . with Bezeal." He
reached out his strange, pale green hand.

"You'd better not be messing with me on this," Archer said. "Or
so help me, Bezeal, I'll use every bit of my Dreamtreader power to
make sure you never make another deal."

The teeth appeared. Archer shook hands and felt a sharp prick on
his palm. When he yanked his hand away, there was a smear of blood.
No, there were two smears. One bright red. The other . . . putrid yellow. Bezeal's blood.

"A bargain in blood must never fail. Even when the Lurker begins
to wail, I hope for your sake your will won't quail."

Archer furiously wiped his hand on his pants leg and sprinted
from the market. With the howls growing louder and more furious,
Archer called up his longboard and let the waves of Intrusion propel
him swiftly back to his anchor.

DREAMTREADER CREED, CONCEPTUS 2

There exist three worlds: Temporal, Ethereal, and Dream.

The Temporal is the Dim Plane, the waking realm where all of humanity now dwells. It is in the Temporal where sight, sound, smell, taste, touch, and thought interpret reality . . . convey existence. Man says, "I think, therefore I am."

How quaint.

But the Ethereal is the true reality, the home from which mankind originated and to which mankind may yet return. The Ethereal is the Forever Realm . . . the final destination. There, and only there, will mankind discover all the senses that are. In Ethereal, living is alive.

And the Dream, well, that is why you have come to the Creeds, is it not? The Dream . . . the Realm Between. Dream is the twilight world intended to remind those dwelling in the Temporal that there is a far better land, a spectacular far-off country, that waits for them in the someday . . . in the plane of the Ethereal. Dream is the nightly nourishing of the part of each human being that longs for a new world . . . their true home. When you awaken to the Temporal, you feel it, do you not? Hauntingly familiar but achingly out of reach? It is the vague memory of life meant to be but . . . yet to be.

A Dreamtreader is a caretaker of the Dream realm. There are always three Dreamtreaders, and together, you will oversee the vast Dream horizon, the Dreamscape. It is no small task . . . because there is an enemy.

He whose will began the Tragedy of Ages is not content to torment mankind in the Temporal, but has built a stronghold in the Dream. His captain is the Nightmare Lord. This being is the one who poisons the resting mind, inflicting all mankind with images and haunts, wicked memories, and crippling fear. You, Dreamtreader, must keep this lord of fear in check.

But beware the Stroke of Reckoning. It is your personal midnight. When Old Jack, the watcher clock, strikes twelve, you must return to the Temporal. You must return . . . or be lost. Tread the stroke of one, two, three, four, five, seven, eight, nine, ten, and eleven. But beware the toll of twelve, your Stroke of Reckoning.

Just as your final heartbeat is the end of the Temporal life, Old Jack's final toll will be your undoing.

EIGHT

DARE TO DREAM

SLEEP WAS VERY DIFFERENT FOR KARA WINDCHIL ON this particular Sunday evening. She found herself in the midst of a pulsing crimson twilight. Stars sparkled vividly overhead, two moons—one full, one a sliver—hovered just above the distant mountains, and a gigantic clock tower loomed high on the horizon. But something troubled Kara.

"Am I doing this right?" she wondered aloud, turning so that the cape of her white cloak whirled and waved. Then, she rolled her eyes. *Of course I'm not doing this right*, she thought.

A moment later, Kara wore a long flannel nightshirt with matching pajama pants. And she was at the mercy of a raging, chaotic ocean of dream scenes. The waves crashed in. Suddenly, an evergreen forest surrounded her, and she stared up at a bright full moon, bigger and brighter than the other two moons combined. Wolves howled in the distance, and she thought she saw a large shadow cross the railroad tracks maybe forty yards away. *Railroad tracks?*

That's when the train came. The five-note chord blast of its horn jolted Kara off her feet. She spun around, and the massive gray locomotive was right there. Its blazing single headlight was blindingly bright, but through its white corona, she caught a glimpse of a clown's face in the train's window. *I hate clowns*, she thought just as the train hit her.

Chaos. Whirling, boiling, writhing, lightning-strike chaos. Kara felt her body thrown around like a toy. She tumbled and fell and finally came to a stop. Wobbly and disoriented, she rose to her feet just when the dragon arrived.

Kara turned around to the gleam of spade-sized, ivory-white teeth inches from her face. Gusts of sewage-smelling wind washed over her. The beast opened its jaws, showing Kara more jagged teeth and a bloodred tunnel beyond. "Oh, this is just not cool," she said.

The dragon roared. Globs of hot spittle pelted Kara.

"Not cool at all!" she yelled as the dragon swallowed her. The jaws closed, the teeth pierced, the blood flowed . . . only it was no longer blood. It was river water. Kara stood on a raft made of lashed palm tree trunks. Her cousin Lindy sat on the other half of the raft. *Gosh*, Kara thought, *I haven't seen Lindy in years.* They were floating down a river the size of the Mississippi or the Nile.

Lindy looked up, flashing those huge blue eyes of hers. *Wait*, Kara thought. Her cousin's eyes were way too big. And they were growing. The eyes continued to swell until they crowded Kara right off of the raft. She plunged into the water . . . only it wasn't water any longer. It was air. Kara plummeted through clouds, into a cold blue sky. Patchwork land far below rushed up at her.

"C'mon, Rigby," she muttered. "I'm getting tired of this."

Kara glared at the surface as it grew larger and closer with each passing second. She could now make out a few structures: houses, roads, a stadium, and lots of trees. A buffalo flew by right beneath her. It wasn't falling. It had wings. Great big Pegasus wings. And it maneuvered the sky with the skill of an eagle. "Hey," Kara said, "that's the critter from that restaurant!"

The winged buffalo was hardly the last oddity to pass her by on the way down. A pizza with antennae whirled overhead and disappeared. There was can-of-Coke blimp, a cherry-red BMW convertible with pumpkin tires, an octopus wearing a polka-dotted party hat, and a yodeling dwarf. Kara wasn't positive, but she thought she saw the Wicked Witch of the West fly by on her broom. The strangest thing, however, was the guy surfing on a touchscreen smartphone.

He wasn't surfing as in bouncing from site to site on the Web. He was standing on top of the supersized phone as if it were a surfboard. And it wasn't just any guy. It was Rigby Thames. He swooped beneath Kara and caught her just a few seconds from impact.

"Whoa," she said, "that was quite a rescue."

"Yeah, sorry about the delay," he said, shifting his hips to steer the phone-surfboard-thing back the way he had come. "You weren't where I told you to wait for me."

"I . . . I wasn't?" she asked. "But I thought . . . well, there were all these crazy dream things happening, and I wasn't sure if I was lucid dreaming or just regular dreaming."

"Oh, you're lucid dreaming, all right," he said. "You just got caught up in the dream currents."

"Dream currents?" she echoed.

"Yeah, yeah, the random bits of other people's dreams," he explained. "Remember? We talked about this."

"I know, I know, but there's so much to learn. It's kind of overwhelming."

"I understand," he said. "I can explain again. Just let us get you to a spot I know." Rigby steered the smartphone-surfboard-thing toward a thick forest at the base of a lumpy, dark mountain. In the center of the woods, there was a clearing. A lone castle tower stood in the midst of the trees. Rigby leaped from the board onto the tower balcony and set Kara back on her feet.

"Much better," she said. "Not that I minded you carrying me so much, I mean. You're very strong."

"Yeah, I guess I am," he said. "In the Dream, that is. C'mon, let's 'ave us a conversation." He led Kara to a pair of ornately carved wooden chairs, and they sat.

Kara ran her hands over the detailed artistry of the armrests. They'd been crafted to resemble the outstretched legs of a bird of prey and ended with sharp talons curling toward the floor. These weren't just big chairs. They were thrones. She liked that. She liked that a lot.

"So, about the dream currents?" she prompted.

"Right," Rigby said. He snapped his fingers and the phone-surfboard floated in through the balcony window and propped itself up on the curving tower wall between the two chairs. "Take a look at this."

The phone's screen came to life, showing a familiar surreal land-scape. "That's here," Kara said.

"Right you are," he said. "But that's here now without the full effect of the dream currents."

"Why'd they stop?"

"They didn't stop," Rigby explained. "But I dampened their impact. See, at any given time, millions—even billions—of people are asleep and dreaming. Those dreams are happening here, all of them, and at the same time. You know 'ow dreams go, right? Herky-jerky things. One moment this, one moment that, and not all of it pleasant."

"Tell me about it," Kara said. "In just a few minutes I was hit by a train, munched by a dragon, and skydiving without a parachute."

"Right useful, parachutes," Rigby said with a grin. Just then, a deep bell tolled. Rigby sat up rigidly and became still. The chimes continued: one, two, three, four, five . . .

Rigby swallowed. He waited a few more seconds and sighed with relief. "You 'ear that bell?" he asked.

"Yeah," she said. "Five tolls."

"Same here," he said. "Those bells come from the big tower you can see from almost anywhere in the Dream. That's Old Jack, the timekeeper for all who enter the Dream. We both 'eard five tolls, so that means we entered the Dream at roughly the same time. Good thing it wasn't six or we'd 'ave to cut this short tonight."

"Why?"

"Later, love," he replied. "Later. For now, the currents. Take a look at this." He gestured to the vast smartphone screen. "This is the Dream realm without dampening the currents."

Kara gasped. The screen showed utter chaos. It was like ten thousand tidal waves, crashing and slamming into each other. It was a kaleidoscope of madness. No one could follow it all. The screen faded to black.

"You can tame all that?" Kara asked.

"Yeah, sure," he replied. "Not all at once, of course. A little at a time. Just enough to keep your local environment safe. I'm going to let up on them a bit. I want you to reach out with your hands. Do you feel them?"

Hesitantly, Kara lifted her arms out. "Oh!" she said. "It's, like, feathery."

"Do you see anything?"

Kara frowned and stared out. At first, she saw nothing. Just her hands. But then, in sync with the feather pulses that she felt, waves of shadow rolled over and around her fingertips. "That's so cool. Strange, but still cool."

"Now, put your hands down," he said. "And feel them with your mind. Close your eyes at first. It helps."

Kara did just what he told her. In her mind, she imagined reaching out as before. She gasped. "I . . . I still feel them. I . . . Oh, that feels so strange. It's like my arms are still outstretched and my fingers are touching the current."

"Precisely," Rigby explained. "It's like a person who's lost an arm or leg in an accident, and yet for months or years he still feels the limb there. The physical flesh is gone, but the mental concept, including all the sensations of experience, are still stored in the mind. It's called phantom limb syndrome, and that's the power of your brain in the waking world. Here in the Dream, more of your brain is at work than ever before. You have a reservoir of power now, power you're not used to using."

"How do I tap into it, the power?"

Rigby laughed. "Here we go, Kara," he said. "You are going to *love* this. Start with your five senses: sight, sound, smell, taste, and touch. You need to activate at least three of them to get something done. More if you can. And they are ready and waiting, Kara. Waiting with ridiculous power. I'm going to release my hold on the currents. You batten them down. See, feel, and 'ear the change, and it will be."

Kara ducked suddenly as a sword swept over her head. The clown again. There were more dangers coming, but Kara didn't panic. She closed her eyes, envisioned the images beginning to dissolve, to fade, and then . . . calm. When she opened her eyes again, the clown was gone. There was barely a shadow of anything recognizable.

"No way!" Rigby exclaimed. He'd stood up from his throne and turned in circles. "You just flattened them, Kara. 'Ow did—? Wait, you didn't just dampen the currents here." He ran to the balcony window. "You've calmed this whole area."

"Is that wrong?"

"No, no," he said. "No way. That's power, Kara. You are seriously strong. The only ones I've ever seen with that kind of power are the Dreamtreaders."

"Who?" Kara asked. She looked down and to the side so that Rigby couldn't see her eyes.

"Subject for another time, love. All I'm saying is you 'ave serious dream muscle, okay? I wonder . . ."

"What?"

"Nothing really," Rigby said, glancing again to the window. "I was just thinking your little display might attract attention."

"Whose attention?" Kara asked. "Or wait, is this another one of those 'you'll tell me later' things?"

He winked. "Yep."

"So what now, then?"

"Now, it's time to meet the club and play a little. But, uh, you might want to change."

"What? Why?"

"You're still in your pajamas, Kara," Rigby replied patiently.

"Well, what can I wear?"

Rigby smiled. "We're in a Lucid Dream, darlin'. You can wear whatever you can imagine."

When Kara reappeared from the castle tower, she wore a completely new outfit. Black steel-toed boots, gray cargo pants, a form-fitting black tank top beneath a half-cinched olive-green military jacket.

"Uhm, that's something," Rigby said, laughing quietly.

"What?"

"Nothing," Rigby said with a dismissive wave of the hand.

Kara looked down at herself. "It's from that zombie show online," she said sheepishly. "You know, that one where those seven teenagers are the last real humans and they have to fight hordes of undead?"

Rigby nodded. "Yeah, sure. *Blood Company*."

"Well, the leader, Crystal Gray, wears stuff like this. It was the first outfit that came to mind. Do I look stupid?"

"Far from it," he said, averting his eyes. He leaped up and landed on his smartphone-surfboard. "Ready, then?"

Kara jumped on behind him. "I can't wait to learn how to do this," she said. "Surfing on dreams. Must be difficult."

Rigby leaned forward, and they were off, surging over the landscape and accelerating. "It's not all that hard," he said humbly. "A lot easier than flying."

"You can fly here?"

"Of course," he replied. "But it's costly. The mental energy required to project yourself through space—manipulating air currents and your own form—it's ridiculously tiring."

"That explains a lot," Kara muttered.

"What's that, love?" Rigby asked.

"Nothing," she said. "Why don't you tell me about the club."

"Don't need to."

"Why not?"

"Because we're here."

Rigby took the smartphone-surfboard into a swoop, descending rapidly toward a vast windswept field that lay in the protection of mountains and towering black trees.

The field itself was alive with activity. Here and there, explosions lit an expanse of grass. There were figures moving all around, colliding and clashing. Some of the figures looked human in shape. But some were larger. Much larger . . . and monstrous. "What's going on here?" Kara asked. "It looks like a battle."

"It is," Rigby said. "Or at least, training for one." He guided the smartphone-surfboard to a feather-light landing a hundred yards from the fighting. Then he hopped off, strode forward, and put his pinkie fingers in the corners of his mouth.

Kara was ready for a high, shrill whistle, but the sound Rigby unleashed was more like an air-raid siren. Before the sound could fade, the combatants, the structures, the fires, the monstrous shapes—everything on the field—vanished. Everything except five dark forms speeding toward Rigby.

They came to a screeching halt, and Kara took an involuntary step backward. Five teenagers approached. Rigby turned and held out an arm. "Kara, I'd like you to meet the Lucid Walkers Club."

Kara's astonished expression mingled with childlike joy. She recognized one of the newcomers. Ultra-straight black hair, anime-large green eyes, and a short but spritely figure—it had to be. "Bree?" Kara said. "Bree Lassiter?"

"Kara!" she squealed, leaping the twenty-foot gap between them. She embraced Kara, then held her at arm's length. "Cute outfit!" Bree said.

"Uhm, thanks," Kara mumbled.

"Oh, you're, like, always so stylish," Bree went on. "You look, like, familiar. Wait, I know: Crystal from *Blood Company!*"

Kara laughed and shook her head. "When did you join this club?"

"Last week after I came to Dresden High," Rigby answered for her. "You and she are the only two from your school. The rest were with me at GIFT when I was there."

Glances were exchanged between the four remaining members—a young woman and three young men—sly glances and quiet laughter. Rigby cleared his throat, and the teens shuffled into a makeshift line.

"Let me introduce everyone," Rigby said. "This fine fellow," Rigby said, referring to a wiry young man with very wide-set, beady eyes and seemingly no neck, "is Bently Aristotle Cumberland the Third."

Bently's hand shot out. He and Kara shook. "Call me Roach," he said.

"Must I?" Kara asked. "I don't care much for bugs, especially roaches."

He scratched at a scraggly patch of dark hair that stuck out like a wing above his ear. "It's an unfortunate nickname, I know," he said. "I got it in second grade because I always finished off everyone's lunches . . . you know, if they were just going to throw them away. The name kind of grew on me."

"Get the charter, would you, Roach?" Rigby asked.

"You got it." Roach scurried off in a blur. He was gone from view in an instant.

The next kid had plenty of neck and a very round head covered in red buzz-cut hair. He had sleepy eyes and a lazy smile. His arms and legs were thick and muscular but very short. Kara thought he looked like a turtle. With the plate armor vest and the heavy-duty combat backpack, he really did look like he could disappear inside it. He held out a stubby hand and said, "Reginald Emerson Hyde. But call me Hyde. Hyde with a *y*."

"As in Jekyll and Hyde?" Kara asked.

He frowned, and his eyelids lowered drolly. "No, far from it," he said, a hint of irritation in his voice. "Hyde as in Nobel Laureate Stanton Romano Hyde's grandson. I take it that you are unaware of my family's contribution to science."

"I'm sorry," Kara said. "But you're right. I'm sure your family is quite exceptional."

"Quite," he said.

The girl standing next to Hyde was a human javelin. She was thin and pointy with the longest ponytail Kara had ever seen. The tremendous blond lock fell almost to her knees.

"And you must be Rapunzel," Kara said, feeling quite clever.

"Like I haven't heard that before," she said, half rolling her eyes. "The name's Bianca Giovanni Piper. I have an IQ above 130, I'm a world-class chess player, and an alternate on the track and field team for the Junior Olympic Games. What've you got?"

Kara crossed her arms and started to speak, but Rigby cut her off. "What she has is enough mental muscle to flatten the rest of us," he said. "If given the right training, that is. She smacked down the dream current on her first try."

Kara felt a little satisfaction seeing the group's raised eyebrows, and especially noting the bob in Bianca's throat.

"Last but not least," Rigby said, "meet the Coopman, the Coopster, the Coop—"

"The name's Cooper Bertram Rutherford," said the plump African American kid with clever eyes and fine, spiky curls that looked like short, tight ringlets flying above his head. "But it's just Coop." He laughed. Rigby laughed. They all laughed.

When they shook hands, Kara found herself feeling instantly more at ease. Coop was just so friendly—and happy—that she couldn't help but relax.

NINE

TEST FLIGHT

RIGBY THAMES'S EYES WERE GLUED TO THE SCREEN OF his phone as he got off the bus. That's why he didn't see his new friend Kara Windchil until she practically tackled him.

"Oh my gosh, I thought you were totally pulling my leg," she said, following him like a giddy puppy. "All those stories about your crazy uncle and his crazy research into dreams . . . well, they were just crazy. But you were right. You were *so* right."

Rigby picked up his phone and carefully wiped it off. Other students filed around them on either side. He glared at Kara and shook his head. "You could'a broken my phone. Do you 'ave any idea the trouble . . . Bah, never mind."

Kara didn't stop smiling. She spun in little circles as if she were in a private waltz as she spoke. Then she drew near to Rigby and whispered, "I'd always hoped Lucid Dreaming could be real."

Rigby slipped his phone into the special holster on his belt. "I told you my uncle wasn't a nutter . . . well, not completely anyway."

"Oh, and the knight," she said. "Better than Prince Charming, and he bowed to me . . . and took my hand! We danced in the clouds. *In the clouds!*"

Rigby stopped walking a moment and drew Kara off to the side of the school steps. "Listen, Kara, who was this fellow? Not one of the club members, eh?"

"No," she replied slowly. "No, it was just someone I met when you told me to go explore."

"I wonder how this man found you," Rigby said. "I purposefully set up our training arena far from populated areas in the Dream. Did this person ask for anything?"

"Only the dance."

"Did he try to give you anything?"

"No," she said. "Why?"

"It bothers me that some dream being found you, that's all," Rigby said.

Kara put her hands on her hips. "It was just harmless dancing. That's all. I was in full control the whole time."

"And you're certain your *dancing* partner wasn't someone you imagined into being?"

"I'm positive," she said. "You're scaring me, Rigby."

"A little fear's not such a bad thing, love," he said. "The Dream can be a perilous place."

Kara rolled her eyes and grabbed his arm. "Can we go again . . . tonight?"

Rigby eyed her warily a moment and said, "Of course we can."

Kara actually leaped for joy. "I'm not going to be able to think straight today at school. Or tonight? I hope I can cross the REM sleep threshold quickly. But what to do? Another planet? Fly on a dragon? Be a queen?"

"Move on!" a teacher called out from the top of the school's steps. "Get to homeroom, people!"

"Tough to decide when anything's possible," Rigby said, taking her arm. After a few steps, he stopped. "Wait, did you just say 'REM sleep threshold'? Where did you . . . 'ow do you know that term?"

Kara blinked a moment but then brightened. "You told me," she said. "You were talking about your uncle's field of research, the REM sleep threshold and all that complicated stuff. Don't you remember?"

"I don't, actually," he said. "Funny, that."

Kara sighed and lightly touched his shoulder. "Rigby, what time can we go?"

"If I finish my homework by nine, I'll hit the sheets around ten." Rigby scratched his head. "It usually takes me about a half hour to get to sleep. I'm sure I'll be out cold by 10:45 or 11:00. I'll come get you after that."

"What are you two talking about?" Bree Lassiter asked, bounding behind them.

Rigby took Kara's arm on one side, Bree's on the other. "The club, of course," he said. "Whatever else is there to discuss?"

It was a rough Monday morning for Archer. The Dreamtreading missions over the weekend had been exhausting. That plus chores and homework were more than enough to drain his batteries. He was late to the bus stop and had to sprint to get the driver's attention. He nodded off in the back of the bus and banged his head on the emergency exit latch. He got off the bus dead last, just in time to see Kara Windchil slam the new kid Rigby Thames with a crushing embrace.

Figures, Archer thought, shaking his head.

"Did you finish the lab write-up for Chem?" Amy asked.

Archer blinked. That little corner vault where half-remembered truths are kept swung wide open. "Awww, man, I took it home but never finished it."

"Archer, it's 40 percent of our grade!"

"Tell me about it," he said. "Dead man walking here."

"Sit with me at lunch," she said. "I'll help you finish."

"I don't want to copy."

Amy slapped his shoulder. "I wouldn't let you copy," she said. "But, I'm better at Chem than you are. I can be . . . your resource, yep."

Archer stopped walking and looked at his friend. She wore her wintery-blond hair back, always. No makeup, ever. Sweats, T-shirts, or jeans . . . and an occasional spring dress, but nothing trendy. Still . . . she was pretty in a mousy sort of way.

He stopped his line of thought right there. This was, after all, Amy Pitsitakas he was thinking about. Longtime friend, reliable, steady as the sun, and twice as cheery. Not quite on Kara's level, but still, a friend.

"Thanks, Amy," he said. "I can definitely use the help. Either that or face Dr. Pallazzo's wrath."

"Wouldn't want that." Amy giggled over her shoulder as she walked away.

As if a TV channel changed, Archer's thoughts went back to Kara and Rigby Thames. He watched them, practically arm in arm, chatting like neighbors as they entered the school's front entrance.

I wish I knew what they were talking about.

Archer wandered to homeroom. He had a lot on his mind and one more day to wait until Gabriel's next expected visit. It was a weighty burden to bear alone. Forty-two breaches one night, fifty-seven the next. Things were getting out of control. And on top of that, he'd been tricked into a blood pact with Bezeal. Gabriel was certain to flip out.

He flopped down into his seat, opened his binder, and skimmed his schedule of classes. American Lit and Math before lunch; Psychology, Gym, and Chemistry after.

"Snot buckets," he muttered. He'd brought the Chem book instead of Math by accident.

He strode up to the teacher's desk. "Mrs. Snodgrass, I need to go back to my locker for a different book."

"Best hurry," she replied. "Announcements are about to start, and you know Mrs. Mears will be doing hall sweeps."

"Can't you write me a pass?"

"It's your responsibility, Archer," she said. "Hurry up."

Archer took off at a trot, ducked through the seniors meandering through he hallway, and charged to his locker bank. He hit his combination without a hitch, reached for his Math text, and froze. Out of his peripheral vision, he caught sight of Guzzy Gorvalec and his entourage of bullies. Archer didn't think they were looking his way, but they were definitely moving in his direction up the hall.

Archer knelt to keep as low a profile as possible and feigned searching for a book. But his eyes kept darting toward the approaching threat. Guzzy looked agitated, angry. The rest of his cronies just looked tough and mean. They were deep in some conversation as they passed behind Archer. He heard snippets of what they said until they'd moved out of range.

". . . better think twice," Guzzy had said.

"Done it before," said another voice, maybe Devery Gates. ". . . do it again."

"You thinkin' Gallows Hall?" a third voice, high and whiny. Definitely Randall Pell.

"Friday," Guzzy said, ". . . right after Gym."

When Archer sat down again in his homeroom, he didn't focus much on the morning announcements. He stood up absently and robotically recited the Pledge of Allegiance. Gallows Hall was the not-so-pleasant nickname students had given to the infamous dark hallway near the gymnasium. If there was going to be a fight or any kind of illicit deal, Gallows Hall would be the place. And if Guzzy and his crew were involved, things could get very bad in a hurry.

It was ten o'clock at night, and Archer couldn't find his father.

"Dad?" Archer called down the basement. "Dad, you on the computer?" There was no answer.

He checked the den. Not there. He leaned over the couch and looked out the picture window. His father's car was there. *Where is he?*

Archer strode out into the kitchen. It was dark. So was the dining room beyond. But light gleamed from the glass doors leading to the screened-in porch. He remembered how his mom, when she was alive, always forced his dad to go out on the porch to smoke his weekly cigarette.

"It's only one cigarette a week, honey," he'd told her so many times.

"It's one cigarette too many," she'd always told him. "Out you go."

Archer moved slowly toward the glass doors. His dad was in his usual chair in the corner. He could stare out over the backyard hill, down to the well. Archer cringed. His father's hand held a still-burning cigarette and trembled. He'd been smoking more than once a week lately, Archer knew, but the tremors were a more troubling development.

Ever since the nightmares started, Archer thought.

He opened the sliding glass door slowly so as not to startle his father. "Dad, it's getting kind of late," he said. "Why don't you come on in?"

His father took a long drag on the cigarette and didn't turn. "Just enjoying the cool breeze," he said.

Archer didn't think his father was enjoying anything at the moment. "It's not a cool breeze, Dad," he said, rubbing his upper arms. "It's cold."

His father shrugged and flicked cigarette ash.

Anchors.

The thought drifted unsolicited into Archer's mind. *Dad's lost his anchors. He's drifting now.* Archer walked around the little glass table so he could face his father. "Dad, look at me," he said.

Archer's father turned his head so slowly it gave Archer the creeps. There seemed to be way too much white in his eyes. He looked terrified.

"Dad, I want you to listen to me," Archer said. "That dream you had the other night. That's a bunch of bunk. You know that, right? You did everything for Mom. You took her to talk to the pastor twice a week. You worked two jobs. You flew her all over to all the specialists. And when she was going, you stayed at her bedside and held her hand."

He blinked exactly one time. "Should have done more."

"Remember what Mom said to you at the . . . at the end?" Archer asked. "She said you were the best man she ever knew, that she'd wait for you in heaven. She never blamed you. Not one bit."

There came such a scream from somewhere in the house that every hair on Archer's neck, arms, and legs stood straight up. It had been a terrible shriek, high and wailing. *Kaylie*, Archer thought at first, but there was something in the pitch or tone. *Not Kaylie. Buster!*

"Dad, that's Buster!" Archer rounded the table and raced for the stairs. His father's slower footsteps followed.

Leaping into Buster's bedroom and hitting the lights, Archer stopped cold. He couldn't make sense of what he saw. There were Buster's feet, flailing frantically by the headboard. There was a sheet waving around, and there was the sound of Buster's screaming and crying, but Buster's head was not visible.

Archer didn't waste another second. He ran to the bed and discovered his little brother had somehow pushed the mattress askew on the box spring and managed to fall through the gap in the headboard. And he was thrashing violently.

"Buster! Buster, stop!" Archer cried out. "Don't! You're going to cut yourself!"

Archer's father appeared. "I've got his feet," he said. "Gentle now. Let's get him out of there."

Archer grabbed one of Buster's shoulders and used his other hand to try to hold his head steady. But it was tough, a lot tougher than Archer thought it could be. Buster was strong, and he was out of his mind with terror. Finally, he slid free. But his forehead was bruised, and his nose bled.

"No, no, no!" Buster cried. "I don't wanna die! No! Please!"

The way Buster said "please" ripped Archer's heart. "Buster, it's a dream!" he said. "Look at me! Buster, look at me!"

Buster finally blinked. His eyes narrowed and he flung himself at Archer. He grabbed Archer so hard that he couldn't breathe. But then Buster slid off of him and flew at their father.

Archer watched them embrace and was glad for it. Maybe a hug was just the thing his father needed. But one thing was certain: Buster hadn't needed that nightmare.

"I was at the beach, Dad, y'know?" Buster explained. "I got caught in a reef and couldn't paddle out. That's when the shark got me. Dad, I saw its teeth bite down on my leg. It wouldn't stop. There was blood everywhere, and the thing just kept biting down. It just kept biting me!"

Archer made fists so hard his knuckles cracked.

TEN

THE LURKER'S TOYS

"A THIRD HAND MIGHT'VE PROVED THE DIFFERENCE," Mesmeera said, creeping up the tunnel behind her Dreamtreading partner.

"What? Archer?" Duncan replied, finishing each word with a huff. "He's a loose cannon."

"If he is a loose cannon," she replied, blowing a sandy-colored lock of hair out of her eyes, "then he is because he followed after you. He's strong. That's all I'm saying. We may miss his mental muscle before we're through."

"Not likely," Duncan replied. He stopped at the fork in the tunnel and worried at the scraggly edge of his red beard. "Most of the Lurker's threat is an overdeveloped legend. After all, he's a Lucid Walker, not a Dreamtreader."

"Still," Mesmeera countered as she crouched beside him. "You know what Master Gabriel would say. He'd—"

"Master Gabriel's Incandescent Armor would go *supernova* if he knew what we were doing right now." Even in the shadowy passage,

Duncan's eyes blazed. "To put it mildly, Master Gabriel would not have approved."

"Perhaps . . . we should have appealed to his greater wisdom."

"Look, we made our choice when we crossed the Archain border. How could we pass up an opportunity to end it, to burn Number 6, Rue de la Mort to the ground forever?"

"But can we trust that weasel?"

A bell tolled, its clear tone rolling up the tunnel. Duncan counted. "Nine bells," he said. "We'd best keep moving."

"Agreed," she said. "But you didn't answer my question."

Duncan made up his mind. "We go left," he said. "And to answer your question, I don't know. Heaven help me, Mes. I just don't know."

The left-hand tunnel wound deeper through the hard stone of the cliff side, rising and falling, opening enough so they could stand or tightening to the point where Duncan and Mesmeera could barely crawl. On and on they traveled until, on a slight incline, Duncan abruptly stopped.

"Not a dead end?" Mesmeera said.

"No, no dead end. Don't you smell it?" he asked.

"Smell what? Other than the musty stone, I—" Her mouth snapped shut. Her eyebrows, cheeks, and upper lip converged, scrunching in the center of her face. "Oh, oh, that's . . . that's horrid. No, beyond horrid. Abominable."

"Few scents are as distinctive as rot," Duncan replied. "There are dead things ahead, but something else too."

"Something sharp," she agreed. "Almost chemical."

"I think chemical is precisely what it is," Duncan said. "The Lurker is known for such things."

"Do we go on?" she asked.

"We are Dreamtreaders," he said. "We rule the Dream."

"Shepherd, you mean, not rule?" she said quietly. "Right?"

Duncan didn't answer. He turned and continued the gradual climb. One toll of Old Jack later, he signaled a halt. "Ten bells," he whispered. "And we've come to the end of the tunnel. There's a chamber here. Ah, the smell is so strong here. Barely breathable." He knelt at the edge and motioned for Mesmeera to join him there. "Careful. Don't overextend, but look. What do you think?"

"Odd for a delved tunnel to empty out so high on a wall," she said, squinting.

"I thought so as well." He peered out of the round, three-foot-wide opening. Outside of the tunnel, the chamber floor was a drop of at least fifteen feet. Likely more.

"That rotten smell is aggressive here," Mesmeera muttered, gazing down into the dark room. "Biting and pungent. I can only imagine what's down—Oh. I definitely don't care for these accommodations."

"What do you see?" he asked. "Your eyesight is better in the shadows."

"You really don't want to know."

"Nonsense, Mes. What's down there?"

"Devices," she said. "Wheels, chains, racks, manacles, and all manner of pointy things. This is a torture chamber."

Duncan swallowed. "Perhaps you're right. I didn't really want to know."

Mesmeera focused her will. A narrow flight of stairs materialized. She clambered out of the tunnel and stood, sweeping her heavy cape behind her. Then, fierce green eyes shining in the twilight, she drew her twin daggers and began her descent.

Duncan lingered a moment. He eased back against the tunnel wall and looked behind him. He'd heard something back up the passage. No, not a sound. It was more of a shift in air pressure, like a pulse.

Mesmeera called in a breathy whisper, "You coming?"

Duncan took one last look down the tunnel, shrugged, and followed his partner into the chamber below.

Each new breath brought a gust of decay. Breathing became a chore. Then, he stopped on the stairs. *I am an incredible idiot,* he thought. He looked down at his hand and willed a little green bottle into being. It was McPhereson's, the strongest cologne he could think of. He splashed it all over his cheeks, under his nose, and even soaked his beard.

He was suddenly overwhelmed with ginger and lime. "That's obnoxious," he muttered. "But better."

On the ground, the Dreamtreaders paused. Mesmeera stared at the floor and strode a few paces. "There are dark stains," she said.

"Blood," Duncan said, catching a chill. "It trails away."

"In all directions." Mesmeera made a deep rumbling sound in the back of her throat. "Still think the Lurker's abilities are just legend?"

"The Lurker chooses to dwell not far from the Lord of Nightmares," Duncan said. "What did you expect?"

"Still," she said. "Something lingers here . . . besides the stains and the stench. It is as if misery is in the air."

"I feel it too" he said. "This may be the best place to anchor."

"Here?" Mesmeera asked.

Frowning, Duncan said, "It is most likely that danger will find us here. Anchor first."

"Anchor deep," she replied.

Only they were not anchoring first at all. The two Dreamtreaders had been in the Dream for ten strokes of Old Jack, but they had waited to anchor.

"A get-out-of-jail-free card," Duncan had called it. His plan: if things got ugly, the anchors would be close by, allowing quick escape.

When Duncan pounded home his anchor, the tall shaft became a miniature lighthouse. It was the Southerness Lighthouse in the village of the same name in South West Scotland. Duncan had such fond memories of the place. His granddad had taken young Duncan there, taught him to fish, and told such incredible stories.

Mesmeera's anchor shaft became the tall rose trellis her late husband had built for her just before his accident. She leaned close and inhaled. "I miss you," she whispered.

Then, intuitively, without another word, the Dreamtreaders split and began to search the room. Duncan tried to ignore some of what he saw there. He failed. There was a table so full of shackles, blades, straps, and chains that he had to turn away lest he imagine their implied use.

But there were also chests and shelves to explore, and Duncan set to it. One glance over his shoulder at Mesmeera showed him that she was doing the same.

"Stay away from the corners of the room," Mesmeera called.

Duncan looked up. "What? Why?"

"The smell," she said. "It's coming from drains in the corners."

"Drains? Drains for what?"

"You don't want to know."

"I'll take your word for it this time," Duncan said, shuddering. His next step, however, did not find solid stone. His booted foot came down on something that squished. He even heard the squish. "No," he muttered. "I don't want to know."

But he looked. Beneath his foot, ruined and dead, was a slender eel-like creature. Against his better judgment, Duncan bent down to examine it more closely. It had pale, globular eyes and a sphincter for a mouth, lined with concentric circles of teeth. "This is a scurion!" Duncan exclaimed.

"What?" Mesmeera called from across the chamber.

"A dead scurion is here on the floor. I stepped on it."

"There are more in the drains," she said. "Big ones. Disgusting."

"Why would the Lurker have scurions here?" Duncan asked, mostly to himself.

"The Nightmare Lord doesn't seem to care where the breaches are so long as there are enough of them to keep us busy."

"Perhaps that is it," Duncan said, his mind much like a parked car idling. The engine was running, but the vehicle wasn't going anywhere. "Remind me, Mesmeera, to mention this to Master Gabriel."

"You mean, after he's finished yelling at us?"

Duncan shut his eyes tightly. "Yes," he whispered. "I mean then."

He quickly distracted his thoughts with the contents of another cabinet. The variety of oddities in the Lurker's chests was certainly distracting. There was something that looked like an eggbeater made in the Middle Ages, but its blades seemed far too large and jagged for simply making breakfast. There was also a tool with a gripping vice at one end and saw teeth at the other. Duncan found the grip fit his hand readily, but when he made a fist, the saw teeth snapped shut like the jaws of a shark. He quickly put that aside and hesitated to pick up any of the other sinister-looking implements.

But a long, segmented tube captured his curiosity. "This looks harmless enough," he muttered. There was some give to it, and he discovered that it telescoped out, stretching to nearly three feet in length. He pulled on it a little more, heard a faint click, and a stark blue flame flared at one end.

"Oh," he whispered. "Oh, dear." The flame disappeared as he collapsed the tube. Then he saw something and gasped. He snatched up a pewter-gray box. "Mes, come here!"

She appeared in a breath. "What smells like stir-fry with lime in it?"

"That would be me," Duncan said. "But look here." He held up the box.

"Is that . . . is that it?" she asked. "It doesn't look silver."

"Tarnished is all," he said. "There's a small hand crank here." He took hold of it and began to turn.

"Maybe you shouldn't do that," Mesmeera warned.

A faint tinkling tune played as Duncan continued to turn the crank. "Nonsense, Mes, it's too small to be any real danger—"

An impossibly large wolf exploded out of the top of the box. Its eyes blazed red. Its sword-sized teeth snapped and gnashed, and hot spittle flew.

Duncan dropped the box and crashed backward. His hammer was pinned, caught between his back and the floor. He reached for his short sword instead, but it was too late. The mountain of muscle, fur, claws, and teeth was upon him.

Gaping wolf jaws filled Duncan's vision. He hopelessly turned his head. He heard a strangling gurgle and thought, at first, that it was his own. He imagined drowning in his own blood as the beast tore into him.

But suddenly the wolf was yanked away. Mesmeera had some kind of spiked chain around the creature's neck. She pulled back fiercely, drawing the beast backward with every strained tug.

"Now would be nice!" Mesmeera yelled.

Duncan leaped to his feet, started to reach for his hammer, but then thought better of it. "Be ready to stand free," he warned. He held his hands high and summoned up whirling fistfuls of molten rock.

Mesmeera released the wolf and dove behind a massive steel chest. Duncan thrust his hands forward, unleashing gouts of lava at the creature. The monstrosity didn't just catch fire. It became engulfed.

Crying out, writhing and shrieking, the wolf seemed to implode on itself. In a fiery blink, the wolf vanished back into the gray box.

"And you called Archer a loose cannon," Mesmeera said, dusting off her leather vest.

"Enough, woman," Duncan muttered. "And thank you."

Mesmeera did not respond but said, "Uh-oh."

Duncan followed her line of sight to the opening of the tunnel from which they'd come. It was gone. No tunnel now at all. Just solid stone. "That can't be good," he said.

The chamber exploded with sound: clangs, growls, crashes, screams, plunks, smacks, and shrill cries. It was coming from all four corners of the room.

"Treader's oath!" Duncan exclaimed. "What is that calamity?"

As if in answer, a hollow, high voice rose above the tumult. "You've discovered my toy chamber!" it cried. "So it must be playtime!"

"I'm going to need this," Duncan muttered, drawing out his great sledgehammer from his back.

Figures poured into the room from all four corners. Fearsome, terrifying shapes, but no one like the other. There was a giant spider with human hands and a lion's head. Bats swooped down, but one had a snake's body. The other, a scorpion's venomous tail. A crab-clawed rhinoceros charged toward the chamber center, and a great eagle with jellyfish tentacles dragging beneath it wafted down from the ceiling.

"I knew this was a bad idea," Mesmeera said.

"Gloat later," he shot back. "Fight now!"

Mesmeera leaped, her daggers flashed, and she shredded one of the bats' wings. The giant spider-thing grabbed the Dreamtreader's ankles and tried to draw her down toward its jaws. Two dagger swipes later, the creature found itself missing two of its hands.

Mesmeera tumbled beneath the spider and thrust her daggers into its bulbous abdomen. She was sorely tempted to yell, "For Frodo!" But in the end, smeared with ichor and gore, she grumbled, "The Lurker has a sick idea of toys."

"Tell me about it!" Duncan yelled, grappling to keep the rhino-crab's claw away from his neck. Duncan thrust the creature away, providing just enough clearance for the hammer. The Dreamtreader turned like a baseball slugger, generating as much force as he could, and slammed the hammer head against the rhino's shell-covered neck. There was a horrendous *Crack!* And the beast went down.

One after the other, they came: creatures, mutated forms, night-marish monsters. A gigantic centipede with feline limbs and an eagle's head, an ogre with a shark's jaws, an entire herd of charging bulls, each with a razorback spine. Mesmeera and Duncan fought them off, but it took its toll on each Dreamtreader's reservoir of mental energy.

A bull slammed into Duncan, sending him cartwheeling through the air. The Dreamtreader crashed to the chamber floor, rolled to his feet, and threw his will at the creature. A fourteen-foot-tall Spanish matador appeared, but it skipped the flourishing red cape and took the beast out with a series of thin swords.

Mesmeera called up a tornado full of bricks to neutralize the ogre but found herself wheezing from the exertion.

"This is so much fun!" the Lurker crowed, still unseen. "What a battle!"

"Show yourself!" Duncan bellowed.

"The creation and the artist are one and the same," the enemy retorted. "I am they, and they are me."

"He really is quite mad!" Mesmeera exclaimed over the tumult of battle. She spun and sent more than a hundred rope lassos to hog-tie the centipede. But even she, with her seemingly endless will and imagination, found herself drowsy and stumbling.

The Lurker called out again, "An epic struggle of two titans! Ah, so good. This is like The Rumble in the Jungle!"

Mesmeera flattened a bull with a concrete fist and sidestepped another just before she would have been gored. The creature disappeared off the edge of a cliff Mesmeera had created.

"Ali, Foreman, going toe to toe!" the Lurker exulted. "Punching, counterpunching—this is grand!"

"What is that lunatic babbling about?" Mesmeera yelled, a pronounced wheeze in each word.

Duncan used a bazooka to take out a pair of dragon-headed gorillas. There was a flash, a hair-sizzling explosion, and then a horrible smell. But it had been a clumsy attack. Duncan had let himself be too close to the explosion. The concussion wave knocked the Dreamtreader off his feet.

He shook off the cobwebs, clambered to his feet, and shouted, "Boxing! He's talking about boxing! Big fight back in the 1970s. Heavyweight bout. Muhammad Ali and George Foreman."

Mesmeera coughed and wiped the dust out her eyes. "Great," she said. "He's a raving mad lunatic and a sports geek." She took a defensive position right behind Duncan just as the sheep arrived.

Duncan blinked and tried to focus his weary eyes. From all four corners of the chamber, sheep by the dozen came wandering in, converging on the Dreamtreaders in the center of the room.

"What is this?" Mesmeera asked.

"I don't know." Duncan stared. They weren't sheep mutations. Just big, dumb cotton balls with little black faces and bright, innocent eyes.

The chamber filled with bleats and brays, snorts and grunts. The effect of the cacophony was dizzying. "Can't get my thoughts to settle," Duncan said. "Can't see straight."

Mesmeera backed into him. They both startled. "Some foul wizardry," she muttered. But the sheep were crowding in on them.

"Wizardry?" the Lurker protested, still unseen. "I do not dabble in witchcraft. I am no warlock. This is the power of the mind. Dreamtreaders should know this above all."

"We should defend ourselves!" Duncan exclaimed.

"Yes," the Lurker replied, his voice gaining a haunting echo. "Yes, you should."

But Duncan couldn't think of a thing to create. No weapon came to mind. Nothing came to mind at all. There were only those confounded sheep. And, as the Dreamtreader watched them, they stopped their wobbly advance. They stopped bleating as well. The chamber fell silent.

"I don't like this," Mesmeera whispered.

"Wait," Duncan hissed. "Something's happening." In the shadowy half-light, the fluffy pelts of the sheep seemed to pulse . . . to blend. It was as if their wool became animated, turning to boiling fog. The dark sheep faces and limbs seemed to melt away. The Dreamtreader felt as if he was standing in a sea of churning white.

What had been the clumpy mounds of sheep began to shred and move independently. Things began to appear in the mist. Skullish, leering faces, vacant socket eyes, and sharkish grins. All at once, the rippling white surged up in a hundred places at once. Ghostly, wraithlike forms shrieked through the air toward the Dreamtreaders.

At the same moment, blackened figures came shambling across the chamber floor. They were as dark as charred meat, bent and knobby, rigid with muscle and horn. They reminded Duncan of the hunched gargoyles that crouched atop the gothic buildings in Glasgow.

A jolt of fear stabbed through Duncan's dazed mind, and just then, he realized that Mesmeera was screaming at him.

"Fight, you ginger lummox!" she shouted. "Wake up and fight!"

Several of the dark shamblers slammed into Duncan, but now the Dreamtreader knew his mind. He willed a pair of sawed-off shotguns into his hands and fired, launching the creatures clear across the room. But the tide of shrieking vapor ghosts came rushing in. He reached up and found the cable he'd just imagined. He triggered the pulley system near the ceiling and let it haul him up, off of the ground.

"That was impressive!" the Lurker crowed. "I thought I had you, but such quick thinking. You live to fight another round. Bravo, Dreamtreaders!"

Mesmeera was flying now. Not hovering or floating. She flew for her life, racing away from the ghostly shriekers. She needed to pull away, give herself enough room to wheel around and fire . . . *something*. Bounding from corner to corner, she finally got the clearance she needed. She spun, braced herself against the chamber wall, and unleashed a torrent of . . .

Piranhas. Big piranhas with exaggerated jaws full of exaggerated teeth. It was an entire school of the creatures, jaws snapping and teeth gnashing as they swam-flew toward the shriekers. But before the first piranha could chomp on an enemy, the whole school began to pulse. One by one, they morphed into something more like giant goldfish.

"No!" Mesmeera cried out. She extended her will, trying to regain control, but found her reservoir of mental energy all but exhausted.

The ghostly shriekers batted the fish aside and streaked toward Mesmeera. She raised a hand to ward them off, and, for a flickering moment, a barbed-wire fence kept the creatures at bay. But the Dreamtreader's will drained away. The fence vanished. Mesmeera slid slowly down the wall.

And there, on the chamber floor, the ghostly creatures surrounded the Dreamtreader. They whirled around her torso and became massive, ponderous chains. They constricted, and Mesmeera groaned. But there was nothing she could do. She could barely breathe, much less do anything to break the chains. She was stuck tight. Captive.

From across the chamber, Duncan saw Mesmeera fall. "No!" he roared. He gathered the precious little mental energy he had left and vaulted over a throng of dark shamblers. He almost made it to her side, but a skeletal claw took hold of his shoulder and yanked him off of his feet. He felt himself weightless for a moment and then sprawled hard on the floor. When he looked up, he saw the Southerness Lighthouse . . . his anchor. For a bewildering moment, he was there again, with his granddad. They sat with their fishing poles, lines dangling in the lake. The sun was going down, and mayflies skittered across the surface of the dark water.

"Precious little time left, eh, Duncan?" his granddad asked.

But the voice instantly warbled into something unfamiliar. With a jostling start, Duncan woke to the reality. His dear granddad was long dead. This wasn't the real lighthouse.

But it was his anchor.

Duncan watched its small lantern rotate once and then looked away. It was no decision, really. He couldn't leave Mesmeera. With some effort, he clambered back to his feet. Old Jack tolled out eleven strokes. *Only one hour left,* Duncan thought through a haze. He wobbled drunkenly for a moment and managed to clear his mind just as two dark shamblers reared up in front of him.

He had little left, summoning a set of brass knuckles. The metal shaped to fit around his knuckles wasn't actually brass, but something closer to wrought iron. They felt heavy in his hands. "I'm gonna go old school on you, lads!" he cried. "This is for Granddad!"

The first shambler clawed for Duncan's face, but the Dreamtreader ducked and fired a bone-crushing blow beneath the creature's swiping arm. Duncan had no idea if the things had ribs, but whatever was there crunched, and the thing went down in a heap.

"Down he goes!" the Lurker exulted. "What a left uppercut by the challenger!"

The next shambler came with both clawed hands for Duncan's throat. The Dreamtreader covered up, defending with his arms and the back of his fists. He felt the shambler's cold talons rake his arms. The sting was fierce and precisely what Duncan needed to wake up a little. He sidestepped, planted his feet to generate leverage, and then launched a succession of jackhammering jabs. The shambler fell backward but couldn't escape Duncan's thunderous right hand. His iron-covered knuckles connected with the creature's face, and the thing went rigid, toppling like a felled tree.

"Astounding right hook by the challenger!" the Lurker shouted. "But . . . can . . . he . . . keep . . . it . . . up?"

The shamblers and shriekers kept coming. Duncan fought on. More jabs, more hooks, more uppercuts, and even a few crosses. Creatures went down left and right. But only for a few moments more.

Duncan's heart felt ready to burst. He breathed in wet gasps. His arms felt leaden. That's when he understood at last what the Lurker was doing to him.

It was called rope-a-dope. Muhammad Ali used it in the Rumble in the Jungle bout, covering up and leaning against the ropes while the hard-punching George Foreman exhausted himself. As soon as Ali saw that Foreman was spent, he bounced off the ropes and tore into his opponent, knocking him out in the eighth round.

"That doesn't bode well for me," Duncan muttered just as a fist the size of a cement mixer knocked him across the chamber. He landed hard, slamming into the wall and collapsing into a jumbled pile of arms and legs. Before he could take another breath, the shriekers surrounded him and formed massive, restraining chains.

"Down goes Duncan!" the Lurker yelled. "Down goes Duncan. Down goes Duncan!"

Duncan could barely keep his eyes open. In his blurry vision, all he saw was a hulking slate-gray mass approaching. The room shook with each heavy footfall. Suddenly a hand thrust outward, and Duncan's lighthouse anchor instantly flattened. Mesmeera's trellis was crushed a split second later.

"Do you have any idea what happens to the human mind when you are trapped in the Dream?" the Lurker asked. "It becomes fused, sealed off from the Temporal forever. It means . . . it becomes *stronger.*"

"I don't have enough left in the tank," Mesmeera whispered, her eyes just quivering slits now. "I cannot free myself."

"Nor I," Duncan hissed back as he slumped. "I can barely keep my eyes open."

"I have lost all functioning there," the Lurker went on. "But the brain does not die. It rewires itself for its new environment. And unlike you Dreamtreaders, whose minds are split between worlds, I am completely immersed in the Dream. Every cell of my brain has become supercharged for power here."

"But you are trapped," Mesmeera said. "You cannot go home."

"This is my home now."

"I am sorry for your fate," Duncan said. "If there were anything I could do to change it, I would. I would spend my life's strength to set you free from this. But you're making a mistake if you keep us here."

"This will only lead to more innocents caught in his net, like you," Mesmeera said. "For the sake of the man you once were, do not do this."

"You are right," the Lurker said, covering his eyes with his bony, gnarled hand.

"We are?" Duncan whispered. He paused. "That went better than I thought."

"Shh!" Mesmeera cautioned. She lifted her voice for the Lurker to hear. "You'll release us?" she asked. "You'll let us go, then?"

When the Lurker lowered his hand, his bulging eyes were bloodshot with tears. But his expression showed no remorse. No sorrow. His grin was maniacal, but it was a grin nonetheless.

"No," the Lurker said, "I will not be letting you go, not until my better comes to claim you. But you are right about one thing: my capturing you will lead to many more reckless souls being snared in the Dream. But they will not be innocent victims, no. They will be guilty, just as I was guilty. They will drink from the same cup of madness, and they will share eternal anguish with me. Misery loves company."

Duncan summoned all of his remaining will, but he could do nothing to impact the chains and manacles that bound him and Mesmeera. And that, Duncan thought, was a terrible shame. Without their hands free, they could not cover their ears. No, they were captives, at the mercy of the Lurker and his insufferable laughter. It was a pulsing, shrieking laughter, and it pierced the Dreamtreaders to the very soul.

ELEVEN

MASTER GABRIEL'S SECOND VISIT

"HEADED TO BED SO EARLY?" ARCHER'S DAD ASKED.

"Rough day at school," Archer said from halfway up the stairs. "Had to bang out a Chemistry lab during lunch. I'm toast."

"That Dr. Pallazzo is a real stickler, isn't he?"

Archer nodded. He was glad to find his father more clear minded and friendly. "It was a huge chunk of my grade. I shouldn't have waited until the last minute, but I think I still did pretty well."

"Well, I guess the good news is that it's almost over. Summer is on the way." Archer's father gave his usual smile, a bit of teeth through the salt-and-pepper goatee, the only smile he'd been able to manage for seven years. Then he turned back to the cable sports show on TV. "Summer," he said once more, the word sounding flat.

Archer lingered on the stairs a few moments. He doubted his father was thinking much about the show. It seemed more a distraction than anything entertaining. White noise.

"Can you look in on Kaylie?" he asked. "Tuck her in, maybe?"

"Sure, Dad," Archer said. "I got you."

Kaylie was not in her room. Patches and her pink blanket were missing as well.

Archer checked the blue bathroom and found it empty. He ducked around the door frame of his little brother's room. "Hey, Buster, have you seen Kaylie?"

"Naw," Buster said, his eyes never leaving the game on his tablet computer. "Whoa! Almost a wipeout."

Archer frowned and called up the hallway, "Kaylie, where are you?"

"In here, Archer," she called. Her tiny voice sounded bright and pixyish. *Dad's room or mine,* he thought. *Knowing Kaylie, probably mine.*

He was right. She and Patches and her pink blanket were snuggled up on Archer's bed.

"Dad says it's time for you to go to bed," he told her. "And aren't you a little too old to be sucking your thumb?

She popped her thumb out of her mouth and said, "It's an acquired taste."

"Right."

"Hey Archer, how come you got ashes on your table?"

"Ashes?" he said. "I don't have any—"

"Right here," she said, pointing with Patches's dolly hand. "See."

Archer did see. There were four distinct irregularly shaped piles of gray-white ash. *The Tokens of Doom,* he thought, *have turned to ash?* He swallowed. It seemed ominous, but what it meant exactly, Archer had no idea.

"Umm, no, I didn't know that," he said. "What are you doing in my room?"

"Nuffin," she replied, popping her thumb back into her mouth.

"Uh-huh," Archer said, scanning the room. "What did you do?"

"Nuffin."

Archer spotted his cell phone sitting at an angle on his dresser. "Awww, Kaylie, not my phone again," he said, turning on her. "You didn't reprogram my phone with some goofy ringtones . . . did you?"

She shrugged and backed up defensively under his covers. Archer pursued. "You know what I'm going to do to you?" He held up both hands and wiggled his fingers.

Kaylie's eyes widened until they looked like big blue planets. "You wouldn't!"

"I would," Archer said, nodding fiercely. Then, he commenced tickling her. He poked at her belly, and she cackled and tried to guard. But as soon as she managed to block her stomach, Archer went after her feet. Even through her footy pajamas, it was too much. Kaylie laughed and squealed and eventually could scarcely catch her breath.

Archer withdrew his dangerous fingers and said, "See what happens when you awaken my wrath?"

She looked up at him, a broad grin and a little rose in her cheeks. "You really ought to have better encryption on your phone," she said.

"What is it going to cost me? Candy?"

She shook her head.

"What? No candy?"

"A story."

"Okay," he said. "Dad wanted me to tuck you in anyway. Come on back to your room. One story coming up."

"Mission accomplished," Archer whispered as he shut his bedroom door. Kaylie had fallen sound asleep before he'd even gotten a third of the way through the story. "Now, to wait for Gabriel." He double-checked the calendar to make sure. "Yup, May 7." In five years, ever since his very first appearance, Gabriel had not missed the seventh day of any month.

And, given all the crazy developments in the Dream, Archer didn't think Master Gabriel would go AWOL on this night. He went to his closet, unlocked the case, and took out *The Dreamtreader's Creed*.

A few minutes later, the blue glow around his bedroom door alerted Archer that his guest had indeed arrived.

"You are studying the Creeds," Master Gabriel said, his voice arriving a moment before he materialized in front of the closet.

"Yup."

"Tell me, Archer, have you mastered the forty-second Conceptus?"

"Uh . . ." Archer looked down at the Creeds. "I've read it but not mastered it."

Gabriel harrumphed. "Tell me, then, of the three districts within the Dream—"

"Forms, Pattern, and Verse," Archer blurted out.

"Yes, yes, yes," Master Gabriel grumbled. "You would have known that by the fifth Conceptus. That is not what I was asking. What I wish to know from you, based on your familiarity with the Creeds, is this: Why were you chosen for the Forms District?"

Archer combed his memory. He'd read about the three districts, of course. He knew where they were in the Dream. He knew the climate of each, most of the towns and kingdoms as well. Forms was the most physically demanding district; the Dreamscape there difficult, even arduous. *But why me?* He didn't know. But he wasn't about to admit it. "I wasn't chosen for Forms," he said, giving his best guess. "When Atticus died, Forms was left open, so I got it."

"It was simply coincidence, then, was it?" Gabriel asked rhetorically. "Clearly you have not read carefully enough. And more troubling still, you do not seem to be aware of your own strengths and limitations. A better answer would have been simply, 'I do not know.'"

Archer closed the Creeds and laid it on the bed next to him. "I am trying," he said.

"Very well," Master Gabriel said with a dismissive wave of the hand. "Tell me about your findings. The breaches?"

"More than I've ever seen before," Archer said. "More than forty most nights, and not just on the outskirts either. They've appeared in the middle of cities."

"The Nightmare Lord is drunk on his recent success, growing more brazen."

"The news concerning Duncan and Mesmeera isn't good," Archer said. He explained everything he'd learned from Lady Kasia and almost everything he'd learned from Bezeal.

"Two moons?" Gabriel echoed reflectively. "It's worse than I feared."

"Master Gabriel, if Duncan and Mesmeera have gone missing, who's repairing the breaches in their districts?"

The Dreammaster did not reply.

"Master Gabriel?"

Gabriel's dark eyes sparked to life. "There have not been any breaches in the districts of Pattern or Verse for two moons."

"Since they disappeared."

"The timing seemed significant to me as well."

"But it's a perfect time for the Nightmare Lord," Archer said. "Why wouldn't he take advantage? Why wouldn't he open up a ton of breaches in Patterns and Verse?"

"I wonder," he said. "What about Bezeal? I want to know more about your interactions with him."

Somehow, Archer knew the conversation would circle back around to the crafty merchant. "Bezeal told me something else . . . about Duncan and Mesmeera."

"Something else? Heavens, lad, tell me."

"Bezeal claimed that Duncan and Mesmeera sought out the Lurker."

"Nonsense," Master Gabriel said. "Bezeal is lying. Why would seasoned Dreamtreaders do something so foolish?"

"They were after a relic, some kind of silvery puzzle box."

Gabriel's armor flared. "What on earth would they want with a puzzle box?"

"I don't think Duncan and Mesmeera wanted it for themselves."

"What do you mean?"

"I think they went after it for Bezeal."

"They—Well, what would possess them to . . . Wait! They made a deal with Bezeal, didn't they? I wonder what he offered them."

Archer thought he knew but said nothing about it. "Bezeal told me I'd find Duncan and Mesmeera if I find the relic. I'm going to try."

"You will do no such thing," Master Gabriel said.

"But—"

"End of discussion," Master Gabriel thundered. "Duncan and Mesmeera went after it and have not yet returned. Do you really believe you could succeed *if* they failed?"

"I don't know," Archer said. "Probably not. But I kind of have to."

"Kind of . . . ," Master Gabriel echoed, ". . . have to?"

"Well," Archer said, "it was part of our deal."

"Treader's oath, lad! You made a deal with that hooded menace too?"

"We made a blood pact."

Master Gabriel's eyebrows shot up so far they nearly left his face. "You did *what?*"

"He held out his hand," Archer stammered. "I didn't know! He had some kind of blade, and it cut me. Him too, I guess."

"Did your blood mingle?" Gabriel demanded.

"I . . . I guess," he said. "There were . . . Well, it kind of smeared on his hand. I . . . yeah, I'm pretty sure it did."

"A blood pact? I told you to beware of Bezeal, did I not? I told you to be discreet. A blood pact is *not* discreet!"

"So now I have to go, right?" Archer asked. "The blood pact means I have to go. It's in the Creeds."

"I know very well it is in the Creeds, Archer," Master Gabriel said, his voice quiet but simmering. "Let me investigate this issue. For now, absolutely do not go anywhere near the Lurker."

"But what—"

"Do not try my patience, Archer. I forbid you to go."

TWELVE

A CHALLENGE

BY THE TIME ARCHER MADE IT TO LUNCH WEDNESDAY, HE was already exhausted. The meeting with Master Gabriel the night before had rattled him to the point where sleep had come in fitful, unproductive spurts. And almost every time he hit even a little REM sleep, the kind of sleep needed for Dreamtreading, Kaylie had woken him up screaming from nightmares. Each time he'd rushed bleary eyed to her room to comfort her until she'd drifted off again. The Nightmare Lord had apparently declared war on Archer and his family.

"If I could only get that relic," Archer seethed under his breath, "then I'd get your secret, and then we'd see."

The Nightmare Lord had certainly won the first couple of rounds. As a result, Archer had nodded off during American Lit and made a ridiculous calculation error (on screen for the entire class to ridicule) in Math. A tired mind was bound to lead to mistakes, Archer knew, but it galled him.

I must look as awful as I feel, he thought with a sad chuckle. Grandma Cho had been extra generous with portions. His tray looked like an otherworldly landscape: a mountain of tater tots, a forest of broccoli,

a vast lake of cheese sauce, an avalanche of chicken nuggets, and rolling hills made of, well . . . rolls.

He munched a cheese-dipped nugget and grumbled, *I am a Dreamtreader.*
I am supposed to go where the danger is. I'm supposed to solve problems in the Dream.
There's something serious going on here, and I can't do anything about it? That's just . . .
well, it's just stupid.

Archer had been in his third season of Dreamtreader service when
he first caught wind of the legendary Lurker. But he had never taken
the stories seriously. They had always been ominous rumors. Tales
of bogeymen, spooks, or other assorted horrors. But Archaia was in
Duncan's district, and the fiery red-beard never said much about it.
And yet, Archer thought, Duncan and Mesmeera had apparently gone
hunting for the relic in Archaia, right to the Lurker's door.

What was the relic, anyway? A puzzle box? What good would
that be? If Master Gabriel had known something about it, he sure
didn't share. Whatever it was, Duncan and Mesmeera clearly thought
it was worth the risk of tromping around the Lurker's backyard. And
Bezeal wanted it so fiercely that he would give up the secret to bringing down the Nightmare Lord.

Could Bezeal be trusted? Not likely. *But if there is a chance, even an*
infinitesimally small chance, to put away the Nightmare Lord for good, don't I have to
take it? No, apparently not. Master Gabriel had, in fact, forbidden it.

Ten tater tots later, Archer had worked himself into a frustrated
state, but the bell rang: time to head to Chemistry. He scarfed down a
substantial portion of the tray's contents and reluctantly dumped the
rest. As he slid the tray into the drop-off window, he watched a crowd
pass by. It was Rigby, of course. And in his train, Kara Windchil . . .
and even Amy Pitsitakas.

Archer shook his head and trudged out of the cafeteria. But once
in the hall, he noticed that someone else was watching Rigby Thames's

procession. Guzzy Gorvalec stood in the shadows next to a bank of lockers. It was hard to see the features of his face . . . except for his eyes. Guzzy's eyes glistened with venom. It was then that Archer felt a pang of responsibility. Being new at Dresden High, Rigby had no clue what might be coming his way.

I'd better tell him, Archer thought. *Maybe during lab in Chem. Maybe.*

Dr. Pallazzo held a book-sized, orange-brown rock up over his glistening bald head and snapped it in half. "Is this unnamed compound most likely ionic or covalent?"

Archer swallowed. He vaguely remembered reading something about one of the compounds being pretty brittle. "Uhm . . . co—"

"Do not guess, Mr. Keaton," the teacher said. "At this point you should know. Mr. Thames, can you tell me?"

Rigby didn't sit up straight. In fact, he seemed distracted by something outside the classroom window. Without looking directly at the teacher, he said, "It's ionic."

"Correct," Dr. Pallazzo said. "And how do you know this?"

Rigby didn't hesitate, nor did he look particularly interested. "Most crystals are ionic compounds," he said. "It's because the ions stack into crystal lattices, right? In addition, you snapped the thing in 'alf with your 'ands. Ionic compounds tend to be rigid and brittle, so there it is. Besides, I recognized the compound as zinc sulphide, which is, of course, ionic."

"Now that, Mr. Thames," the teacher said with a sideways glance at Archer, "is what I call a confident answer. Correct!"

Archer sank down in his chair and fumed. It was the third time in the block Rigby had shown off his (admittedly stunning) intellect.

By the time the lab started, Archer was so sick of Rigby that he completely forgot about Guzzy and his stooges.

Of course, Kara was paired up with Rigby. Everyone seemed to find partners right away, leaving Archer gazing around the classroom like some abandoned puppy in a pet shop window.

"Ready to get started?" Amy said, tugging on Archer's black lab apron. "C'mon, this is an easy one, yep."

Archer sighed in relief. Amy to the rescue. "Nothing's easy in here, Amy," he said. "But thanks all the same."

"Sure it is," she said, gesturing for him to join her at the microscope. "See, look at the crystalline structures, the little boxy shapes. That means it's ionic." She went on to explain more key differences between ionic and covalent compounds.

Archer listened intently to Amy at first, but soon Rigby's smooth English wafted over. Archer glanced across the room and saw that, as usual, Rigby had a small crowd gathered around him. Dr. Pallazzo didn't even say anything about the distraction. He just walked around nodding as if he were responsible for Rigby's superior intellect.

Archer went back to the microscope. "So how come you're not still following Rigby around?"

"I was never following him around," Amy contested. "Not really. I mean, sure, he's interesting, yep. And smart. And funny. And—"

"Forget I asked," Archer said.

When the lab was over, Dr. Pallazzo ushered the students back to their desks and put a new slide up on the digital overhead projector: "Battle of the Brains."

"What's Battle of the Brains?" Garret McCormick asked.

"Nothing you need to worry about," Gil Messchek said.

"Quiet," Dr. Pallazzo commanded. "As you know, your final exam will be on June 2. It is a significant part of your grade. So to help you study, we will engage in mortal combat. Intellectually, that is." He paused and gave a stack of papers to Kara to pass out. "This is your list of topics. You will challenge one another on any three."

"Great," Archer muttered to himself. He knew Chemistry but . . . to be tested against another student . . . in front of everyone in the class? That sounded like a recipe for humiliation.

But as the opponents chose each other, things went horribly wrong. Kara chose Bree Lassiter. Emy Crawford stole Amy right before Archer was about to claim her. Two by two, the students all paired off. No one seemed to want to challenge Rigby Thames.

Archer looked around for anyone else to oppose. There was Gil Messcheck, but that would be a mistake; he was one of Guzzy's crew. Who else? A little more desperate now, Archer bounced from person to person. The only other one left was that girl who always smelled like cigarette smoke and had a screechy voice. What was her name? Felicia? Felicia Dudka? Or was it Dooda? He couldn't recall.

That wouldn't turn out well, Archer thought. *No. That vice would drive me up a wall.*

Dr. Pallazzo said, "That's almost everyone. But will no one challenge Mr. Thames? How about you, Mr. Messcheck?"

Gil had apparently found something riveting on the floor to look at. He gave only the subtlest shake of the head. No.

Wait, Archer thought. *What am I afraid of? Someone's got to put this new hotshot in his place. Why not me? If I'm going to take down the Nightmare Lord, I ought to be able to handle Rigby.*

Before his brain caught up to his mouth, Archer said, "I'll do it!"

"Mr. Keaton?" Dr. Pallazzo said incredulously. "Are you sure?"

In his periphery, Archer saw Amy's wide eyes. For some reason that emboldened him all the more. "I'm sure," he said. "I think I match up pretty well with Sir Rigby, actually."

Archer ignored the giggling in the room. *Wouldn't that be the day?* he thought. If he could show up Rigby in front of everyone—in front of Kara—that would be, well . . . epic.

"Is this agreeable to you, Mr. Thames?" the teacher asked.

Rigby said nothing. He smirked and gave a subtle nod of the head.

"That leaves Mr. Messcheck and Miss Dutka."

"Awww, mannnn!" Gil whined.

On the way out of Chemistry, Rigby Thames slid up close to Archer. "Oi, Keaton," he said. "Bravo to you for challenging me. Better than most of the gutless wonders in there."

"You'll probably kill me," Archer mumbled. He hadn't expected any kind of approval from Rigby.

"Maybe," Rigby said. "I do have advantages. I went to GIFT. And I had a semicrazy master chemist for an uncle. But you never know . . . underdogs are often fierce opponents. You seem like that type too."

"Uh, thanks," Archer said. "I guess."

"So . . . what say we make this so-called Battle of the Brains a bit more interesting?" Rigby said, his voice friendly and eager.

"What do you mean?"

"A little wager," he said. "Fancy that?"

"I don't gamble," Archer said.

"No, no," he said. "Nothing like that. I had something in mind though. You have any chores you hate? I know I do. We have . . . er . . . quite a few pets. Feeding them and cleaning their cages is right vulgar, it is. Let's say, if I win, you come over to my place, do that chore for me . . . for a week."

"I dunno," Archer said.

"Surely you've got some business your folks make you do, but you can't stand it."

One popped instantly to Archer's mind. Ever since his mom died, there'd been a ton of new work for all of the kids. But one stood out as particularly hated. "Well, maybe . . ."

"That's the spirit. What is it?"

"It's laundry. I do the whole family's laundry."

"You don't play around, do you?" Rigby said. "Right, then. You win, I'll do laundry at your place for a week. I win, you've got my pet duty."

"But not on Sundays," Archer said. "We go to church on Sundays."

"Church . . . how quaint." Rigby rolled his eyes. "Ah, to each their own." He held out his hand.

Remembering Bezeal, Archer hesitated for a moment. *Stupid,* he thought. *Rigby's not making a blood pact here.* The two shook.

"Done and done!" Rigby started to walk away.

"Oh, hey," Archer called, but Rigby held up a hand. He reached for his holster, yanked out his cell phone, and put it to his ear.

"What are *you* calling me at school for?" Rigby asked.

Archer had no earthly guess as to who might be on the other side of that call, but the way Rigby said the word *you* was nothing short of venomous.

Rigby turned sideways to Archer and walked away. Not meaning to eavesdrop, Archer couldn't help but hear a little more of Rigby's end of the conversation.

". . . told you it's going to cost a lot of money up front. Right, right. No . . . you don't seem to understand. There's nothing else . . ."

That was it. Archer heard nothing more. A few moments later, just before Archer disappeared into the gym, Kara caught up to him.

"Are you crazy, Archer?" she said. "Rigby will have you for lunch."

"Thanks," Archer said. "That's nice."

"You know what I mean."

"Yeah," he said. "I think I do."

"Look," Kara said, "I know you're probably tired of Rigby's new-kid cool routine. I am too. Kinda."

"Are you?" Archer asked. "Could've fooled me. Word is, you've been spending a lot of time with him."

"Have you been asking around?" Kara shot back.

"I've seen you two, Kara," he said. "Just the other day, you were walking away from the bus arm in arm. What's that about?"

Kara put her hands on her hips. "Archer Keaton, you sound jealous."

"Jealous?" he echoed as if the word had just beamed down from another planet. "Why should I be jealous? We've hardly talked since the storm."

"Don't worry, Archer," she said. "I've still got your back. But listen: Rigby is really, *really* smart. What are you going to do?"

Archer stopped at the locker room door. "Actually, I know what I'm going to do," he said. "I have an ace in the hole."

Kara looked at him strangely. "Your ace better have a degree in Chemistry."

"Close enough," Archer said. "But it's going to cost me a *lot* of candy."

THIRTEEN

A NEAR THING

"BOOYAAAAH!" ARCHER CRIED OUT AS HE SLID DOWN the wispy, whirling vortex, entering the Dream once more. From this height, the view was breathtaking: all the colors in the sky, the two half-moons, the other vapor tornados, and the rich and varied land beneath. It was extraordinary.

Archer came to the bottom of the funnel and hit the ground running. "Razz!" he called. A puff of fur and purple smoke, and there she was. "Ready, boss!" she said, saluting and almost knocking her acorn hat off.

"I'm not your boss," he said. "Hop on. We've got a lot more to do tonight than usual."

"More breaches?" she asked.

Razz hopped up onto Archer's shoulder and got herself steadied. "Let's rock!"

Archer called up his longboard, released his deflective hold on the Intrusion waves, and raced off.

Their first stop wasn't far. A line of breaches flared on the outskirts of Varta. Pieces of the Dream fabric began to unravel at the breach's edges. It had taken Archer and Razz until the stroke of four to finish closing that one up. After that, Archer and Razz surfed south through the rocky crags of Farnham Tor, repairing breaches as they went. At Riverford, in the deep south, they found a massive cluster of eighteen breaches. That took toward seven tolls.

When they'd finished their assessment and repair of the twenty-one fiefdoms in Archer's districts, it was already ten. He'd purposefully planned their route to hit Cold Plateau last, as it was just across the border from the moors of Archaia.

Even so, there just didn't seem to be enough time. Archer lay his longboard aside and sat on the edge of a vast ringed tree stump.

"What's wrong?" Razz asked.

"Everything."

Razz leaped into the air and glided back and forth in front of Archer's nose. "Seems to me we did a bang-up job tonight. What's the worry?"

"If you'd come with me to see Bezeal, you'd know."

"Ohhhhh, I should have guessed it had something to do with Bezeal. How did he trick you?"

"You assume he tricked me."

"Didn't he?"

"Well, yes." Archer explained the blood pact, what Bezeal was after, and what it could mean for every being in the Dream.

"Really?" Razz said. "Do you think it's possible? Can the Nightmare Lord himself be defeated?"

"I don't know," he said. "But if there's a chance . . ."

"What are we waiting for?" Razz squeaked. "Let's go get that puzzle relic thing!"

"What about the Lurker?"

"We'll deal with him if we have to. You have plenty left in the tank, don't you?"

"Yeah, sure," he said. "But there is one more thing."

"Uh-oh."

"Gabriel told me not to go, not to get the relic."

"What? Why?" Razz drifted to the stump and curled up.

"He wouldn't tell me," Archer said. "But I think he's worried about me getting hurt."

"I guess that settles it then," Razz said.

"You don't want to go now?"

"Are you crazy?" Razz yelled. "No one, and I mean *no one*, defies Master Gabriel."

"Apparently Duncan and Mesmeera did," Archer argued.

"You don't know that," Razz said.

"Well, I know they went looking for the relic and haven't been seen since."

Razz squeaked and said, "Maybe they were on a secret mission for Master Gabriel."

"That makes no sense at all. Why would Master Gabriel send Duncan and Mesmeera and then forbid me to go?"

Razz looked sideways. Her nose twitched. "Do you really need me to explain it to you?" she asked.

Archer crossed his arms on his chest. "Yes, actually. Tell me why."

"You're just not ready yet," Razz said, rolling her eyes. "Duh."

Archer sighed. He'd been so hopeful that Razz would travel with him. "I have to do it," Archer said. "I have to try. The Nightmare Lord has been going after my friends, my family, even Kaylie. I've got to stop him."

"Yes," Razz said, "we do need to stop him, but not by ignoring

Master Gabriel's commands. He's just looking out for you, Archer. You're not strong enough yet."

"Of course I'm strong enough," Archer said, his voice sharp. "I'm going."

Razz frowned, leaped into the air, and flittered in Archer's face. "Well, you can count me out then. I won't cross Master Gabriel. Not now. Not ever."

There was a crackling and then a puff of purple smoke, and Razz was gone.

Archer hopped up onto his board and caught a wave north across Achaia's border. *This is probably the biggest mistake of my life,* he thought, seeing the moors just ahead.

"I've got to time this just right," he said. "I don't want to get too far away from my anchor."

One does not simply surf into Archaia.

Archer caught a huge Intrusion as he went over the border, but that just made the fall even worse. The wave slammed into something Archer hadn't seen. Suddenly, there was nothing under the longboard. It happened so fast that the Dreamtreader didn't have time to call up anything to cushion his fall. He slammed into the ground chin first and ended up tumbling over himself several painful times. When Archer came to rest in a jumbled heap, he had a mouth full of peat moss and blood.

The Dreamtreader jumped to his feet and brushed himself off. He'd had worse spills but few quite as awkward. He looked back, but there was nothing there that seemed likely to cut a wave of Intrusions out from under him. Then it hit him. There were no inbound Intrusions at all. He reached out with his senses. Nothing. Nothing anywhere. Archer had never found a region of the Dream where Intrusions did not roll. It was peculiarly still. The whole thing sent a ripple down his spine.

Archer shrugged it off as best he could. "Razz, you're really missing out here." The Dreamtreader turned back to the north. The treeless, mossy, gray-green terrain undulated forever. Slate-colored shards of rock punched up frequently, and there were abundant craggy outcroppings of stone. As Archer looked on, a writhing tide of mist poured over the lip of a jagged stone rim, slowly drifting down into a dell about a hundred yards away.

With one last look at the distant face of Old Jack, Archer called up a gnarled driftwood staff and strode forward. He kept the pace as brisk as the uneven footing would allow and aimed as best he could for the center of the region.

"*To find them and it, seek the rotten core, the home of evil out on the moor.*" Bezeal's words. *Rotten core*, Archer thought, adjusting his course to aim for the dark ridge where the mist flowed.

Scraggly dead plants grasped at Archer's ankles. Here and there, the moss and soil gave way under his feet. Once, his boot sank up to his shin in the gray mud. The temperature had dropped and it seemed to be getting darker. The Dreamtreader hit the upslope and waded through waist-high, reedy grass. Altogether, it was a miserable slog. *This is like Scotland*, he thought. *Only worse. Much worse.*

The vaporous wisps of the fog slithered like indistinct serpents, trailing over and around the stones and clumps of tall grass. Soon, they spilled down at Archer's ankles. He found himself mesmerized by the rippling motion of the mist. In the Dream, nothing was ever as it seemed.

Archer slammed the butt of his staff to the ground. An iris

opened in the mist around his legs, but it was short-lived. The gray-white shreds surged back in. Archer had little choice but to keep walking in the midst of it.

The incline steepened. The mist thickened. Archer's pulse quickened. The black ridge of stone loomed ahead. It was more of a rocky overhang than Archer had first thought. He stopped again, scanned the extent of the craggy horizon. It would be quite a trek to get around it on either side. It would—*What . . . was . . . that?* his mind demanded. The sound had been faint, but in the mist-dampened stillness, it was loud enough. Archer sucked in an icy breath. He stared at the darkness beneath the overhang. More than just volume, it was the form of the sound. Like a moaning, wailing shriek: high and desperate. Frightful.

Nothing moved but the ever-swirling mist. The gloom played tricks with Archer's mind. The overhang almost looked like an archway of some kind.

The shriek again. This time, it rang out in the air and seemed to rattle the world. It was such an urgent, agonizing wail that Archer squinted and covered his ears. When it stopped, the mist withdrew back toward the overhang. Shred by ghostly shred, the sea of fog vanished over the ridge. Then the world really did begin to tremble.

A deep rumbling tremor began. It sounded like an avalanche or maybe a stampede. Archer stared up at the ridge of stone. Was that an archway? Was it some kind of doorway? If so, what was making that noise? What thunderous thing would come bursting forth?

As the rumbling grew louder, Archer raised his staff with both hands to a defensive position across his body. The roar continued to grow louder. It carried with it an aura of pressure that squeezed at Archer's inner ear as if he swam in deep water. The Dreamtreader stared so hard at the ridge that he felt his eyeballs might burst. For a moment, everything stopped. All was silent, except for a single, solitary breath.

Screaming, wailing white skulls surged over the ridge. It was like a tidal wave of ghosts bearing down on Archer. The Dreamtreader yelped involuntarily and braced himself. The bone-rattling rumble, the ear-splitting shrieks—it was so painfully loud that Archer could scarcely think. But he had to protect himself against the coming onslaught.

It was a stupid idea, but it was the only thing that popped into his mind in the moment. Just as the spectral tsunami would have bowled him over, Archer created a phone booth. It was one of the old British police call box structures made of wood and iron and painted royal blue. Archer held on inside for dear life as the spectral wave hit the phone booth. The windows rattled and leaked howling shrieks. Archer held on as the fearful ruckus made his thoughts swim.

The moment the vibration stopped, Archer charged out of the booth. The ghostly wave of mist flowed away but reversed itself. The faces reappeared, scowling and wailing at Archer as they raced back. Archer threw his staff like a javelin at the oncoming spectral host. The Dreamtreader called up the strength of his well-trained mind and caused his airborne staff to change.

It grew a black nose cone. It sprouted stabilizer fins, two sets of four. A fiery engine suddenly propelled it faster. It hit the oncoming ghost wave and exploded in a dazzling spray of liquid fire. Like a wash of gasoline, it spread through, around, and over the specters. As their shrieks rose in pitch, Archer fell to one knee and clutched his ears. He gathered his focus as best he could and prepared for another strike.

But the shrieking wail faded to a distant, echoing moan. Archer rose to his feet but saw the threat had died out. Only a series of rippling circles made of still-burning pools of white fire remained. A distant bell began to toll eleven strokes.

Archer charged up the hill toward the stone ridge. He knew the archway was something, and he had no time to lose. He skidded to a stop in the ridge's dark shadow and stood before a massive, arched, dark iron door. *"Knock not once but twice on the Lurker's door."* Bezeal's command came ringing back to Archer's mind. He lifted his fist and gave two sharp raps to the metal. Each blow sounded like distant thunder. One side of the door swung inward.

"Highly respectable effort," came a high, crazed voice. "Or you would'na have passed my wraithlings, would you? No. Come in, come in, Dreamtreader. Come and join my little collection."

"Sword," Archer muttered. He reached over his shoulder and loosed the blade from his back hanger. Blue flame crawled up its cutting edge, but very faintly. When Archer stepped through the door, over the Lurker's threshold, the flame went out altogether.

Yellow torches lit a curling tunnel winding into the stone.

"Come on, come on!" the voice taunted. "We have'na got all day. I suppose I should say you have'na got all day, right, Dreamtreader?"

Archer took a deep breath and nearly choked. A smell filled the air as if something had died and been left to rot. Yet there was little else to do but go forward.

Each torch flared once as Archer passed by. An even brighter light was somewhere up ahead, shining golden upon the curving stone.

Archer came into a vaulted chamber that looked very much like a laboratory. There were a dozen stuffed bookcases and twice that many shelving units holding jars of every size, shape, and hue. Small burners lit various beakers and cylinders on vast tables, but there was no sign of Duncan or Mesmeera.

"You said I was joining your collection," Archer called out. "Where are the other two Dreamtreaders? Do you have them?"

"They visited me, yes," the voice answered. "They came to call on the Lurker. Wasn't that nice? And nice of you to drop by. Won't you stay?"

"I don't think I should," Archer said. "It would be rude to take advantage of your hospitality."

"Well-spoken, aren't you, Dreamtreader?" There was coarse, hacking laughter. "On the contrary, it would be rude t'leave so soon. Can I get you something? A little refreshment, perhaps?"

Archer stared into the corner where the bright light's glow seemed to originate. There was movement in that light, a shadow shape intermittently swallowed up by the light. "Well, maybe something, I suppose. I'm looking for a silver puzzle box. Do you know of it?"

The hiss that came out of the light made Archer feel as if his skin were shriveling.

"You seek the Karakurian Chamber!" the Lurker howled. "I was afraid of that. Now, unfortunately, you will *have* to stay."

Archer turned but couldn't take a step. Heavy chains appeared out of the ground. Faster than he could think, they curled around the Dreamtreader's torso and constricted. "You . . . you're killing me!" Archer cried out, struggling in vain.

"Not yet," the voice said. "Sands of the hourglass will serve your fate, and we will forever have something in common. Forever!" The voice trailed off, and the shadow shape in the light became more distinct as it came closer. It took on the shape of a man. An impossibly large man.

A bell tolled in the distance. Archer sucked in a sharp breath. "No," he whispered. "No, it can't be time already."

The bell tolled again. And again. Old Jack had tolled eleven just before the attack of the mist. That left one toll left: the Stroke of Reckoning. There came a fourth toll.

"Oh, dear, how unfortunate," the voice said, and the tall shadow began to withdraw. "I am afraid you'll have to wait until later for my attentions."

"No, no, wait!" Archer yelled. "Let me go! You can't leave me like this!" The bell tolled a fifth time. Archer summoned up all his focus and tried to will sections of the confining chain to split apart. But nothing happened at all.

"I am afraid I must," the Lurker said. "I will return once I've dealt with the hounds."

"Hounds?" Archer mumbled. Old Jack struck six. But no more came.

Wait, he thought. *No wonder the Lurker heard the tolls too.* Never had Archer been so glad to hear Sixtolls. Sure, that meant that the Nightmare Lord was unleashing chaos into the Dream, in effect, turning every dream to nightmare, but at least time still remained before Archer's Personal Midnight. But not much time.

Archer heard a tremendous metallic thud. The Lurker had gone. *Out to deal with the hounds?* That struck Archer as very strange, but he didn't have time to ponder it. He tried to free himself again with the full might of his will, but the chains didn't even move an inch. They were as tight as ever, and as heavy.

"Razz!" he called. "I could really use some help here!"

No puff of purple smoke. No sudden fuzzy appearance.

"Razz? Come on! This is no time to be fickle! I'm in trouble here!"

"Think, Archer," came a voice. But it was not Razz. It startled Archer until he remembered where he'd heard it before: this was the deep womanly voice that had helped him back to his anchor after he'd failed to take down the Nightmare Lord. "Use your mind."

"I've tried that!" Archer grumbled. "It didn't work."

"Think chemistry," the voice said. "Consider the chain's properties."

"Chemistry?" Archer muttered. "What? What do you—solids, liquids, and gasses. Solid, for sure. And a metal. No, wait." Archer paused, thinking. He held up his one free hand. "Welding torch," he said. "Mask!"

A shaded-visor mask fell down upon his head. An industrial-grade acetylene torch appeared in his hand. He went to work on the chain immediately, working the outer links to keep the heat bleed from burning his own flesh. The first began to redden. Soon, he had sheared the link in half. Some of the chain's length fell away, but not enough to free him. Twisting his upper body painfully, he set the torch to another link on the opposite side.

When that link melted open, the rest of the chains fell. Archer leaped up out of the coils and started to race back the way he'd come.

"The puzzle box," he whispered, stopping hard. He darted back into the laboratory and searched frantically. There were strange objects and artifacts in every nook and cranny of the place, but no silver puzzle box, the Karakurian Chamber, or whatever the Lurker had called it.

"I don't have time for this!" Archer grumbled. He cast himself about the chamber, going to the bookshelves and cabinets. Still nothing promising. He couldn't linger much longer. Who knew when the Lurker would return? Who knew when the Stroke of Reckoning would sound?

At last, Archer came to an odd cabinet made of bamboo with tortoiseshell handles. He pulled open the door and found . . . another cabinet. It was made of the same materials in exactly the same style, but it was scaled down one size. He slung open those cabinet doors and found . . . another cabinet.

"Really?" Archer blurted.

He opened that cabinet, and the next, and the next, until there was one cabinet about ten inches high and seven wide.

Expecting to find yet another tiny cabinet, he opened the small doors. There was no cabinet, but there was a small silver cube. It was ornately carved with all manner of figures and symbols. The puzzle box. It had to be.

Archer snatched it up and sprinted out of the lab. As he raced out onto the moors, he heard Old Jack begin to toll once more.

"*No!*" he yelled, pouring on the speed. He used up every last bit of will to propel himself forward. He was running, but barely touching the ground, a blur on the moors. He crossed the border out of Archaia with two strokes of Old Jack remaining. He dove for his anchor.

Before leaving the realm of Dream, his last thought was about the relic . . . the puzzle box he'd taken from the Lurker. What would happen to it? Would it fall back to the ground in the Dream where any idiot could pick it up? Had all his efforts been for nothing?

But when Archer opened his eyes and sat up in his bed, he still clutched the puzzle box in his hand.

Dreamtreader Creed, Conceptus 3

The difference between life and death is a matter of small details. And so, over the ages, Dreamtreaders have made painstaking observations about the nature and boundaries of the Dream in such precise measures that they have detected nine laws at work. Learn them, Dreamtreader! Your life and the lives of those you love may depend on it.

The Laws Nine

Law One: Anchor first; Anchor deep. Construct an anchor image that is rooted in a deeply powerful emotion. It must be dear to you.

Law Two: Anchor where you may return with ease, but no one else can. If your anchor is destroyed or otherwise kept from you, your time may run out.

Law Three: Never remain in the Dream for more than your

Eleven Hours. Your Personal Midnight is the end. Depart for the Temporal . . . or perish.

LAW FOUR: Depart for the Temporal at Sixtolls or find some bastion to defend against the storm. The Nightmare Lord will open wide his kennels, chaos will rule, and the Dreamtreader will be lost.

LAW FIVE: While in the Dream, consume nothing made with gort, the soul harvest berry. It is black as pitch and enslaves your body to those with dark powers.

LAW SIX: Defend against sudden and final death within the Dream. Prepare your mind for any number of calamities that may come, or else be shut out from the Dream forever.

LAW SEVEN: Never accept an invitation from the Nightmare Lord. Not even to parley. He is a living snare to the Dreamtreader. There is no good–faith bargain. With him, the only profit is death.

LAW EIGHT: By the light of a Violet Torch, search yourself for tendrils, the Nightmare Lord's silent assassins.

LAW NINE: Dreamtread with all the strength you can master, but never more than two days in a row. To linger in the Dream too often will invite madness. Temporal and Dream will be fused within you and shatter your mind.

FOURTEEN

THERE ARE RULES

KARA WAS ALREADY WAITING WHEN RIGBY ENTERED THE
courtyard. No surprise. The girl was practically giddy about the
whole thing. *Can't say that I blame her,* Rigby thought, *but, sheesh, look at her.*

Kara sat on one of the white stone benches in the center of the
courtyard, though *sat* wasn't the right word. She was bouncing. The
contents of the school lunch tray on her lap threatened to tumble into
the grass.

"So far, you've handled the club's duties wonderfully," he said.
"You're a natural, really, and you're strong. But going solo is a different kettle of fish. You really think you're ready, then?"

"Ready?" she asked. A tater tot actually did hop out onto the
grass. "Are you kidding me? I've been ready for this my whole life!"

Rigby held a finger to his lips. "Not everyone's ready for this.
Not until the club's ready to expand, that is. Until then, it's a very
select few."

"Including me," Kara said. It wasn't a question.

"And anyone you choose," Rigby said. "I trust you."

Kara looked down a half second and said, "Thank you . . . that means a lot."

"But this is about experience, not trust," Rigby explained. "You've only been, what, six times now?"

Kara huffed and looked away. "I know how to get in," she said. "I know how to create, how to navigate, and how to disguise."

"It's more than that, love," he said. "There are dangers you know nothing about."

Kara lifted her hands in the air. "Then tell me about the danger. Honestly, Rigby, what kind of trouble do you think I'll get into?"

"You want honesty, do you?" he asked, his voice deeper. "Well, there's plenty of trouble a novice can get into. Also, I'm concerned about the white knight you keep mentioning. I've more than a little suspicion that this Prince Charming type is actually the Dream King in disguise. He took out a Dreamtreader once that way."

"I didn't know that," Kara said quietly. "And Dreamtreaders are—"

"As strong as they come."

"I can finish my own sentences," Kara muttered. "And I can take care of myself. So what if this white knight is the Dream King? He's done me no harm. And it *is* his world. Kind of makes us guests, doesn't it?"

"Guests," Rigby said with a laugh. "Yeah, like parasites. I don't know, but I think he'd just as soon be rid of us."

"Rigby, please," Kara argued. "I want this. I need this. I'm begging you."

Rigby was still and quiet for several long moments. He turned away from her to avoid her eyes. He sighed heavily. "Right, then. If we're going to get you in solo, you need to understand that there are rules."

"Fine," Kara said, frowning. "But I thought anything goes in a dream."

"Almost," he said. "But there's a give-and-take. It's kind of like being on the moon. Sure, you almost ignore gravity and jump higher and farther than on earth, but there's that little thing called air that you rather need."

"Okay. So in a dream, I can do many things I could never do in reality, but the environment forces me to think about other threats."

"That's right," Rigby said, his eyes narrowing a moment. "That's exactly right. You really are quite smart, you know that?"

Kara blushed. "So what are the rules, then?"

Rigby glanced left, right, and over his shoulder. He turned to face Kara and said, "Rule number one: you've got only eleven hours of dream time. You'll hear the chimes of the big clock in your head. One to twelve, that's all."

Kara's eyebrows went up. Then she squinted. "Wait, you said we have eleven hours, but the clock tolls one to twelve. That's twelve hours."

"Right, but your clock, the one in your head, never tolls six."

"Why?"

"The Dream King made it that way," Rigby said. "If you ever hear the clock strike six, it's 'is time. That's rule number two: if the clock strikes six, you get out and wake up as fast as you can."

"Okay, you got me again. Why get out? If the Dream King is the white knight, he doesn't seem so terrible. He's actually been kind. Benevolent, even. He danced with me in the clouds."

"My experience has been a little different," Rigby said. "No benevolence and certainly no dancing. The guy's a dictator, and there's nothing he can't rule over in the world of dreams. He has another name, you know? Nightmare Lord."

"He's not a nightmare," she said. "Not to me."

"Listen, Kara, don't get too close, right? He can't be trusted."

Kara sighed. "Fine. Have it your way."

"It's not my way. It's the safe way. Lucid dreaming is a fantastic opportunity, but . . . it can be dangerous."

"But it's a dream, right? Not real, so how can it hurt you?"

"If you are captured or willingly stay past eleven hours, your personal stroke of twelve on the clock, you'll . . . ." Rigby paused. "You'll go away."

"What does that mean?"

"It means you won't wake up here again, ever. In the real world, you'll go away in your mind and never come back. You'll be in a coma for the rest of your life."

Kara ate a tater tot and mumbled, "Next rule?"

"You don't seem too worried about dying."

Kara shrugged. "I'm not worried. I'm just not going to let it happen."

"Well, good," Rigby said. "But don't even cut it close, not if you can 'elp it. Rule number three? Do not Lucid Dream more than two days in a row. If you do, you may start to warp. That means you'll begin to lose touch with reality. It'll become more and more difficult to tell the world of dreams and our world apart. Do it too often, you'll go mad. Trust me on this one."

Kara paused, connecting the dots in her mind. "Your uncle?"

Rigby nodded. He cleared his throat. "It wasn't pretty. Especially toward the end."

"I'm sorry."

"Yeah, well . . . pioneers often make the most sacrifices." Rigby's cheek twitched. He scratched absently at one of his sideburns. "If not for Uncle Scovy, we wouldn't be having this conversation."

"His research . . . well, he really made the breakthrough, didn't he?" Kara asked.

"Yeah, yeah . . . he's the one who came up with Anchor Theory. He discovered the Cerebral Countdown too." Rigby looked up at the exterior clock. "Lunch is almost over. We should finish this up some other time."

"C'mon. I don't want to wait another day. Just go fast. I won't ask any more questions."

"You sure?" Rigby asked. "We could talk after school."

"Yeah, I know," she said. "Just try."

"Rule number four: do not eat or drink anything that is black. It was most likely made or seasoned with something my uncle called gort. It's a kind of berry, I think. It can turn you into something like a zombie. You'll still be aware, but you'll be controlled by others more powerful, possibly even the Dream King, if he chooses."

"But eating's part of the fun," Kara said. Rigby gave her a look. "Got it," she continued, demure. "Nothing black."

"Rule number five is one you already know: Place your anchor in a place you can easily return to."

"Right. I remember."

"Rule number six: always check yourself for tendrils. Always. As soon as you get back. You know the light I gave you?"

"Yeah," Kara said. "I wondered about that. It looks like some CSI thing."

Rigby smirked. "Tendrils are like invisible leeches. You won't see them without UV light. You won't even feel them. They latch onto your thoughts and can manipulate them. If you come back to your anchor and leave without getting rid of them, you'll think you've woken up, but you'll really still be asleep. I don't need to tell you that that can be bad."

Kara's eyes widened. "So, yeah, I see. You think you're awake, but you're still there, so you miss your deadline. You stay in too long."

"Scary stuff. You usually don't pick up tendrils unless you're in a dream forest for a stretch of time. I don't know why. It's prob—"

The bell rang, signaling the end of lunch.

"Is that it?" Kara asked, standing up with her still-full tray. "Did we get through them?"

"Not quite," Rigby said. "One more. Rule number seven: don't get killed in the Dream. It doesn't kill you in real life. That's a bunch of Hollywood nonsense."

"So what does it do?"

"It keeps you from having a Lucid Dream ever again," he said. "The human body is an amazing thing, right? The mind protects itself. If you get killed in a dream and actually experience the life leaving your body, your mind seals off the nerve passages that make Lucid Dreaming possible. It's quite extraordinary, really."

"But I can get shot or stabbed or blown up?" she asked. "I mean, I know I'm in a dream and that it's not really happening."

"Sure," he said. "Yeah, so a guy pulls a gun on you in the Dream world. You see it. You know it's a gun, but you know it's a dream, so the bullets hit you. It takes a moment for your brain to catch up. You might bleed a little, but you can make it go away."

"Right, right," she said. "But?"

"But if something happens suddenly, without warning, say, like a beheading, your mind doesn't catch up. You feel yourself fade out. You can't come back. Uncle Scovy had a research partner that happened to, so that's 'ow he figured it out."

"What happened to him?"

"You don't want to know," Rigby said, heading for the door to the cafeteria. "C'mon, we have to get to class."

"No, tell me," Kara said. "Please."

Rigby stopped, sighed, and put his hands in his pockets. His intense brown eyes seemed to withdraw within themselves. His usually too-cool, sideways smirk vanished. "It was like the guy was an addict," Rigby said at last. "Going through withdrawals because he couldn't experience Lucid Dreams any longer. It was horrible: panic attacks, the shakes, paranoia. Eventually, he went mad and jumped off a bridge."

In a sightless chamber, where the cold lingered and the air was as still as a grave, two figures sat crouched in the dark.

"It was foolish," he said.

"Seeking to aid someone in dire need is never foolish," she replied. "How long will you distress yourself? Isn't the torture from our captors enough?"

"No, Mesmeera," he said. "It's not. It was my folly that drove us both on that beady-eyed little maggot's errand. It was my folly that took us into the forsaken moors of Archaia. And it was my folly that led us into the Lurker's torture chamber."

"Look at me, Duncan!" Mesmeera hissed.

"I cannot look . . . at . . . you."

"Right." Mesmeera released a caustic sigh. "I know that. Imagine me, then. Imagine my face, stern and indignant. Imagine my green eyes flashing with anger . . . *and* compassion. *Listen* to me. It is not noble to rob me of my responsibility in this matter. I wear these chains now, not because you led me to them. I did. I chose to follow. I made a decision at every turn. It was my folly as well as yours!"

Mesmeera let out fierce cry and shook her fists. The heavy chains rattled, their weight forcing her arms to drop.

Duncan scratched quickly at his beard. "There is wisdom in what you say. But I led you, Mesmeera. I led—"

"Lead, follow—what difference does it make? It's all a choice. There's no escape in blame, no comfort in shirking responsibility. We all make choices. We must all face the consequences of those choices."

"Even when it means we both knew better, that we both knowingly broke almost every rule of Dreamtreading? Even when it means that we will never see the waking world again? Even when it means we will forever be at the mercy of utter wickedness . . . even then?"

"Yes, Duncan. Even then." Mesmeera sighed. "The truth may hurt, but it is never so agonizing as the dagger of lies we tell ourselves." She was quiet a moment, resting her head on her cuffed wrists upon her knees. Then she said, "Besides, we need to use our thoughts for something more productive, like getting out of here. I'm not ready to believe we don't have a part to play in this yet."

"Shhh!" he whispered. "Someone's coming."

"Yes, I am coming to visit you," came a rasping voice, seasoned with a peculiar buzzing, almost like hornets. "I have brought nourishment, meat and bread." Footsteps grew nearer.

"Well, now, that's a relief," Duncan quipped. "More dream food. You know it does us no good."

"Oh, it will now, Dreamtreaders."

The voice was just outside the cell bars, but Duncan and Mesmeera could see nothing in the inky black of the chamber. "What do you mean?" Mesmeera asked.

"This food will nourish your minds. Take. Eat."

Duncan recoiled as a hunk of bread was pressed into his hand. He hadn't heard the cell door open. But someone was in with them now.

Mesmeera let out a yelp.

"Mes!" Duncan called.

"I'm okay," she said. "Just startled me is all. Gave me the food."

"Same here," Duncan said. He lifted the bread to his nose. It smelled fresh. It smelled spectacular. Cinnamon for sure. Maybe nutmeg. He took a bite and found it was something like raisin bread. There were little pieces of dried fruit within the flaky flesh of the bread.

"Thank you for the food," Mesmeera whispered, her eyes straining to pick up some form, some figure outlined against the thick darkness. She saw no contrast. Only pitch-black. "Hello? Are you still here?"

"Yes. Still here."

"You said this food nourishes our mind. How so?" she asked.

"Your minds are forever in the Dream," the voice said. "They will need stimulation. My food can do that for you. But I wonder if someone will take such good care of your physical bodies in the Temporal."

"Don't you worry about that," Mesmeera said defiantly. "We have plans in place."

There was laughter from the darkness, but it was not pleasant.

"You've kept us in darkness all this time," Duncan said. "Why all the hiding?" There was no answer. "At least tell us where we are?"

The laughter stopped abruptly. "Now that you've eaten, I suppose you'll have the strength to bear it. So I will tell you about your new home. It is called Number 6."

FIFTEEN

GALLOWS HALL

Archer had a problem. Lots of problems, actually, as usual. This was a new one, however, and as he tried to soldier through a droning Chemistry lecture, this fresh issue vexed him. He'd brought Bezeal's coveted puzzle box, the mysterious Karakurian Chamber, back from the Dream.

He hadn't meant to. He'd meant to take it straight to Bezeal and be done with it. But the Stroke of Reckoning had sounded, and there had been no way to get back to Kurdan in time. Still, when the Dreamtreader hit his anchor, he hadn't expected the puzzle box to come back with him. That's not how things worked.

On one of his first Dreamtreading trips, Archer had found a six-inch, superfuzzy, talking caterpillar. He wanted to keep it as a pet, so he held on to it when he touched his anchor. The caterpillar did not enter the waking world. Archer had repeated the experiment with metals, stone, paper, leaves, jewels—even food. Nothing came back. Ever.

Yet the Tokens of Doom had come back. Somehow the Nightmare

Lord had attached them to Archer before he went to the anchor. That was the first time. Now the puzzle box.

". . . hope you are all preparing well for the Battle of the Brains," Dr. Pallazzo was saying. "Monday will be *A* through *H*. Tuesday, *I* through *P* . . ."

Archer bolted upright. *Tuesday? Tuesday! I haven't started studying. Rigby is going to slam me.* No, that wasn't quite accurate. *Rigby is going to beat me fiercely about the head and shoulders, drop-kick me into the lower atmosphere, and then slam me.*

Archer shook his head. *Okay, so I have two problems. I'm going to fail Chemistry. And I've brought back some kind of powerful relic from the Dream.* A little voice in the back of Archer's mind whispered that there was a third problem that maybe trumped them all: he'd defied Master Gabriel. Inexcusably. Directly. Absolutely. Archer rushed that voice back into a dark mental corner.

The bell rang, emptying classes out into the halls. Kara pushed by Archer to catch up with Rigby. She didn't say a word. All Archer could do was shake his head.

Amy appeared at Archer's elbow. "You getting ready for the big match versus Rigby?" she asked, bubbly as usual.

"Kaylie's on board," he said dismally. "But there's only so much she can do. After all, it is Chemistry, and I am, well . . . me."

Amy laughed. Archer laughed too, his snorts inspiring new rounds of snickers and giggles.

"I *love* your laugh," she said. "You sound just like Elmer Fudd, uh . . . with snorts."

"You love my laugh?" Archer asked. "Most people think it's annoying."

"How can anything that makes you laugh be annoying?" she asked. "Laughter makes the world go round."

Just like that, Amy was gone, off on her way to Tech Ed. Archer had a random thought about Amy, but tossed that one quickly into the same mental corner as his imprisoned worries about Gabriel.

Puzzle box! Think! Archer wondered what it was. Why did Bezeal want it so badly? Why had the other Dreamtreaders gone after it? Had they also been tempted by the offer of a sure-fire way to dethrone the Nightmare Lord? That was the only answer that made sense. Duncan and Mesmeera were not stupid. They didn't take unnecessary risks. Still, they had gone after the puzzle box.

Archer wasn't thinking about his path to Gym class. He came to the T-junction in the hall. To go left was the long way, around the auxiliary gym. Going right was much shorter, past the custodial offices and supply rooms, and up the hallway known as Gallows Hall.

Still puzzling over the puzzle box, Archer turned right.

The best thing to do would be to contact Gabriel, confess his lack of obedience, and give him the puzzle box. If anyone knew what to do with it, Master Gabriel would. If anyone could see through Bezeal's deceptions, Master Gabriel could. And if anyone could banish Archer into some nether-region hole in the ground, Master Gabriel could. Archer chucked that idea into the already crowded corner.

That led to an even more frightening thought. What about the Superior? Would the Superior be upset about Archer's lack of obedience?

Suddenly, Archer stopped walking. The light in the hall dimmed ahead. It was not a gradual thing either. It went from full light to a little light . . . to no light.

"Gallows Hall," Archer muttered. "Why did I come this way?"

He looked ahead. The Gym entrance was the very last door on the right at the very end of the hallway. Prior to that, there were two alcoves on the right: one to the girls' locker room; one for the boys' locker room. There was one gap on the left-hand side for restrooms and two drinking fountains notched between. Even on a blazingly sunny day like this one, all three of these areas were in almost complete shadow.

There had been more fights and so-called "jumpings" in this hall than all the other halls in Dresden High put together. The principal and assistant principal did their best to patrol the area. They published a newsletter saying that the school had ordered new track lighting, but the Board of Ed had frozen school funds until a district shortfall could be taken care of. The result: Gallows Hall stayed Gallows Hall.

And it was Friday. Archer had heard Guzzy and his cronies talking about something going down on Friday in Gallows Hall, but what, and exactly when? He couldn't be certain, but he couldn't help but wonder if it might be some form of payback to Rigby.

"I should probably at least mention it to him," Archer muttered as he stepped into the shadows of Gallows Hall. He passed the guys' locker room, moving a little to the right as he passed the restrooms, and back to the left as he passed the girls' locker room. He could handle himself. Dreamtreader training had been heavily dosed with hand-to-hand combat. Archer wasn't really worried about a fight for himself, at least not one-on-one.

And Rigby had pretty much disabled Guzzy with one strike, though it had been an unexpected blow. But taking out several very strong, very devious guys would be a lot more dangerous.

Archer passed through Gallows Hall without incident and headed into Gym. Mr. Gant and Ms. Simmons divided up the classes into six soccer teams and turned them loose for the block. Archer loved soccer, but his mind was so busy with other issues that he all but phoned in his effort. Worse still, Rigby was on a different team, and they never played against Archer's.

But after class, Archer was determined to catch up to Rigby. The locker room was crowded, and Archer raced through the other boys trying to get to his locker. He passed Rigby's row and was about to turn in and talk to him, but three senior football players plowed right past and blocked the row. Archer figured he'd change first and then catch Rigby. He ducked under a towel battle and finally found a clear path to his own locker. He changed faster than ever, feeling very much like Superman ducking in and out of a phone booth. But unlike the Man of Steel, who usually arrived on time to save the day, Archer zipped around two banks of lockers to find Rigby already gone.

"Did you see which way Rigby went?" Archer asked Chris Hopper, whose locker was close by.

"Nah, man," Chris said. "But he has Physics last with Mrs. Shapiro."

"Thanks," Archer said, racing out of the locker room.

The bell had rung and so the hallway just outside the gym was flooded. Archer hopped up and down as he passed through the throng, looking for Rigby. He wasn't headed the safe way, not unless he was ducking down for some reason while he was walking. That meant Gallows Hall. And that meant trouble.

Archer reversed course, pushed his way through the crowd, and started to duck down Gallows Hall. He felt a hand on his shoulder.

"Whoa, where are you going in such a hurry?" Kara Windchil asked.

Something in the back of Archer's mind mentioned that this was the first thing Kara had said directly to him all week. He was tempted to ignore her.

"Archer?" Kara said.

But then again, Archer thought, maybe she could help. "There's something going on," he told her, freeing himself from her grip to keep up his momentum. "Get a teacher, would ya? It's Guzzy in Gallows Hall."

Archer pressed on and passed into the shadows. He slowed just a step, wondering why he was wandering into Gallows Hall when he knew good and well that Guzzy and his buddies would be waiting. He heard the deep voices before he saw anyone. One, slightly annoyed, perfect diction, and an English accent: Rigby. The other, hoarse, gravelly, full of mischief: Guzzy.

Not thinking of what he was doing, Archer drove ahead. He passed the door to the girls' locker room, finding the group in the twilight near the restrooms. Archer skidded to a halt and instantly took in the situation. It was four against one: Rigby surrounded by Guzzy, Dev Gates, Gil Messchek, and Randy Pell.

". . . think you can just step off the boat and be the man?" Guzzy was saying, the rasp in his voice thicker than ever.

"Look," Rigby said, "I don't know what you think you know, but I'm not about takin' over your territory, right? Just startin' a club, that's all. I'd let you boys join, but I don't think you have the brainpower to handle it."

"Is he sayin' we're stupid?" Dev mumbled.

"Shut up!" Gil hissed.

Guzzy fumed. "Whatever, man, but you cheap-shotted me, made me look bad. You made it personal."

"That hurt, did it?" Rigby taunted. "Well, there's more where that came from. You and your boys better back off, or I'll do far worse than that."

Archer was initially frozen by Guzzy's speed. In a blink, he'd lunged at Rigby and launched a right cross. Rigby spun with the blow, but when he looked up, his lower lip was split and bleeding.

"That was a mistake," Rigby said, his voice quiet and menacing.

Dev surged forward, taking a wild swing, but Rigby slipped the punch and caught his attacker's forearm. With blurring speed and agility, he seemed to swing on Dev's arm, leaping up and hooking his lower legs on either side of the kid's throat. The move threw a ton of weight on Dev, felling him in a split second. Rigby rolled off, leaving his attacker gasping for air.

That was apparently enough of the one-on-one approach for Guzzy and the others. They came at Rigby from three different directions. That was also enough for Archer. He launched forward and performed a perfect base-stealing slide, taking Randy Pell off his feet.

"Keaton?" Randy breathed. "What're you doin'? Stay out of this!" Gil had awkwardly grabbed Rigby from behind in some kind of improvised wrestler's hold. Guzzy smashed a heavy fist right into Rigby's midsection. Rigby coughed, but must have been feigning because he used the blow and drove Gil backward into the hall's brick wall. Stunned, Gil let go, but Dev jumped up and thundered his cinder-block fist into Rigby's jaw.

All Archer could do was watch out of the corner of his eye as Randy came back in, ready to fight. Unlike Gil's wild punches, Randy's quick jabs seemed to have some real skill behind them. It was all Archer could do to duck and dodge them.

Back in the center, Rigby shrugged off Gil's heavy punch, but there was a lot of blood around his mouth. Gil and Guzzy seemed to be converging on Rigby.

A flash of movement, and Archer ducked two of Randy's quick jabs to the head. The uppercut that came next might have knocked out Archer had he not twisted his trunk to catch the punch in his shoulder. It still hurt, but Archer was able to hold on to consciousness.

At that point, there came shouts in the hall, but it wasn't a teacher, as Archer had hoped. Somehow high school students turned their fight-recognition-radar on all at the same time. Even half a school away, students could sense the buzz or tension in the air and come running to watch. On a Friday, it was all the more keen. As Archer ducked and bobbed and darted around Randy's relentless attacks, he saw the crowd gathering. This would not end well, no matter what.

Finally, the moment Archer had been looking for came. Randy had thrown so many shots that he'd grown weary, his breath ragged and heavy. He'd also missed with most of his jabs, turning his face red in anger as well as effort. Randy's next swing was clumsy and put too much of his weight forward. Archer kicked out his leg, hooking Randy's, spinning his opponent sideways before driving a side kick into Randy's ribs. Randy went down in a gasping heap.

When Archer looked up, the crowd of teens were yelling, Gil was on the ground clutching his elbow, and Rigby and Guzzy were slowly circling each other. Archer's blood ran cold. Guzzy had a knife.

"Move aside!" came a very loud, nasal voice. It sounded like the assistant principal, Mr. Bohrs. Archer wasn't sure that he would make it in time. "Let me through!"

Guzzy's nose and lip were bleeding. The corner of his right eye had a red, golf ball-sized welt growing. His face was a mask of fury. He brandished the knife as if he'd used it before.

"That changes things," Rigby said.

"Do that martial arts stuff now!" Guzzy hissed.

"Guzzy, don't!" Archer yelled.

"Should've minded your own business, Keaton," Guzzy said, never taking his eyes off Rigby.

"Are you certain you want to cross this line?" Rigby asked. There was something different in his tone now, something Archer hadn't heard before. There was an odd inflection on the end syllables of every word, almost as if there was a second voice speaking Rigby's words but ever so slightly off in timing.

"You started this!" Guzzy snapped.

"Look around," Rigby said. "There are fifty witnesses. Put the knife away now, maybe no one says anything."

"Everybody! Move! Now!" Mr. Bohrs yelled, still too far away.

Guzzy tightened the circling. He lowered the knife hand to his side. Archer thought for sure he would strike. Less than a yard lay between the fighters.

"Are you sure you still have a knife?" Rigby asked, his voice still strange. With a rippling of his fingers, Rigby made a gun with his hand and pointed.

Archer blinked, stupefied. He blinked again, but what he saw, well . . . it was still there. Instead of a knife, Guzzy now held a bouquet of bright yellow daisies.

"What . . . ?" Guzzy's mouth dropped open. He dropped the flowers, and his knife clattered to the floor.

"I can do things," Rigby whispered as he lunged forward. "You don't want to mess with me. Ever." Guzzy retreated so far that his back hit the wall.

Just then, the crowd parted and Mr. Bohrs lumbered forward. He slammed Guzzy up against the wall and simultaneously put his rather large foot on the knife. "This is it, Guzzy!" the assistant principal rumbled. "This is a weapons violation. You'll be expelled . . . if you're lucky!"

Kara was suddenly at Archer's side. "You fight pretty well," she said. "I never knew."

Archer didn't know what to say. "Thanks for getting Mr. Bohrs. This was getting ugly."

"I didn't get Mr. Bohrs," she said. "Not sure who did."

"You . . . but I asked you . . ."

"And miss the fight?" she said. "Are you kidding?"

"Keaton, Pell, Gates, to my office!" Mr. Bohrs yelled. "Now! And someone call the nurse for Messchek!"

SIXTEEN

Trading in Fate

"Suspended?" Archer's father erupted.

"It's the school's zero-tolerance thing, Dad!" Archer argued, pacing the den. "I didn't start the fight. It was four against one and I was trying to help!"

"But we taught you violence doesn't solve anything."

"I know, Dad, I know. I'm sorry."

"Suspended? Really, Archer?"

"I didn't know what else to do," Archer said. "I didn't want to see . . . well, I just didn't want to let . . . ." His voice trailed off.

Archer's dad dropped his hands from his hips. He'd already run out of fight. He plopped down in his armchair and stared straight ahead. "Guess you did right, Son . . . but still."

"I know," Archer said, stopping near the stairwell. *That's it, Dad? I get suspended for fighting, and that's all you got?* It was crazy to think that way, Archer knew. He honestly didn't want more consequences. He just wanted to see his dad show a little spirit, a little more . . . life. Maybe he just needed a little prompting. "So how long am I grounded for?"

His father didn't answer at first.

"Dad?"

"No," his father said. "You got suspended. That's enough."

Archer shook his head. "It's just Monday. Anyway, I guess I can use the extra time to study Chemistry."

Archer trudged up to his room and flopped down onto his bed. He had a burning urge to summon Master Gabriel. After what he'd seen Rigby do with the knife or flowers or whatever, well, it was mind boggling. In the Dream, Archer could turn a knife into a water buffalo if he wanted to, but in the waking world? How did Rigby do that? Was it some kind of sleight of hand? Some kind of hallucination? Archer had no idea.

That was exactly why Archer needed to talk to Master Gabriel. But Archer also had in his possession the Karakurian Chamber, the puzzle box he'd been forbidden to seek. And that was exactly why Archer couldn't summon his master.

For the whole weekend, Kaylie tutored Archer in the fine points of organic chemistry. Archer's chosen topic was "States of Matter." Rigby had picked "Atomic and Electronic Structure." Kaylie knew both . . . very well. Archer didn't. Needless to say, it was a long weekend.

It didn't help that Archer had an exhausting Dreamtreading adventure Saturday night. There had been more breaches than he could finish before the Stroke of Reckoning. Which meant Archer had to go back Sunday evening.

He sat on the edge of his bed and held the Karakurian Chamber in his palm. The Smurfs' song suddenly rang out from his cell phone.

"Kaylie," Archer grumbled, punching the cell's green-lit button. It was a text from Kara.

Sorry about Friday, she wrote. *I hope you didn't take it the wrong way.*

Archer rolled his eyes. As if there were a right way to take what she'd said. *I asked you to get help,* Archer texted. *All you did was bring a mob to watch the fight.*

Everyone likes to see the fights. Well, we don't want anyone to get hurt, but it kinda livens up the day.

Archer shook his head. *Really, Kara? That was just fun for you? People could have been injured.*

Not you and Rigby. You two can seriously fight. What was that? Kung fu?

"No, no," Archer mumbled to himself. He was not going to get sucked in by the compliment. He typed, *Look, Kara, I gotta run. I'll see you in school Monday.* He remembered and texted, *I mean Tuesday.* Then he shut down his phone and turned back to Karakurian Chamber.

Since the stupid puzzle box wouldn't fit in the case with the Creeds, Archer didn't know where to keep it. It was perfectly square and just too big to fit anywhere safe, and too odd to hide in plain sight. All six surfaces were made of a silvery metal so smooth that it looked like a liquid, almost like mercury. The images etched into the metal were intricate and captivating. One side had a ship with nine sails. Another side had skeletons dancing. The last side showed a rising sun with rays radiating out to two crescent moons.

Each side seemed to have its own story to tell among its hair-thin grooves. Certain pieces even looked like they might be movable. But who knew what this thing was?

An image flashed into Archers' mind . . .

He was tinkering with the puzzle box, flipped a small lever, and suddenly, there was a blinding white flash and a fiery mushroom cloud.

. . . but the Dreamtreader shook that thought out and went to his closet. He put the Karakurian Chamber on the second shelf and pushed it as far back as it could go, past the drawing pads, past the cans of pencils and markers, to the very back corner. It wasn't the best spot, but it was better than nothing. Only then could Archer relax on his bed. Duty called.

For once, sleep came quickly. One second, Archer was blinking at the alarm clock. The next, he was falling toward the canopy. A crimson tornado gave him a ride past Old Jack and deposited him in a gully that looked like a dried-up creek bed.

"No water?" Archer said. "No problem." He summoned his longboard and raced away in search of breaches to mend. The Dreamtreader began where he left off the previous evening: in the rocky crags of Farnham Tor. Just after he'd repaired his sixth breach, a familiar puff of purple smoke blossomed near his shoulder.

"Did you tell him?" Razz asked, seemingly doing the backstroke in the air.

"No, I didn't," Archer said, tying off a final stitch. "Not yet."

"Why?" she asked. "It's only going to get worse the longer you wait."

"I want to see if I can wrangle some information out of Bezeal first."

"Whatever would you want to do that for? He'll only feed you a pack of lies."

"I'm going to challenge him on the terms of our deal," Archer said. "Duncan and Mesmeera were not where Bezeal said they would be."

"Surprised?" Razz made a spluttering sound. "Bezeal is a liar."

"I know that, but he's bound by the blood pact. And I need more information."

The night went on, but by the eighth bell, all the breaches in Archer's district had been dreamwoven back to safety. Archer had plotted his course so that he could finish in Kurdan and go looking for Bezeal. Finding the peculiar merchant wasn't nearly the challenge that it might have been. The Dream sun was up, a blazing yellow-gold oval that seemed to hover too close to the landscape. It brought light and warmth, and the Kurdan Marketplace was hopping.

As Archer suspected, Bezeal was right in the center of all the action. "Sold!" the merchant cried. "This lovely grelsh cub with the tricolor horn, playful from the day he was born, to the Celosian shopper, shrewd Calgorn!" Bezeal clapped his hands for the local he'd just sold the creature to. His eyes glimmered as he spun around. The moment he saw Archer, he stopped.

"So, you've returned from dangers untold, a venture both noble and naturally bold, deliver my prize before Bezeal grows old."

"Not so fast, Bezeal," Archer said. "We need to talk. We can go somewhere private, or I can shout to the entire market how terribly you ripped me off."

Bezeal blinked. Honestly, Archer wasn't sure if it was a blink, but his light-point eyes went out for a moment. When they popped back on, Bezeal raised his voice and called to the crowd, "Good day, fine shoppers, and good afternoon. I have business away, and I must leave soon. But tonight I'll be back before the stars or the moon!"

The undersized merchant nodded for Archer to follow, leading the way through the crowd to a small shop at the edge of the market. Archer didn't remember it, really. It was one of a thousand little shops and taverns. This one seemed to feature its baked goods. Bezeal ordered a muffin dotted with large black seeds. He offered one to Archer, but the Dreamtreader knew better. They sat at a candlelit corner table, and Archer said, "That was a pretty low attempt, even for you."

Bezeal's Cheshire grin appeared for half a moment. "You Dreamtreaders have so many rules, it's hard to keep track. You can eat something blue, but never eat black. I'm surprised that you ever dare to come back."

"Look," Archer said, placing one hand flat on the table. "You told me I'd find Duncan and Mesmeera in the same place as the puzzle box. I found the puzzle box, but my friends were nowhere to be seen."

Bezeal gasped. "You . . . you found it? The box?"

Bezeal's unrhymed reaction took Archer a little off his game. The little man really wanted that box. It was time to switch tactics a little. "I've got the box, Bezeal, but to tell you the truth, I'm beginning to kind of like it, especially the side with the ship of many sails."

"Ohhhh," Bezeal sighed. "You do have it."

"Yes, and I'm going to keep it. Or maybe I'll destroy it . . . unless you tell me where my friends are."

Bezeal leaned forward far enough that his hood slid down to nearly cover his eyes. "How dare you challenge me. That's no way to act. You shook my hand. You made a blood pact. Leave me be and return with my prize intact."

"You tricked me into the blood pact," Archer said. "I didn't agree to bleed over the deal. And then you lied about the other Dreamtreaders. This is barely a deal at all. But I'm still willing to give you the box. You need to tell me where my friends are, and you need to tell me how to destroy the Nightmare Lord."

Bezeal lifted a muffin to his hood. There was a sickening suction sound, and half of the pastry disappeared. When he spoke again, his words hissed between his teeth. "If you would learn the Dreamtreaders fate, perhaps they were taken; perhaps, escaped. But in the end, it was far too late."

"Wait," Archer said. "Are you telling me that Duncan and Mesmeera might have escaped? That makes no sense. They would have contacted us by now. And what do you mean by too late? Too late for——?" Archer's mouth snapped shut. With hopeless clarity, he realized what Bezeal meant.

Duncan and Mesmeera had stayed past the Stroke of Reckoning. Archer shook his head. "How could this happen?" he muttered. "They were too smart for that."

"Bezeal knows not what kept them too long, but in this world many things can go wrong. I suspect the tendrils and their illusion were strong."

"Tendrils," Archer whispered. Icy cold conviction sliced down his spine. Those things were the bane of all Dreamtreaders. If it was already close to Duncan's and Mesmeera's Stroke of Reckoning, and they carried tendrils back to their anchors, they would believe they'd awakened. They'd have gone about their lives, never realizing that they were still in the Dream until it was too late.

Archer hung his head. "What about the Nightmare Lord? How can he be defeated?"

Bezeal's smile appeared for just a flash. "He is terribly strong and knows his world well, but there is a secret within that fierce shell. Until you bring my treasure, I will never tell."

Archer was about to unleash two days worth of pent-up anger when Old Jack began to toll. Bezeal didn't seem to hear it, and it tolled past five to seven, stopping at eleven. The Dreamtreader didn't have much time to get back to his anchor, but he didn't want to let Bezeal off so easily. Archer summoned half of the mental strength he had left and readied to create. "I don't trust you, Bezeal," he said. "No one in the Dream trusts you. Now, I warned you once, and you crossed me. Do it again . . ." Archer paused and waved both of his hands.

A massive oak-beam and wrought-iron guillotine materialized, crushing Bezeal's chair. The merchant stumbled forward and came to rest with his neck in a very awkward spot.

". . . And I'll finally get to see just how ugly your head really is." Archer nodded, and the huge, razor-sharp cutting blade began to fall.

Bezeal shrieked. "No, no!"

Archer raised his hand, and the blade vanished just inches from beheading Bezeal. A second later, the entire guillotine was gone, and the merchant was back in his chair. "Don't forget," Archer said.

Bezeal adjusted the collar of his hooded robe. "Bezeal never, ever forgets, but kill him, and you'll have such dreadful regrets. You'll never stop the Nightmare Lord's threat."

Archer glared once more at Bezeal and stepped outside. But then, a memory of Lady Kasia flickered, something she'd said. He turned back through the doorway. "Bezeal, I heard you violated the Inner Sanctum of—"

". . . ing weary of this part," Bezeal was saying. His voice was different, confident and ringing of power. At first Archer thought maybe someone else had been talking. After all, he couldn't see Bezeal's lips moving, not in the inky black within his hood.

"Who are you talking to, Bezeal?" Archer asked.

"Speaking to myself, oh Dreamtreader supreme. Imagination it was, I deem. Perhaps your time has come to leave the Dream."

Archer frowned and left the café. *Maybe I was imagining,* he thought. *But that was weird.*

When Archer awoke, there was bright sunshine in his room, and Kaylie was all dressed for school.

"Playing hooky today, huh?" she asked, a little bounce in her pigtails. She sat at Archer's desk with her backpack toward the bed.

Archer rubbed his eyes. "I got suspended," he spoke through a yawn. "There's a difference."

"Is your Battle of the Brain still tomorrow?" Kaylie asked.

Archer squinted. "Yes, unfortunately."

"Means just tonight left to study," Kaylie said. "But don't worry. I'll help you."

Kaylie still didn't turn around.

A little puzzled, Archer stared at her. "Whatcha doin?" he asked.

"Playing," she said.

"With what?"

"Your little game," she said. "You know, it's good that you've been playing with this. It really does challenge your mind . . . for a little while, anyway."

"Kaylie, show me what you have. Turn around."

Kaylie shrugged once and turned in her chair. In her hands, there was the gleam of silver in the sunlight. She held the Karakurian Chamber. And it was open.

SEVENTEEN

THE BATTLE OF THE BRAINS

"WHAT IS IT?" KAYLIE ASKED. "I MEAN, BEYOND THE OBVIOUS?"

"Kaylie," Archer said, his words clipped with tension. "I want you to put that into my hands . . . right . . . now."

"But it's fun," she said, turning the box at different angles to reflect a sunbeam.

"Look, I don't know how you got that open," he said, "but truth is, it could be dangerous. Very dangerous. Please, Kaylie, give it to me now."

"Oh, fine," she said, wriggling out of the chair. She gave the puzzle box to Archer.

Kaylie had managed to open the Karakurian Chamber, but it was so intricate that Archer wasn't certain what he was looking at. Three of the sides had unfolded into platforms, each with multiple gears and components.

"What did you mean, Kaylie?" Archer asked. "What did you mean when you said . . . 'beyond the obvious'?"

His sister shrugged. "It's a toy."

Her hand moved to some lever on the side of it that Archer hadn't even seen.

There came the tinkling of bells, a very pretty birdsong trill, and one of the platforms began to transform. The skeletons frozen in their dance came to life, each one raised on a tiny wire and spinning round and round. Then, one after the other, each skeleton leaped up and disappeared as though falling into a hole in the platform.

Archer leaned forward as Kaylie reached out and depressed another latch. The ship with nine sails emerged from another platform. It was all metal, that was certain, but the sails undulated and shimmered as if filling with trade winds for a voyage.

"This is incredible," Archer whispered.

"See, I told ya it's a toy," Kaylie said. "Where'd you get it?"

"Wait," Archer said. "Wait. Can you close it?"

Kaylie's fingers danced over and around it like flesh-tone spiders. There were more chimes and tinkling sounds, pieces of silver slid this way and that, and things collapsed into each other. In a few moments, the Karakurian Chamber returned to its initial form.

"Kaylie," he said, "this is a very rare artifact, and . . . it doesn't really belong to me. And like I said, it might even be dangerous."

"Don't be silly," Kaylie said. "What could be dangerous about it?"

Archer shook his head. "Please, Kaylie, just promise me that you won't touch it again."

Kaylie hesitated a moment, but nodded. She tilted her head sideways. "Oops! Time for me to go to school. Bye, Archer! Enjoy playing hooky!"

The violent cyclone gave Kara Windchil a splendid view of the Dreamscape. It was constantly changing: alpine one minute, desert the next, and so on in every imaginable environment. That was one thing Kara hadn't quite figured out. *How can you protect your creations when there are billions of other people dreaming their stupid random nonsense all night long?*

This was one of a few important remaining questions. Questions to be dealt with later. For Kara, for now, it was time to play. To play like she had never played before. Once the vortex deposited her safely upon the Dreamscape surface, Kara did a cartwheel. Then she flew.

There was nothing on earth like flying. Watching the multi-colored surface fall away, soaring ever higher, and gliding among the mountaintops or even up to the great old clock. Kara couldn't help but giggle as she dropped to stand upon the great tower. Her time was all before her. Nearly eleven full hours. She'd never felt so happy or so free before. She yelled, "Now—at last—I finally know the rules!"

Kara stood at the very edge of the clock tower and raised her arms. The boiling clouds above, the massive churning banks that spawned so many tornadic vortices, responded to Kara's call. And so did the lightning. Great sparking blades of electrical light shot down to the Dreamscape. *"Yes!"* Kara exulted. "Exactly like that!"

Kara closed her eyes and leaped from the tower. Not to fly. She plummeted instead, soaked in the acceleration. Then, she altered the Dreamscape into an open sea beneath her. Eyes wide open now, she pulled up and set herself to running across the water. The whitecaps felt cool on her toes, and the spray chilled her face, but she did not sink. She ran and grinned, the rain pelting her face, pelting every inch of her. Lightning flashed and thunder clapped overhead, and Kara laughed aloud. "I know the rules!" she cried out and punctuated her words with another fierce lightning strike.

Something came to her in that moment, something her parents

had drilled into her ever since she was little: rules equal freedom. To enter a Lucid Dream without knowing the rules meant constant fear and worry. It meant never knowing what you could and could not do. It meant a complete diminishing of the entire experience. And Kara Windchil would not have anyone or anything diminish her experience.

"Live now, live fast!" she shouted at the waves even as she leaped through them.

Kara leaped off the surface of her sea and flew once more, this time taking a more direct path. She blasted through mist and low-hanging clouds, speeding north where she wanted . . . snow. *Yes, I would like snow.*

The sky became a mantle of slate gray, and the air filled with ten trillion dizzying eddies of wind-whirled snowflakes.

Whoa, Kara thought, blinking sleep and snow from her eyes, *that took a lot out of me.* But Kara knew her destination was coming up soon. She navigated the mountains north and west of Shadowkeep, looking for the white fortress built high upon a cleft. The stronghold was a massive barrel-shaped vault hewn from the natural stone but was often hard to spot due to its pale color and the frequent snowfall. Yet Kara found it with little trouble. As if drawn to it magnetically, she sailed in one of the long rectangular windows and seated herself at the table within.

"This will never work," she said. The sole reply was her echo. Kara pounded a fist on the table. A crackling fire roared to life within the corner hearth. Torches sprang up even as tapestries rolled down the chamber walls. Music chimed throughout the hall, music from the strangest ensemble ever formed: lute, harpsichord, electric guitar, bass, synthesizers, brass, and percussion—all played by multi-colored monkeys. The table, now overlaid with a brilliant white silk cloth, adorned itself with a feast fit for a king, queen, and quite a few other members of a court. Kara sighed contentedly and sampled a little bit of everything: roast duck, a dollop of braised potatoes, a piece of chocolate layer cake that was more than a foot tall.

"Yummm." It had been an exhausting effort to create it all, but it had been worth it. Kara entertained herself for hours, always carefully noting the exact time. She sat by the fire and sipped from a pewter goblet. It was quiet contentment at its finest.

Not long after, Kara felt she had regained all of her strength, that is to say, her mental energy. She was considering another swift flight across the Dreamscape when the great clock began its warning. Only it did not ring out eight bells as it was supposed to. It rang out six.

Sixtolls.

When Kara stood up from the table, she wore a dazzling white ballroom gown. "I won't be running home," she said, taking to the air. "I am going dancing."

"And after six rounds," Dr. Pallazzo announced to the class, "our two parolees are virtually tied."

Parolees, Archer thought. *Very funny.* Ordinarily, he might have been resentful of the teacher's quip, but not today. Today, Archer was too busy feeling pretty extraordinary. He was holding his own against the GIFT kid himself: the brilliant, the high and mighty Rigby Thames.

On top of that, Kara Windchil looked as though she'd gotten a pretty healthy dose of what-goes-around-comes-around. She looked positively awful. Her normally silky-straight black hair was tousled, and her makeup was smeared. She looked bleary-eyed and sniffled a lot, like she had a cold.

"The next question will be from Mr. Thames's category: Atomic and Electronic Structure. This will be the deciding question. Are you ready?"

Rigby nodded. Archer nodded also. Thanks to Kaylie's expert instruction, he didn't even hesitate. The Chemistry class went silent.

"Electrons gather around the nucleus in quantum orbitals following four very basic rules. We call these rules . . ."

Archer's thoughts rolled away. *Kaylie showed me this on the chart paper. She had written it in pink crayon at the top of the third page. Elbow Principle? No, no. But similar—*Archer slammed his hand down on the desk.

"Mr. Keaton?" Dr. Pallazzo shifted his gaze. Even Rigby looked impressed.

"It's the Aufbau Principle," Archer said.

"Yes, yes," Dr. Pallazzo confirmed. "That is correct, and now, as per the full question, you must state the four basic rules of the Aufbau Principle."

There wasn't a hand large enough in the universe to deliver the kind of facepalm Archer felt like he deserved. *I didn't listen to the whole question!*

"Mr. Keaton?"

"Uhm . . ."

"Aww, really?" Rigby said. "You're messin' with me now, right? Dodgy sandbagger."

Archer wasn't messing with anyone. He didn't remember the four rules. It had something to do with electrons filling up orbitals, and two of the rules were pretty much the same. But it didn't matter. He released an enormous breath and said, "I can't remember the rules."

"No way," Rigby said.

"The rest of the question goes to you, Mr. Thames," Dr. Pallazzo said. "Answer correctly, and the contest is yours."

Rigby gave the sly sideways grin and slowly recited all four rules from the Aufbau Principle. Half of the class sighed. The other half cheered.

Archer hung his head and went back to his seat.

After the bell rang and the Chemistry class emptied into the hallway, Archer headed for Gym as quickly as he could. He almost made it when Rigby sidled up. "You've surprised me twice, Keaton," he said.

"That's me," Archer said. "Full of surprises."

"First with Guzzy and his pals, then in the Chem battle today. You're quite the understated bloke. So, uh, anyway, about our bet . . . you don't have to do the pets. They're nasty and, well, really I think I owe you."

"No, I agreed to it," Archer said. "I'll follow through. Something I've learned the hard way lately. So, when do I start?"

"Tell you what," Rigby said. "Just start tomorrow after school, through Friday, if it's okay with your folks. Let three days be it."

"Okay, thanks. I'll let ya know."

"Need directions to my place?"

"The old Scoville Manor? Looks like something from *The Addams Family?*"

Rigby laughed. "Yeah, that's it."

"I know it. Pretty scary place . . . to live in, I mean."

"It's scary, all right," Rigby said. "Just wait until you see all the beasts you need to clean and feed. That's when you'll really be afraid."

"I'm pretty good with animals, so I'll make do, but . . . I wanted to ask you something."

"Sure," Rigby said. "Shoot."

Archer looked around. He and Rigby were like tall stones in a stream. Other students were everywhere. The hall traffic was especially congested. There was no way he could talk to Rigby about . . . about how he'd done the knife and flowers trick.

"Y'know," Archer said, "it can wait. I'll just talk to you at your house tomorrow."

Rigby squinted at him. "You're right cool, but a little weird too."

"You have no idea," Archer mumbled.

EIGHTEEN

SCOVILLE MANOR

SCOVILLE MANOR WAS A SHORT BIKE RIDE AWAY FROM Archer's home. To say that it sat on a hill was quite an understatement. It dominated the hill. It consumed the hill. Even the scraggly, dark trees in its yard refused to grow as tall as the old building's main spire.

Archer parked his bike at the bottom of the hill. He snapped his fingers twice. "They're creepy and they're kooky. They're absolutely spooky . . ."

No, he thought. *The Addams Family would be afraid to live here.*

The Victorian mansion looked as if the builders got carried away and forgot where the structure was supposed to end. All dark wood siding, irregularly shaped windows, and dragon-scale shingles— Scoville Manor was a sight to behold. There were three stories, two broad gabled roofs, two tall brick chimneys, some kind of attic sub-roof, and a widow's walk. Oh, and the spire had a dark, wrought-iron weather vane in the shape of a galloping horse.

Archer trotted up the hill via a set of wide stone stairs. Then six more traditional wooden steps to the front porch. As he expected, they creaked with every step. He pushed the doorbell and heard a melodic chime that reminded of him of something, though he couldn't quite remember what it was. Besides, the moment the bell sounded, there was an explosion of barks, yaps, and chittering.

"Leapin' loogies!" Archer exclaimed, taking a step back from the door. "He's got a zoo in there." The front door swung open, groaning on its hinges at a consistent, slow speed. And there was no one standing there.

"O-kay," Archer muttered, stepping backward almost to the point of teetering on the porch's edge.

There came a shriek, a blur of motion, and a tremendous thud. It was all Archer could do to keep from falling backward down the stairs. There stood Rigby just inside, grinning.

"Got ya!" he shouted. "You should've seen the look on your face. Sheesh, Keaton, you're quite the jumpy one."

Archer laughed at himself. "Yeah, well, next time you plan on doing that, give me a heads-up so I can bring an extra pair of boxers."

Rigby smirked. "Come on in," he said, leading Archer between a staircase and a sitting room and into a kitchen. The interior wasn't nearly as neo-Gothic-haunted. It was actually quite modern, especially the kitchen, which was all brushed silver appliances, spice racks, and high-end cookware. It looked like something out of that cable cooking show: *Master Chef*, or *The Iron Spatula*, or whatever it was called.

"Can I get you something to drink?" Rigby asked. "A snack? You got here pretty fast after school. Can't imagine you 'ad much time to eat at 'ome."

"That's okay," Archer said, though his stomach was rumbling.

"You sure?" Rigby asked. "My mom left a bunch of those huge gourmet cookies. You know, the thick ones with hunks of chocolate instead of chips?"

Archer changed his tune instantly. "Well, a few of those couldn't hurt."

"That's the spirit," Rigby said. He went to the refrigerator, which looked to Archer like it could double as a guest room, and took out a gallon of milk. He poured two glasses, set them on the table, and came back with a platter of gigantic cookies.

"Uh," Archer said, "do we eat these or play catch with them at the beach?"

"I know, right?" Rigby said, digging in.

They munched cookies in relative silence, but it was an awkward thing. They exchanged glances, and Archer thought Rigby had a bit of a scientist-thing going on. Archer felt like he was being analyzed . . . measured. It was unsettling.

"Where are your folks?" Archer asked.

Rigby blinked. "Dad's out of town. He's a currency exchange specialist for investors, venture capitalists, that sort of thing."

"Venture capitalists?"

"Bunch of rich guys who don't know what to do with their obscenely large piles of money. So they look for poor inventors willing to give up the rights to a great new idea for a bunch of cash."

"Ah," Archer said. "And your mom?"

"At the tennis club," Rigby replied. "As usual." He drained his glass. "Guess we best get to it then, eh?"

Archer finished his glass and nodded. He wondered how to bring up the knife-flower incident. Maybe not just yet.

The basement stairs emptied into a T-shaped hallway. Rigby led Archer to the right, but Archer couldn't help glancing to the left. It was a short stub of a path drenched in shadows, with a single formidable-looking door at the end. Archer swallowed and said a silent prayer that there wouldn't be any animals he needed to take care of behind that door. He shuddered and turned his attention quickly back to following Rigby.

The smell hit Archer first. It was a combination of dry straw, mulch, dog food, and stale poop. When Rigby turned a corner, the yips, yelps, barks, and cries began again. "Yes, yes," Rigby said, "we've come to feed you. You can calm down now."

When Archer turned the corner, he stopped walking and found himself staring down the first of several aisles of cages, pens, hutches, and other pet enclosures. "Snot rockets!" Archer exclaimed. "You have a pet store down here."

"It was a passion of my late Uncle Scovy," Rigby said. "He collected rare and exotic pets for quite some time. We didn't have the heart to get rid of them. Come see."

Archer strolled down the aisle and gaped at almost every cage. A huge pair of golden brown eyes stared up at Archer from a network of branches and leaves. The eyes belonged to a fist-sized clump of fur with floppy triangular ears, a tiny peach-colored nose, and skinny knob-knuckled fingers. "What on earth is this thing?"

"Ha. Actually, it's not found on earth," Rigby said, retracing his steps. "Well, not many of them, anyway. This is a pygmy tarsier, quite rare, actually. We call him Herby. Now, take a look at his neighbor."

The next pen held a cross between a mop and a gray wig . . . with really dark eyes and a twitching nose. "Is . . . is this a rabbit?" Archer asked.

"Angora rabbit," Rigby said. "Folks in some countries make hats out of them. But not old Flops here."

The tour continued, revealing a squat creature with a tapered snout. Its shell was covered in a mixture of yellow and rose-colored scales. It scurried when it saw Archer and began burying itself in the thick straw of the crate.

"A pink fairy armadillo," Rigby said. "But you can call him Tex."

"Oh, man! Kaylie would love this thing!" Archer said.

"Who's Kaylie?" Rigby asked.

"My little sister. She is completely nuts over animals, especially cute ones."

"You should bring her with you tomorrow."

"Really?"

"Sure," he said. "Most of these beasties crave attention, well, except Tex there. He's shy."

Even in a zoo, Archer had never seen so many strange and interesting animals. In the Dream, sure, but never in the waking world. Rigby's family had a lemur, a tapir, a fennec fox, a sand cat, and even a red panda. There were dozens of animals, some quite cute and others, not so much.

"You sure you want to do this?" Rigby asked. "Now that you've seen how many there are?"

"Bet's a bet," Archer said. "So how do I take care of them all?"

Rigby grinned. "You have no idea what a relief it will be to not have to do this for a few days." He patted the top of a hutch, and the two gray ferrets that had been tangling inside instantly separated and darted away to hide. "Okay then, the one thing they all have in common is that they need water . . ."

So began an intensive half hour of curious creature care. Aside from the universal water need, these animals had completely peculiar diets: everything from premanufactured food pellets to tiny frozen mice to bamboo leaves. And, of course, there was the matter of cleaning out the cages.

Some of the pens had little trays that slid out from under to allow relatively easy dumping of critter poop, but others were much more complicated. A few required Archer to physically climb into a pen to get at the offensive animal droppings. Once, a lemur named Sherlock got hold of Archer's dark red hair and started to chew on it. That had been mildly alarming, but a sweet-natured female barn owl made up for it by perching on Archer's shoulder. She seemed perfectly content to ride there while Archer did his rounds.

"Whoa, Doctor Who really likes you," Rigby said. "She's normally pretty shy."

"Reminds me of Razz," Archer muttered half to himself as he admired the beautiful bird.

"Who's Razz?"

"Uh . . . just an old pet of mine."

Rigby raised an eyebrow. "What kind of pet?"

Archer didn't know what kind of creature she was. She was just Razz. But Rigby was waiting for an answer, and it would seem odd not to know. "Kind of a flying squirrel," Archer said.

"Really? Well, that's one creature we've never had here." He paused thoughtfully for a few moments. "I suppose that's pretty much it. You good? I've got a bit of running around to do. You don't have to lock the door when you go."

"You're leaving?"

"Yeah, why?" Rigby asked. "You're okay down here, right?"

Archer frowned. "Well yeah, sure. Doctor Who and I can handle things."

"Right, then," Rigby said. "See you tomorrow in school."

"Uh . . . hey, Rigby?"

"Yeah?"

"The other day, during the fight," Archer said, "I saw you do something."

Rigby's smile vanished for a split second, but then it was back.

"Oh, oh, that's Krav Maga," he said. "It's Israeli martial arts, actually a combination of all kinds of—"

"Not your fighting style," Archer said. "Not really. Some of the strikes were the fastest I've seen, but I'm talking about what you did to the knife."

That took care of the smile. "I didn't do anything to the knife," he said. "I never touched it, and Mr. Booring or whatever his name is took it."

"How'd you do it?" Archer asked. "How'd you turn the knife into flowers like that?"

Rigby laughed. Hard. "Look, Archer, I don't know what you think you saw . . ." His voice trailed off. His eyes flicked back and forth, and he frowned. Then, the smile was back. "Listen, I've got to get going, but . . . ah, tell ya what. I'm got a club going here at school. That's where I'm headin' now. Maybe you could come sometime, and maybe we could talk about what you think you saw." He didn't wait for Archer to answer. He turned and walked away.

Archer listened to Rigby's retreating footsteps in the hall, on the stairs, and then somewhere overhead. After that, other than the non-stop chattering of the animal kingdom, Rigby's house was silent.

Club? What did Rigby mean by that? Then, Archer laughed as a new thought occurred to him. *Son of a gun, he's starting a magic trick club. That's how he did it. Man, he's fast.* It made sense now. Given how quick Rigby could throw a punch or strike, it was clear that he'd used that speed to switch the flowers with the knife.

No, Archer thought. Part of his mind wasn't ready to let that slide. *I'm not buying that. It's not like Rigby was carrying flowers around all day just in case he could switch them with someone.*

There wasn't much he could do about it at the moment, so Archer set to work. It gave him time to think about something besides Rigby Thames. So many variables paraded through his mind: the puzzle box, Bezeal, the confession to Master Gabriel, Kara Windchil's most recent attitude changes, the ever-increasing number of breaches in the Dream, the missing Dreamtreaders, the mysterious Windmaiden, and more. Even Amy Pitsitakas made a suprise visit to Archer's thoughts. What was that about?

Through steady efforts, Archer finally finished his new chore routine. It really wasn't all that bad, actually. Well, the fecal disposal really *was* all that bad. But other than doodie duty, Archer enjoyed working with the animals. They seemed to accept him, especially Doctor Who. He had a hard time putting her back into her cage just before he left.

He bid the animals farewell and made his way back up the long hallway to the stairs. But at the stairs, he paused a moment. There was something about the door at the other end of the hall. Archer glanced up to the first floor, listened intently for a few ticks, and then slipped around the corner into the darkness.

With just a few steps, Archer stood directly in front of the door. It was metal, some kind of thick metal with riveted panels. There was a vertical handle and a digital keypad. It was obviously locked, but Archer tried a gentle push anyway.

It didn't budge. Not a centimeter. The handle had a slight vibration to it, and Archer took his hand away. *What on earth is behind this door?* It certainly wasn't normal. Rich people did have a reputation for being eccentric, but what was it? A bomb shelter? An international spy center? A hidden crypt full of vampires?

Okay, Archer thought. *Where did the vampire thing come from?* He quietly laughed at himself. He was about to leave when an absurd idea entered his mind. He crept closer to the door. Then, ever so slowly, he leaned his head close. Closer. Now his ear actually touched the cold metal of the door.

The whole basement seemed to go silent. Archer pressed his ear flat against the metal and squinted. He thought there was nothing at first, but then he heard it. It was a faint pulse of air, kind of a shoosh-ing sound. But there was something else too, a quiet, steady beeping.

For no reason that Archer could explain, he felt suddenly very afraid. He pulled his head away from the door and took to the stairs. He left Rigby's home, hopped on his bike, and didn't look back. There was something behind that door in the basement. Archer felt certain that whatever it was, it wasn't good.

NINETEEN

MASTER GABRIEL'S THIRD VISIT

"TIME TO FACE THE MUSIC," ARCHER MUTTERED, SHUT-
ting his bedroom door. He'd let it linger on his conscience for too
long already. Before he could talk himself out of it, he went straight
to his closet and took down *The Dreamtreader's Creed*. In the back of the
heavy book, there was a pocket containing a single white feather. It
was only for emergencies, but it was the only way he could contact
Master Gabriel on his own terms.

Archer sat down on his bed and removed the feather. He glanced
at his bedside table, at the lumpy piles of ash still there, the ominous
remnants from the Tokens of Doom. Two leaves, a black feather, a
segment of chain, now all turned to ash. What could it mean?

Archer was about to toss the "messenger" feather into the air
when a mental sledgehammer struck him a glancing blow. He stared
down at the white feather . . . and thought about the black feather.
*If the Nightmare Lord planted the tokens on me before I touched anchor, could the
black feather be a kind of messenger feather?* But to summon whom? Archer

swallowed. What would have happened had Archer thrown that feather up in the air? It was time. Archer tossed the white feather into the air. There was a small burst of sparkling light, and the single feather became a pair of small golden wings. They fluttered and spiraled up to the ceiling and vanished.

Archer shook his head. "This is going to sting."

"What is going to sting?" Master Gabriel asked, appearing just a foot from Archer's shoulder.

Archer caught his breath. "That was rather sudden," he said, trying to slow his racing heart.

"You do not often summon me, Archer," he said. "I felt I had better hurry."

That comment immediately added three more bricks to the weight Archer had already been carrying on his shoulders. He sighed.

"What has gone wrong?"

"*I* have, Master Gabriel," Archer said, closing *The Dreamtreader's Creed* and laying it beside him on the bed. "I've gone wrong."

"What do you mean?" The old master's dark eyes grew large. "You have not attempted another one-man storming of Shadowkeep, have you?"

"No, not that."

"I suppose not, or you probably would not be here."

Archer took in a deep breath. "I defied your command."

"Ah, I understand your original comment now. Yes, this will sting. Which command, Archer?"

Archer stood up and went to his closet. He came back with the silver puzzle box and handed it to Master Gabriel.

There was a moment of strangling tension, and Master Gabriel said, "I see."

"I'm sorry, Master Gabriel," Archer said. "It's just, I'd made a deal with Bezeal, a blood pact, and honestly, I just wanted to strike some kind of blow that matters in this fight. So I went into Archaia, I faced the Lurker, and I took the silver puzzle box."

"I know," Master Gabriel said simply.

"I wouldn't have escaped . . ." Archer's mouth snapped shut and he blinked. "Wait, you know?"

"I have tried to explain to you, Archer, that my vantage is different from yours. I have sources you know nothing about. I took the liberty of confronting Bezeal about the 'blood pact.' Even for him, that was a low play. I forbade him to force you to honor that pact, and that was when he revealed that you had already done so . . . to a point."

Archer sighed. "Oh, oh, man," he said. "You have no idea how relieved I am to know that . . . well, that you know. I felt so guilty and—"

"Foolish novice!" Master Gabriel said, his voice suddenly like a cannon blast. "This issue is not about making you feel at ease. In this action, you have sent a rippling wave through the Dream, and who can say where it will crash? You may have done yourself and others irreparable harm."

"Master Gabriel, I—"

"Archer?" The voice, high and soft, sweet with curiosity—shut off all other conversation. Master Gabriel vanished in a brief sparkle. Archer turned, and there stood Kaylie in her footie pajamas.

"Kaylie?" Archer said, staring back and forth between her and the door frame. "What are you doing still up?"

"It's only 9:30," she said. "Who's Master Gabriel?"

Archer fought back the urge to shout. "I . . . well . . . you know . . . it's . . . what?"

"When I opened the door, you were talking. You said, 'Master Gabriel' something or other. But no one else is in here . . . is there?"

"No, no, Kaylie," he said. "You're right, of course. No one's in my bedroom, except you. Oh, hey, hey, glad you came in. I wanted to ask you something."

"Really?" She put her doll in the crook of her arm and clapped. "What, what?"

"You kind of like weird animals, right?"

"Only the cute ones," she said, nodding emphatically. "Did you know that some sloths are so slow that algae grows on their coats?"

"Uhm, no," Archer said. "I didn't know that. But listen, Kaylie, how would you like to see a ton of rare animals? Bunches of cute ones too?"

Kaylie actually bounced. "Really? Really, Archer? Are you going to take me to the zoo?"

"Close enough," he said. "This new kid I've been hanging out with at school, he has a ton of pets. I mean a *ton* of pets. And they are some of the wildest, coolest things you've ever seen. Especially this barn owl named Doctor Who."

"Oh, I get it," she said. "Who, who!"

"Exactly," he said. "So what do you think? You want to go over and see the animals with me tomorrow after school?"

She didn't answer but padded across the bedroom floor and slammed a hug into Archer's legs.

"I'll take that as a yes," he said. He knelt down to be at her level and gave her a hug back. "Now, Kaylie, you know you're always welcome in here, but when the door's shut, you need to knock, remember?"

"I'm sorry," she said. "I'll remember next time."

"Okay, thanks," he said, ushering her out of the bedroom.

As Kaylie departed, Archer heard her say, "That glowy stuff around the door was cool. You need to show me how to do that."

Archer shut the door and swallowed. Master Gabriel appeared two heartbeats later. So did his ethereal door sealant.

"Your sister?" he asked.

Archer nodded. "How'd she get in? No one's ever gotten in before when you're here. Is something wrong with your power?"

Master Gabriel scowled. "Nothing is wrong with my power! The foolish notion!"

"Well, how did Kaylie open the door, then?"

"I . . . well, I do not know. That should not have happened. Only a chosen Dreamtreader can break a dreamseal. Could it be that you did not shut it flush initially?"

Archer went to the door. "It does stick sometimes . . . in the summer. Especially when it's humid." His voice trailed off. "It wasn't that hot today, though . . ."

"Be that as it may," Master Gabriel said. "We have a discussion to finish."

Archer's shoulders sagged. "I am sorry, Master Gabriel," he said. "I shouldn't have defied you. I know it now. I know it. It's just that, with Duncan and Mesmeera missing, I'm all alone out there. Razz is cool, but she's not another Dreamtreader." The next thought he would not speak aloud, but it was something that had bothered him for years. *I wouldn't be alone, Master Gabriel, if you'd come with me . . . and fight.*

Master Gabriel's expression softened. Something like sadness or regret rode on his brow like an unwanted hitchhiker. "So, then, there was no sign of Duncan nor Mesmeera in Archaia? They were not captives of the Lurker?"

"I don't know for sure," Archer admitted. "I never saw them. The Lurker spoke as if they'd been there, but then Bezeal said something about them escaping. But then they hit their anchors without checking for Tendrils. But Bezeal was holding something back. I don't trust that story, but I don't know what else to believe. Perhaps this has something to do with the Windmaiden . . ."

"Windmaiden?" Gabriel echoed sourly. "What are you talking about?"

"I've never seen her," Archer said. "But she speaks through the air. She guided me to my anchor that time . . . that time I faced the Nightmare Lord. If it weren't for her . . . I don't think I would have made it."

"I do not know this Windmaiden," Gabriel said slowly. "If indeed she did help you, I am grateful, but, Archer, you should know that there are Walkers about in the Dream."

"Walkers? Like something from the Nightmare Lord, something new?"

"No, something old," he replied. "Very old. They are called Lucid Walkers. They are people, not Dreamtreaders, but people entering dreams consciously. Like common thieves, they break in. They have no right to manipulate the world within the Dream, and yet they do. And no good comes of it. It never does. This Windmaiden may be such a one."

"But she helped me," Archer said. "There was no evil intent."

"So far as you know," Master Gabriel said. "Understand that every time these Lucid Walkers enter the Dream, they tear breaches larger than those of the scurions. If you meet one, even this Windmaiden, you must convince him or her to return to the Temporal and never Walk again. Explain to them the damage they are causing, the tragedy of a rift."

"Okay," Archer said. "Okay, I will."

"I need to depart. Stick to your schedule, Archer. Stick to it tightly. Weave as many breaches as you can."

"I really don't want to ask this," Archer said. "But is that it? No consequences for defying you? I deserve—"

"You have no idea what you deserve," Master Gabriel said. "As for your consequences, I give you the most severe of any: you will have to see this through. You take the silver puzzle box to Bezeal. Resolve your pact and be done with it. But know that the consequences may be dire."

DREAMTREADERS CREED, CONCEPTUS 4

Concerning those who call the Dream their home:

The three districts of the Dream are home to many races, creeds, and cultures. The flora and fauna are as rich and distinctive as any on earth. And the corral of creatures is especially full. It is an odd reality that, of the creatures dreamt up by the billions of sleepers on any given night, the vast majority of them are monstrous. This is no doubt due to the influence of the reigning Nightmare Lord.

From time to time, the creatures become so prolific that all three Dreamtreaders must stray from their normal activities. They must go forth on hunting expeditions to reduce the numbers of the most dangerous of these creations. We call this the Festival of Calling, but it is hardly a holiday. This is an extremely perilous task, for the beasts of Nightmare are brutal and vicious and numerous. That said, the rewards earned for a successful Calling are, quite literally, beyond one's wildest dreams.

TWENTY

PATCHWORK

ARCHER WANTED TO GO STRAIGHT TO BEZEAL, BUT THE number of breaches evident when he arrived in the Dream wouldn't allow it. There were whole new patches in almost every fiefdom. With Razz's help, he managed to sew them up by the eighth toll, leaving very little time for travel, a search for Bezeal, and any confrontation that could ensue.

Archer surfed to the outskirts of Kurdan and leap-walked the rest of the way. By ten tolls, Archer found the marketplace absurdly busy, ten times more than usual. In the central market, a mob of people gathered to make a mad run for some product being sold. Archer leaped from rooftop to rooftop until he could get a better look at what was happening. From the ledge of a bell tower, he saw that there was someone speaking on a huge platform that was piled high with small chests.

"Step right up, do not be shy," said the speaker. "You too can patch up breaches if you're willing to try. Ten golds are all you need for one of these kits of mine!"

It was Bezeal, of course. Who else spoke in rhyming triplets?

"Unbelievable," Archer muttered. "What a con artist."

"You're not going down there, are you?" Razz asked.

"Of course I'm going down there," Archer said. "He's ripping those people off. Ten golds? Are you kidding me?"

Razz's face reddened. "I don't think I want to be here for this," she said. "But call me if you need me." She vanished in a squiggly puff of purple smoke.

Archer leaped off of the bell tower and floated slowly downward until he came to a soft landing right behind Bezeal on the platform.

"A plague of breaches is upon us, you see?" Bezeal was saying. "And the Dreamtreaders aren't doing enough to help us stay free. So that means it's up to people like you and me!"

The crowd cheered heartily, but apparently it wasn't the roar Bezeal was expecting because he warily turned to look behind him. He jumped and his eyes flashed when he spotted Archer. "Whu-whu-what? Archer, why you . . . you're here. Look, good people, a Dreamtreader has come near! Now we know we have nothing to—"

"Save it, Bezeal," Archer commanded. The crowd gasped. "What are you selling these people for ten golds? Huh? What kind of scam are you running?"

"Shrewd as I am, I am not the heartless kind. I've invented a dream fabric patch that is so sublime. With it, anyone can mend a breach in very little time."

"Prove it," Archer demanded.

Bezeal's ultrawhite toothy grin appeared, and suddenly Archer felt as if he might have just become part of Bezeal's new advertisement campaign.

The small hooded merchant fished around in his robe pockets and at last removed a sealed glass jar containing a frantic scurion. He held it up for the crowd, causing titters of discussion. When Bezeal broke the seal and opened the jar, the customers standing closest to the stage drew back hurriedly.

Bezeal dumped the scurion onto the stage. It wasted no time, but arched up on its tail section and leaped into the air. It caught hold of dream fabric with its front mandibles and began to chew. Slowly, its head disappeared and light plasma began to flow. A breach had been opened. A small one, but a breach nonetheless.

Bezeal waited until the scurion's head poked back out. Then, with a pair of strange forceps, he grabbed up the wriggling, snapping scurion and tossed it back into the jar. He sealed it immediately and dropped it into his robe.

He raised his little green hands on either side of the breach, and the crowd responded with an appreciative muttering. "Now watch and be amazed," he said. "Do not avert your gaze. For we shall now subdue the blaze!"

He took a chest off the mountainous pile, opened it up, and removed two objects: a phial of some opalescent liquid and something that looked like a wire hairbrush.

Archer laughed openly and crossed his arms. "This ought to be good," he muttered.

Bezeal unstoppered the bottle, held it up just above the breach, and began to pour out its contents. The liquid sparkled as it drizzled over the breach, but it didn't pour through. Not a drop. It pulsed and surged and began to coat the breach. Bezeal emptied the rest of the liquid and then went to work with the brush. Lo and behold, the brush spread the liquid like spackle on drywall.

The enthusiasm of the crowd rose as Bezeal finished up. They cheered when he put down the brush and held up his hands victoriously. They pressed toward the stage with wads of golds in their fists.

"Me first!" one cried out.

"I'll take three!" someone else shouted.

"You aren't going to run out, are you?" came a third.

Archer bent at the waist and stared at the seemingly mended breach. There was still a tiny strand of leaking light plasma, but other than that, the breach was sealed. "I don't believe it," Archer said. "Bezeal, you evil little genius, you've done something extraordinary here!"

Bezeal's eyes flashed. He grinned, and strange pink glows appeared just where his cheeks would be . . . if he ever lowered the hood.

Archer continued, "I mean, this stuff won't hold indefinitely. It does let some plasma through, but . . . but this is genius. Can you repeat the recipe? Can you make it in great quantities?"

Bezeal grinned again. "Yesss, yess, as long as the golds keep flowing, my pocket to feed, I'll take some time off from my usual greed, and work hard, to make as much as you need."

"That is the best news I've heard in a very long time, Bezeal," Archer said. "But the price of ten golds is far too much, especially since it is no trouble to make more."

"But—"

"No, no, Bezeal," Archer said. "I'm already part of your show here. Let me do the talking."

"But I—"

"People of Kurdan!" Archer cried. He used his Dreamtreader creativity to both deepen and amplify his voice. The crowd hushed. "Bezeal here is a true patriot of the Dream!" Cheers from the audience. "For he has come to all our aid in this time of great need!" More cheers, growing dizzy with joy. "This brilliant invention may not completely mend the breaches that beset us, but they will bind them tightly until a Dreamtreader can permanently weave them shut! And you, good people and your neighbors in the other fiefdoms, must take up the fight against the breach plague!" Hysterical cheers. "And Bezeal, may his eyes ever shine brighter, has agreed to lower the price to two golds per kit!" The crowd erupted.

"T-two?" Bezeal spluttered. "But—"

Archer held up a hand. "No, no, Bezeal," he said. "I won't let you make the price any lower!"

"L-lower?"

Archer ran to the piles of small chests and began tossing them out to the crowd. "Here's yours!" he cried. "And yours!" One after the other, he launched kits to the villagers. "Razz, you won't want to miss this."

Poof! Razz was there in a puff of smoke. "What's up?"

Archer told her. She glanced mischievously at Bezeal. "Right," she said. "I'll help!"

Bezeal ran back and forth across the stage and collected golds from the people's willing hands. In less than an hour, Bezeal was completely sold out.

Back in Bezeal's rented cottage, he and Archer sat across a table and glared at each other for several minutes before either spoke.

"You just cost me a fortune," Bezeal said, his lack of rhyme obvious.

"Nonsense, Bezeal," Archer said. "I believe I just made you a fortune. I stopped counting golds in the thousands."

"It might have been tens of thousands," Bezeal hissed.

"Think of it this way," Archer said. "Do you know anyone who gets around the Dream like I can?"

Bezeal's bright eyes widened.

"I didn't think you'd take long to think it through," Archer said. "Now, this breach patch you've created is incredible. Like I said, it's not permanent, but it could be the key to stopping a full-scale rift. With your leave, I will carry news of your invention to every kingdom in the three districts."

Bezeal leaned forward and knocked over his tea. "All . . . all three?"

"Yes, Bezeal. Can you see the profits mounting now? If you want, I'll even tell them that each district must send you a brick of chocolate every moon."

Bezeal clapped his green hands. "Yes, yes," he said. "A thousand times, yes! Chocolate and golds unending sounds good, I confess!"

"Now, Bezeal," Archer said, reaching into the deepest inside pocket of his leather duster. He placed the silver puzzle box on the table and slid it across the surface. "As per our bargain, I have brought your coveted relic."

Bezeal reached for it, but it leaped into the air just out of his grasp. "What?" he gasped.

"For this, as well as for my services today, you owe me."

Karakurian's Chamber slowly dropped into Bezeal's hands. The merchant clutched it to his chest and howled with joy. Archer had never seen his white smile so wide. "At last, at last!" Bezeal exulted. Then slowly, he eased the box back onto the table. His fingers roamed it instinctively, and the puzzle box's panels began to shift and move. The silver sailing ship popped up, and the nine sails seemed to ripple and shimmer as they had when Kaylie had activated them.

"Now, more than ever," Archer said, "I need you to tell me how to destroy the Nightmare Lord."

Bezeal's smile vanished. His eyes shrank to a tenth of their normal glimmering size.

"No tricks, Bezeal," Archer warned. "Your blood mingled with mine, remember? And no rhymes either. Tell me plainly . . . and tell me . . . right . . . now."

Bezeal's fingers danced on the puzzle box, and it closed itself up. "Very well," Bezeal said, his voice a clear, careful whisper. "Destroy his throne, not once but twice, but the one who does will pay the price, in blood and pain and sacrifice—"

"I said no rhymes!" Archer's voice was a thunderclap.

Bezeal jumped, jarring the puzzle box. He caught it just before it fell. "I am sorry. The throne must be destroyed, Dreamtreader. It is the seat of his power. But you must destroy it twice."

"What does that mean?"

"In his stronghold, he has a massive stone chair, his throne. Shadowy as night and dark as pitch. Destroy that first. But travel then to his courtyard. There is a second throne there between two very unique trees. You must utterly destroy that seat as well, but the only way you can do it is by burning up both trees."

"Two trees," Archer muttered. "Does one have teardrop leaves; the other's more like bat wings?"

Bezeal's eyes flashed. "Yes, yes," he said. "How did you know?"

"Just finish, Bezeal."

"Burn the trees, burn the roots," he said. "Not one sliver of green wood or leaf may remain."

"Why?"

"They are the Trees of Life and Death," he said. "Leave one, the Nightmare Lord lives forever. Leave the other, and the Nightmare Lord can never be killed. But . . . once the trees are gone, the Nightmare Lord will be at your mercy. Now, Dreamtreader, I have revealed to you a secret known only to me, a costly secret. Leave me!"

As if on cue, Old Jack struck out eleven chimes.

Archer stood and pointed at Bezeal. "This had better be the truth, Bezeal."

Bezeal looked away and began to fidget with his silver prize.

TWENTY-ONE

CREATURES GREAT AND SMALL

WHEN ARCHER GOT HOME FROM SCHOOL THURSDAY afternoon, he was surprised to see Amy Pitsitakas following him away from the bus stop.

Maybe she's taking a different route home, he thought. He kept walking.

But when he turned the corner onto Allen Court, he knew something was up. Amy should have gone straight, across Pekoe Street and onto Earl Grey Road. Archer turned around in a huff. "Are you stalking me, Amy?"

Her hands flew to her chin. "Why, yes, Archer Keaton," she said. "You've caught me. But, in a way, it feels good that you finally know." She ran to him suddenly and threw her arms around his neck. "Marry me, Archer Keaton!"

Then she fell away, cackling. She even rolled on the ground. Archer got over his shock at last and erupted into a series of his own honking, nasal laughter.

"Oh my gosh!" he said with a snort. "You freaked me out!"

He helped her to her feet, and eventually the laughter diminished and they wiped their eyes.

"But really," he said, "what are you doing?"

"Kaylie must have told you," she said.

"Uhm . . . no, she didn't say anything to me."

"She said you were taking care of Rigby's exotic animals," Amy explained. "She texted me, I guess around lunchtime. She told me I should come. I asked Rigby. He said he didn't care."

"Oh, well, that's beautiful," Archer said. "More hands make less work. I have to feed, water, and clean up, you know?"

"That's no trouble," she said. "I love animals. Kaylie knew that. How come you didn't?"

Archer looked at his wrist. "Oh, look at the time," he said, rushing toward his house.

"No you don't!" Amy ran after him.

They charged up Archer's front steps and into the living room. Buster and Kaylie were both already there.

"Brosef!" Buster said. "I can't wait to see these gnarly critters."

"Kaylie!" Archer said, pacing the living room. "This was supposed to be just you and me."

"I know, Archer," she said, her pigtails bouncing. "But Buster wanted to come too. Besides, he plays too many video games!"

"Dude," Buster said, "so not cool."

"Well, she's right," Archer said.

"Bogus," Buster said.

"So, can Buster come?" Kaylie asked.

"I guess so," Archer said.

"It's a party, then," Amy said.

"Starting to look that way," Archer said. "I hope Rigby's got enough cookies."

"Did you say cookies?" Buster asked. "Rock on!"

With Doctor Who alert on his shoulder, Archer barked orders to his new helpers. At first, he had to repeat himself quite often due to the volume of gasps and explanations.

"Gorgeous, yep! Just gorgeous!" This from Amy.

"Righteous lizards!" Buster.

And lots and lots of "Awwww!" from Kaylie. Eventually, everyone settled into actually feeding, watering, and cleaning. "Amy, put some extra bamboo into the red panda pen. He eats more than you'd think. Oh, and make sure the heat lamp is on medium."

"Medium," she repeated. "Got it!"

"Dude, these guys are crazy!" Buster said, tossing mealworms into the meerkat pen. "Archer, come look."

Archer wandered over and peered inside. To him, meerkats looked like big weasels or mongooses. *Wait? What is the plural of mongoose? Mongeese?* Archer had no clue, but the four of them were some cute little devils. They liked to stand up on their hind legs, and their faces, with dark brown eyes and constantly sniffing little pug noses, took on the most curious expressions.

"Watch this!" Buster said. He tossed in a mealworm. A meerkat snatched the food right out of the air.

"Whoa," Archer said. "That *is* cool."

"Check it." Buster tossed in several mealworms at a time. The meerkats bobbed and darted, snagging each one before it could reach the safety of the bedding below.

"That is amazing!" Archer said. "Oh, and hey, did you try to take out the . . . uh . . ."

"The poop tray?" Buster asked.

"Yeah, the poop tray. Was it too heavy?"

"Naw," Buster said. "It's all good."

Archer moved on to see how Kaylie was doing with the fennec foxes. He found her sitting on her knees, absolutely captivated by the big-eared desert dwellers. "I fed them the beetles like you said," Kaylie explained. "They made a crunchy sound when they ate. Kinda gross, huh? I wouldn't eat a beetle."

"I don't know," Archer said. "Probably high in protein."

"Ewww," she said. Then her eyes traveled to Archer's shoulder. "Oh, ohhh! Is that Doctor Who?"

"Sure is," he said. "She's a barn owl."

"Tyto alba," Kaylie said. "The common barn owl. Wait, did you say she?"

"Yeah, she's a pretty little lady, isn't she?"

"Those black button eyes and the soft white feathers, and gosh, she has a heart around her face."

Archer cocked his head sideways. The owl did the same. Sure enough, Doctor Who had a very distinct, tawny-colored heart outlining her pure white face.

The afternoon went on like that, and it wasn't long before the crew finished its chores. Surprisingly, it didn't feel like a chore to Archer. And given the way the others were chattering excitedly, it probably didn't feel like a chore to them either.

After making sure all the pens, cages, hutches, and tanks were secure, the group funneled out into the long part of the hallway. They turned at the stairs, but Archer lingered. "Hold up a sec," he said. "Amy, c'mere. See that door?"

"Yep," she said. "I wear glasses but can't hardly miss something like that. Why?"

"I don't know," he said. "But there's something weird about it. Kaylie and Buster, head upstairs for a minute." He led Amy over to within a foot of the door. "Do you hear anything?" Amy listened, slowly moving her head closer to the door. "I . . . don't hear . . . Wait," she said. She put her ear to the door and waited, her expression first curious, then uncertain, finishing out with a dose discomfort. "That's kind of creepy."

"I know," he said. "Wish I knew how to get in."

"Eww, really?" she said. "I don't like that faint beeping sound. Makes me think of a hospital."

He shrugged, and they went back to the stairs to begin their journeys home.

Archer lay in his bed and looked forward to a night of regular old dreaming. He'd done Dreamtreading two days running, so he needed at least a twenty-four-hour break. There was a faint knock on the door.

"Come in."

The knob slowly turned, and a pink fuzzy slipper appeared, followed by the rest of Kaylie. "Nighty night, Archer," she said. "Thank you."

"Night, Kaylie," he said. "Thanks for what?"

"Taking us to see the animals. I loved it." She ran over and gave Archer a huge fuzzy footie-pajama hug.

He let her go, smiled, and patted her shoulder. "See you tomorrow," he said.

"I can get you in," she said.

Archer sat up. "What?"

"That door in Rigby's basement," she said. "I know how to get you in."

TWENTY-TWO

BENEATH THE SURFACE

THE SECOND MOON HAD RISEN JUST HIGH ENOUGH OVER
the windswept moors of Archaia to paint the incline a frozen silver.
The ever-churning mists wrapped around shrub and stone, shreds
of it moving in odd directions as if more than one air current flowed
there.

Movement flashed beneath the ridge of dark stone, where the
jagged rocks in silhouette made it appear that a host of demons and
devils had perched. A sinewy figure worked carefully at an arched
door of stone. He stepped inside and pulled the door shut, dust rain-
ing down upon his wild shock of white hair. The large man laughed,
the sound high and manic. "Won't be gittin' in this way agin, no!" he
said. "Not without ringin' the bell."

There was a slight hitch in his gait, an uneven measure in his
knobby legs that made him seem lopsided as he passed the torches,
his many shadows even more misshapen. The hall opened into his
favorite room: the laboratory. His fingers clicking as he worked, the
man adjusted the height of one burner's flame, lowered another. He
switched out flasks at the end of one section of tubing and drained

another. Finally, the man came to the end of a very busy machine and checked the level of a deep holding cistern built right into the floor.

He cackled again and clapped. "He, heh, hee! Production's well ahead of schedule. Grand, isn't it?" He reached into the lowest pocket of his coat and pulled out a handful of shriveled black berries. He tossed them into his mouth, chewing vigorously enough that their juice drizzled down his lips. "Grand, indeed."

The man left the laboratory and came to a semi-hidden door. He grabbed the nearest torch from its sconce, checked over his shoulder, and then disappeared through the door. Stairs led down and down. Fifty feet from the bottom, he could already hear their clicking and gnashing. Of course he could. The man didn't breed them for serenity.

At last, near the bottom of the stairs, he stopped and gazed over the edges of the six massive breeding tanks. They were filled near to the brim with teeming, wriggling black shapes, hundreds of thousands of scurions. But these were special scurions. They were blind, sure, but they had other ways to sense where they were. And they were voracious.

The man came to the bottom of the stairs and looked curiously down into a hay-strewn pen where several lambs lay sleeping. "Not this one," he muttered. "Too skinny." He walked around the waist-high fence, wobbled a moment, and then said, "You'll do." He curled his long knobby fingers around a rather plump lamb's neck. With little effort, he yanked the lamb off the ground and carried it back to the stairs.

The man snorted and cackled. Then he tossed the lamb into the vat of scurions. The teeming and snapping in the tank sprayed a mist of water into the air. The sound was something like a driving rainstorm combined with a brick of firecrackers.

"My, can they eat," the Lurker whispered.

He scuttled the rest of the way down the steps and used his torch to light other torches all around the room. Then, he began the arduous task of opening all the pipeline valves. It took several tolls of Old Jack, but in the end, it would clear the way for his little beasties to travel great distances, deep beneath the surface of two districts.

Three strains had gone in already. This was the last one. It wouldn't be long now, the Lurker knew. He went to the breeding tanks and, one by one, turned their wheel valves to open. Scurions flooded out into the pipeline system.

"No, it won't be long at all."

A melodic tinkling bell drifted down the stairs. The Lurker looked up, grumbling. "Hmph, a bit early." He took a large blackened-metal snuff cap and went round to put out the torches. Back through the percolating laboratory and up the winding hall, he trudged, breathing more heavily than he would have liked.

The bell rang again, this time loud and shrill so close to the door. The Lurker rolled his eyes and adjusted his wire-rim glasses. Then, he swung wide the door and said, "Evening, Nephew."

Kara pushed herself away from her grand dining table. She couldn't possibly have eaten even a single bite from each main course she'd created. It was enough food for a small army. But she didn't care. It was so easy to create things she'd already created once. Like cheesecake, for instance. Coop had given her tips, and her cheesecake now was just as tasty. Maybe better. And all this was guilt-free too, she remembered. No calories in the Dream counted toward the waist in the real world. Even so, she was too stuffed for cheesecake.

Kara stood and wandered once more to her favorite chair before the fire. She was about to plop down for a rest when she remembered something. Something she hadn't realized before.

Rather than sitting, she wandered over to the door she'd "installed" the other day. There was no handle or ring presently. She fixed that and yanked the door open, or rather, she nearly pulled her arm out of socket. "Why did I make this so thick?" she grumbled. But she knew why. She remembered. That was what she noticed the lack of this time. No screams. No complaints. No crying out.

Kara reduced the thickness of the door and opened it rather easily. She stepped to the threshold of a long set of darkened stairs. She listened for a long moment and heard nothing. "Hello, down there!" she called. "You're awful quiet lately. You are still alive, aren't you?"

She waited. Still no answer. No movement. Nothing stirring.

The thought hit her like a bolt of lightning. But they couldn't have escaped. They were too weak. Too delusional. The bonds too strong.

No, she realized, *not an escape. He'd come for them at last.*

TWENTY-THREE

THE BASEMENT DOOR

"ARE YOU SURE WE'RE STILL ON ZOO DUTY?" AMY ASKED. "I didn't see Rigby at school."

"I really don't know for sure," Archer said. He led them up Rigby's front walk to the porch. "Rigby didn't text me."

"He better be here," Kaylie said. "I want to see the animals."

Archer shrugged and rapped lightly on the front door. The Rigby who opened the door that Friday afternoon looked tired. *No*, Archer thought. *Tired would be an understatement.* The young man who usually oozed cool and roguish charm had dark circles under bloodshot eyes, frizzy hair, and rumpled clothing.

"Whoa," Archer said. "Aren't you a portrait of stunning good health."

"That's why I stayed home from school today," Rigby muttered. "Guess I've come down with something."

"I can see that," Archer said.

"Should we come back another day?" Amy asked.

"Noooo," Kaylie whined quietly.

Rigby held the door open wide. "No, no," he said. "It's nothing that bad. Please, come in. You're doing me even more of a favor by takin' this off my hands."

"You sure?" Archer said.

"Yeah, yeah, come on in," Rigby said, stepping back. "But, ah, we're fresh out of cookies, I'm afraid."

"No big deal," Archer said. "Let's hit the zoo, gang."

"Ha," Rigby said. "You're callin' it a zoo now, are you?"

"It's better than a zoo," Kaylie said. "Zoos are so mundane. Your animals are so diverse and magnificent."

"Quite the vocabulary you have, Miss Kaylie," Rigby said, his charm turned up a notch.

"I'm kind of smart," she said, blushing.

"So I've noticed," he said. "From what I've heard, I'm surprised you're not a GIFT kid."

"Yeah, well . . . we should probably get to work," Archer said, avoiding an awkward conversation about money. He moved quickly toward the basement door. Amy and Kaylie followed. Then, Archer called back, "Rigby, you . . . uh . . . you going out or just crashing?"

"Actually," he said, "I'm feeling a little better now. I might just go out. Yeah, can't let the lads down, now can I?"

"Lads?"

"The club, Archer," Rigby said. "I mentioned it to you before. We'll have a talk about it sometime. I think it might be right up your alley."

Okay, Archer thought as he led the way to the basement, *what was that?* He was used to Rigby looking sly or smug, but this look was different. Rigby had a gleam in his eye, an eagerness that bordered on hunger.

They'd been working diligently on the animal care for about thirty minutes when Archer heard footsteps overhead. He thought he tracked them pacing across the kitchen, up the hall, and to the front door. He wasn't positive, but he thought he heard the front door open and close.

So Rigby decided to go out after all, Archer thought. Doctor Who, in her usual spot on his shoulder, cocked her head sideways. Archer knelt to scoop some feed into the angora rabbit's hutch. He heard Kaylie and Amy talking a row or two over.

"Buster was stupid not to come," Kaylie was saying. "Video games are stupid."

"He's a boy," Amy said. "He's wired differently, yep."

"You mean he's stupid?"

"No," Amy said, giggling. "Buster's quite smart. Not as smart as you and not in the same ways, but still smart. He just, well . . . boys find the action in those games stimulating."

"I find these animals stimulating," Kaylie said. They laughed.

Archer was only half listening. His thoughts turned to the strange metal door on the other side of the basement. It wasn't just simple curiosity. In some ways, Archer really didn't want to know what was behind the door. There was a very strong sense of foreboding related to the door. Everything from the strange pulsing vibrations felt through the metal to the odd shooshing sound to the faint, thin regular beeping—it all felt wrong. Dangerous, even. But, for whatever reason, this felt like a danger he should know something about. Like knowing a rattlesnake waited a few feet away, it was better to know it was there, rather than stumbling onto it later.

Archer finished feeding the rabbits and went on to the next task. He tried not to think about the door.

"I guess that wraps things up, yep," Amy said.

Archer didn't reply. He sat on a stool near the meerkat pen, deep in thought.

"Archer, you ready to go?" Amy asked.

"What, huh?"

"Where's your head?" Amy asked. "I said, I think we're finished here. Ready to go."

"Uh, yeah, sure," Archer said, knowing that he couldn't have sounded any more reluctant if he'd tried. He stood, trudged slowly to Doctor Who's cage and let the barn owl hop onto its perch.

They left the basement, but Archer stopped in the kitchen. "Rigby?" he called. "You back yet?" There was no answer. "Rigby?" Still no answer.

"Archer, what are you doing?" Amy asked.

"Actually, Amy, there's something else Kaylie and I need to do," he said. "But you can go on home."

"You sure?" she asked. "I don't mind staying to help."

"You've been a huge help, seriously," he said. "But I'll catch up with you in school on Monday."

Amy shrugged. "Okay, then. See ya."

With Amy gone, Archer turned back to the basement steps.

"You want me to open that door," Kaylie said. "Don't you?"

"Kaylie, I would never ask you to do something that might get you into trouble," he said. "But this door . . . there's something about it that worries me."

"Curiosity killed the meerkat," Kaylie said, looking over her shoulder back at the zoo.

"Don't remind me," he said. "But it's really more than curiosity." He led Kaylie back down the stairs. "There's something suspicious about Rigby. He lives in this big house with his mom, he says. But I've never seen her. He leaves GIFT in May? No one changes schools in May. And honestly, I wonder about his uncle. The circumstances around his uncle's death are peculiar."

"Think Rigby killed him?" Kaylie asked.

Archer looked at his sister. "Have you been sneaking peeks when Dad's watching murder mysteries?"

"No," Kaylie replied, half pouting. "I've been reading Sir Arthur Conan Doyle."

"Okay, Sherlock," Archer said, "I don't know what it all adds up to, but it feels wrong. My gut tells me there's something important behind this door. I mean, who has a door like this in their basement? It looks like a hatch to a space station."

They turned left and came to the door. Archer put his ear to the metal. Same vibration. Same shoosh. Same faint beeps. "Think you can do it?"

"Uh-huh," she said, nodding. She went to the keypad and stared at it for a long time, several minutes at least. Then she started pushing buttons. After each sequence, the keypad made a tone, and a little red light blinked once. "You might want to sit down for a bit, Archer," she said. "It might take me a little while."

Archer sat on the bottom step and tried to listen for any sign that Rigby might be returning. He watched Kaylie working and let his mind roam.

Then he heard a muted buzz.

"Yes!" Kaylie said.

Archer was up in an instant. The keypad light now shone bright green. "Kaylie, how on earth did you figure it out?"

"This is where Sherlock would say, 'Elementary, Watson,'" she giggled. "See, look at the keypad. The numbers that are most worn out are 1, 3, 7, and 5. At first, I thought for sure the code would be at least six numbers, so I tried all kinds of doubles. But nothing worked. Then I thought, well, he's a boy. He wouldn't want a long combination, so I went to five numbers. And then just the four. He's tall, so I figured the higher numbers first. I was right. It was 3-1-5-7."

Archer nodded, impressed. "Stay behind me. No idea what's in here." When Kaylie stepped back, Archer turned the latch handle and pushed the door inward. There was a faint hiss of compressed air, and all the sounds from within grew much louder. The shoosh, the beep, and a light tip-tapping that he hadn't heard before. The door was open now a few inches, but other than a few small lights, it was totally dark inside.

Archer swallowed and pushed the door again. It swung slowly away from him. There was a faint plinking sound, and fluorescent lights snapped on overhead. In that moment, several things happened in quick succession:

There came a terrible ruckus from above.

Heavy footfalls pounded down the steps.

Kaylie screamed.

Someone yelled from behind, "What have you done?"

Kaylie screamed again, and Archer nearly jumped out of his skin. He spun around and put Kaylie protectively at his side. "Rigby? I . . . I thought—"

"You thought I was gone, so you hack in, is it?" His face turned blistering red. "What, you got your little sister to crack the code, did you? Could'na been you. You're not smart enough."

"It's not her fault, Rigby," he said.

Rigby's face churned between exhaustion, rage, and anguish.

His voice sounded weak when he said, "You shouldn't 'ave opened that door."

"You wanna explain what I'm seeing?" Archer demanded, pointing inside the room.

It was a laboratory, but medical in nature. There were all kinds of machines and monitors, keeping track of various vital signs. And in the room's center, lying on a mechanically adjustable examination bed, was a very tall man. He was much older. His straggly wisps of hair were white, and his skin was wrinkled and very stretched. He wore a plain hospital-style gown. His arms, legs, and head were all strapped down.

"Well, Rigby?" Archer yelled. "What is this?"

Rigby sighed. "*This* is my Uncle Scoville."

TWENTY-FOUR

NO TIME

"IS HE . . . IS HE DEAD?" KAYLIE ASKED, ON THE VERGE OF
tears.

"No, he's in a coma," Rigby said. He pushed past Archer and
Kaylie into the room. He wandered over to a bank of monitors, clicked
a mouse a few times, and said, "He's doing about as well today as he
has for the last five years, but some of 'is major organs are beginning
to wear out."

Archer walked into the room. Seeing Rigby's uncle up close was
not a pleasant experience. In the sterile fluorescent light, his flesh had
a greenish quality as if it might begin to peel away from the bone.
"What . . . what happened to him?"

Rigby sighed. "He stayed too long."

Archer frowned. *Stayed . . . too long. The Laws Nine.* When the reality
finally hit him, it was like a thunderclap. "He was a Walker," Archer
whispered.

"A what?" Rigby asked, squinting.

"A Lucid Walker," Archer explained. "Your uncle studied dream
science, didn't he? He figured it out, how to have Lucid Dreams?"

"Listen, Archer," Rigby said. "Are we going to beat around the bush here, or are we going to lay all the cards on the table?"

"Huh?"

"You *are* a Dreamtreader, aren't you?"

"I . . . How do you know that term—"

"Don't try to deny it," Rigby said. "I know that you are. I was there, in the Kurdan Marketplace . . . at the Reliquary. You were looking for Bezeal, remember?" Rigby's face seemed to change, his eyes darkening. When he spoke again, his voice had changed, "He's fresh meat, ain't he?"

Archer felt the blood drain from his face. "That . . . that Scarecrow person was you?"

"Well, in disguise, anyway," he said. "Easy to do, in the Dream."

"Archer," Kaylie said, her voice thin . . . worried, "what is Rigby talking about?"

"I'll explain it later," Archer said.

"But why did Rigby say his uncle was dead if he was just comatose? There's a difference. Why?"

"Something I mean to find out," Archer said. "Now, go look in on the meerkats. Rigby and I need to talk."

"But why did Rigby call you a Dreamtreader?" she persisted. "A treader is one who treads or travels. Who walks on a dream?"

"Kaylie!" Archer thundered, and then felt terrible because he saw Kaylie jump and then shrivel. And feeling guilty just made him angrier. "I said, go check on the meerkats!"

"Okay . . . ," she mumbled through quivering lips. And then she was gone.

Archer turned back to Rigby. "So your uncle was a Lucid Walker. And now you are. I should have figured it out. When Guzzy attacked you . . . with the knife, you did something, something with the . . . Did you make the knife turn into flowers?"

Rigby laughed acidly. "Yeah, I was wondering if you'd come back to that." He shook his head angrily. "I don't know how that happened. I mean, I can do all kinds of things in the Dream, but not here. That was a first. I was so upset, so scared, it felt like something in my mind slipped. And boom, the knife turned into flowers."

"You're messing with things you don't understand," Archer muttered. "Breaking into the Dream is dangerous."

"I don't break into dreams," Rigby said. "It's lucid dreaming, same as what you do."

"Not the same," Archer said.

"Oh, that's right. Dreamtreaders are chosen." Rigby glared. "You're not better than me, Archer."

"I never said I was."

"No?" Rigby coughed into his hand. "Well, mostly it's implied by your kind, isn't it? Dreamtreaders are the chosen guides, the mediators, and the justice. I saw you there, Archer. I know what you're capable of."

"But do you know what you're capable of?" Archer fired back. "You Lucid Walkers are ripping holes in the dream fabric."

"You lying—" Rigby's voice fell to a low snarl. He took a step toward Archer.

"It's not a lie," Archer said, watching Rigby's hands. Better than getting a flat-hand strike to the throat. Archer knew how quick Rigby could attack.

"You Dreamtreaders just want to have the Dreamscape to yourselves," Rigby contended.

"You Lucid Walkers just want to go where you don't belong.

Look at your poor uncle. He stayed too long in the Dream, didn't he?" Rigby didn't answer at first. "Didn't he?"

"Past his eleven hours," he whispered and then was silent for several moments. The life support machines continued their faint beeps. The respirator filled and emptied. Rigby went on, "The first time it happened, he came back. It was maybe just a little more than twelve hours, that's all. But he was acting a bit strange . . . kind of aggressive. We didn't think much of it. My mum thought it was an old age thing, but Uncle Scovy, I think he knew something had gone wrong. The next time he went in . . . he never came back out. He slipped into a deep coma. It destroyed me. Uncle Scovy . . . well, he was like a father to me."

"I can imagine."

"Can you?" Rigby asked, the words sizzling contempt.

"My mother died of cancer when I was seven," Archer said quietly.

Rigby's mouth hung open for several heartbeats. "Maybe you can imagine, then," he said. "Rough."

"You said your dad was overseas, right?"

"Oh, yeah, yeah, he's overseas, all right. And not coming back. He was never happy with the move to the States . . . or us."

"I'm sorry," Archer said. "That's a lot to have to endure."

"All of it, yeah," Rigby said. "But see, I'm going to do something about it. I'm going to bring Uncle Scovy back."

"I . . . I don't think you can," Archer said. "I've been reading *The Dreamtreader's Creed*, and I don't see any way to do it."

"There is a way," Rigby said. "Kill the Nightmare Lord. He's behind all the death and misery that comes out of the Dream. We knock him off, it'll free up the Dream for good. We'll have the power then to bring Uncle Scovy back."

"We?" Archer said.

"You're a Dreamtreader," Rigby said. "And the Nightmare Lord is your enemy?"

"Right on both counts."

"Then, we're fighting the same battle. There are three Dreamtreaders, aren't there? With all three of you, with all your experience, we could—"

"The other two Dreamtreaders are missing," Archer said, his tone flat.

"No . . . way." He shook his head and stared at his uncle's still form.

"I don't know what happened to them, Duncan and Mesmeera. They were my friends. Strong, smart, fierce . . . I can only imagine what could take them down."

"That's horrible news, mate," Rigby said quietly. "But it explains a lot. Things are getting dicey in the Dream. You've seen it too, right?"

"Breaches everywhere . . . If something doesn't change soon, a rift will occur."

"Rift?" Rigby's eyes narrowed. He seemed to be looking inward. "What are you talking about?"

"A rift is like a gigantic breach, only worse, it spreads, and if it can't be closed up, the Dream and the Temporal will mix. That could be the end of . . . well, everything."

"Temporal?" he asked. "You mean this world too?"

Archer nodded. "Can you imagine if people could no longer tell whether they were dreaming or awake?"

Rigby's expression flattened and became unreadable. "Yeah, I can imagine it. All the more reason we should join forces. I got friends, Archer, friends from GIFT . . . and a few from Dresden 'igh. We've been training for a while."

"What? More Lucid Dreamers?"

"Yeah, yeah, and we're good. We can use what the Dream gives us. We can take the fight to the Nightmare Lord, but to 'ave you join us? Well, you might just be the difference in this fight."

Archer thought about the wisdom he'd learned from Bezeal. "I need to talk to someone first."

"This can't wait long," Rigby said. His eyes narrowed. "Wait, you listen to me, Archer. You're not planning on ratting me out to your superiors, right? You . . . just can't do that. My uncle . . . I have to try this, for him."

"There's just one superior," Archer said. "And I have to tell him. The last time I kept something from him . . . it didn't work out so well."

"Put in a good word, then," Rigby said. "You tell him we can all fight the Nightmare Lord. We might even be able to help you find the other two Dreamtreaders."

"I'll tell him that," Archer said. *But Master Gabriel doesn't like to negotiate.*

TWENTY-FIVE

Master Gabriel's Fourth Visit

Archer was ready to explode. Of all the nights for his father to want to talk. Ordinarily, it would have been the best thing to happen. Archer wanted to talk to his dad. He missed talking to his dad. But on this night, there were forces at work that needed to be addressed.

"I miss her, Archer," his father said.

"I know, Dad," he said. "I miss her too."

"You know, it'll be seven years in August."

August. A memory came unbidden. His mom had been suffering so much, and so often she'd complained of the summer heat. Archer had gone to the well. He'd weighted the pail so it would drop all the way to the bottom of the well. He got his mom a bucket of the purest, coldest well water. He'd been thrilled to give it to her, but when he came upstairs, he heard sobbing. And baby Kaylie was screaming. Archer brought the cold well water for his mother. But he was too late. She was gone.

"Yeah, Dad," he said. "I remember."

"It's just these . . . these dreams," his father said. "I've never had dreams like these. Never! They're so vivid. It's like every night, I'm getting my heart broken all over again."

"Dad, look, I'm really sorry. But I just can't go there tonight, okay?"

"Son?"

"No, I can't. I'm going upstairs. I'm going to bed."

"But . . . Archer?"

As he turned the corner and ascended the stairs, Archer felt like a piece had torn free from his soul. His father wanted to talk. He *needed* to talk. But Archer swallowed down the guilt and went to his room.

Archer sat on the bed and opened *The Dreamtreader's Creed*. He took out the white summoning feather and tossed it into the air.

"I was coming tonight anyway," Master Gabriel said. His Incandescent Armor was brighter than Archer had ever seen it, and it flared as he spoke. His face appeared more fierce as well. "Things in the Dream are reaching a boiling point."

"It doesn't seem to matter which way I'm looking," Archer said, breathing heavily. "You always appear somewhere else."

"Enough small talk, Archer. Your news first."

Archer wasn't sure where to begin. "Okay, I went to Kurdan, like you said I should. I gave Bezeal the Karakurian Chamber."

"And what did you gain in return?"

Archer explained about the thrones and the two trees. He told Master Gabriel everything Bezeal had said.

When Archer was finished, Master Gabriel stroked his beard once and said, "I have known the Creeds from the beginning," he said. "And I recall nothing about the thrones and trees. But . . . the Tokens of Doom, the leaves twain . . . that could be a connection.

Perhaps it is not the doom of the Dreamtreaders after all, but rather the Nightmare Lord himself. Perhaps. It is something to consider. Something to ponder deeply."

"There's something else," Archer said. "Bezeal has developed a patch."

"A what?"

"He's concocted some kind of chemical or herbal, well, I'm not sure what it is. But it's a kind of pasty liquid patch that will temporarily seal up breaches. The patches let some plasma through, and they won't last forever. But it'll slow down the breaches from widening and give me a chance to weave. Bezeal has even developed kits that villagers . . . the everyday folk of the Dream can use to help us stem the plague of breaches."

"That is news, indeed," Master Gabriel replied. "Though it is unlike Bezeal to do something helpful."

"Well, he's made a fortune on it."

"That certainly sounds more like him. This may provide a critical cushion of time. But we must remember, as you say, it is temporary. Any news on the other Dreamtreaders?"

"Bezeal thinks they missed their eleven-hour deadline," Archer said. "But he didn't explain it. I don't know anything else."

"That is grave news, but not completely unexpected," Master Gabriel said. "It could not have come at a worse moment. The Dream is unstable. And while this patch of Bezeal's may hinder the Nightmare Lord, time is ultimately running out. If we do not take more direct action against the enemy, I am afraid a rift is inevitable."

"Funny you should say that."

"There is nothing funny here, Archer."

"Figure of speech." Archer shifted his weight and stared at his bedroom window. "I met a Walker."

"A Lucid Walker?" Master Gabriel's armor flared.

"Yes, but he's a friend. He's on our side."

"No Lucid Walker is on our side, Archer. The very act of them entering and exiting the Dream causes new breaches."

"But this one wants to throw down the Nightmare Lord too. He's been training other Lucid Walkers."

Gabriel's hand flew to the hilt of his sword. "He has an army?"

"Well, no, I don't think he has an army. More like a team. But they know how to operate within the Dream, and they all want to take out the Nightmare Lord."

"At what cost, Archer? At . . . what . . . cost? The very act of ushering Lucid Walkers into the Dream could trigger the very cataclysm we are struggling to avoid!"

"They know," Archer contended. "Or, at least their leader knows. But he said he'd help us find Duncan and Mesmeera, if we'll fight together against the Nightmare Lord."

"I fear Duncan and Mesmeera may be . . . beyond finding."

"Dead?" Archer gasped. "No!"

"I am not certain," Master Gabriel replied quietly. "But they have been missing for so long . . . well, it is possible that death might be a mercy."

"I don't understand," Archer said. But then he did. It hit him, and it was as if the gravity in the room had increased exponentially. If Duncan and Mesmeera had missed their Personal Midnights . . . they'd be trapped forever in the Dream. Rigby's Uncle Scoville, wasting away strapped to the table . . . the image was difficult to bear.

Then Archer remembered what Rigby had said. "Master Gabriel, the Lucid Walker I met . . . he's researched this quite a bit. He's convinced that the Nightmare Lord is the source of the . . . that is, he's what's keeping people stuck in the Dream. If we destroy him, we might . . . well, we might be able to bring people back."

"A curious notion," Master Gabriel said. "But the Creeds speak nothing of anyone coming back. Ever."

"Okay, maybe not," Archer said. "But we still have to try, right? You said yourself that we need to take direct action."

Master Gabriel opened his mouth to speak, but Archer cut him off. "I'm sorry," he said. "I've overstepped again. You'd think I'd have learned by now. I will abide by whatever you decide."

Master Gabriel remained silent for a long time. His armor flared intermittently as he paced Archer's room. At last, he pounded a fist into his palm and said, "So be it, Archer. You cannot do this alone. Take up with these Lucid Walkers, but be wary of them. The opening of the imagination, the expansion of the brain's capabilities, can often lead to trouble."

"Should we go tonight?"

"No," Gabriel said. "Not tonight. Tonight, make plans, organize, and prepare. Go tomorrow night. And may Shadowkeep fall to your attack!"

"Master Gabriel," Archer said. "There's something I've wondered for a very long time. But, honestly, I've been afraid to ask you."

"Hmmm," he said. "Perhaps it is better left unasked. Those kinds of questions can be very dangerous."

He turned to leave, but Archer grabbed his arm. "At this point," Archer said, "it seems worth the risk."

"What, then? Speak, Archer. Ask your question."

Archer took a deep breath and said, "Well, Master Gabriel, what I want to know is . . . why don't you ever come to the Dream with us, with the Dreamtreaders, I mean? You are obviously very powerful. I feel like there are battles we lost . . . that we might have won if you'd been with us."

Master Gabriel's armor flared white hot.

"I mean, I know you have your reasons," Archer added quickly. "You've said again and again that not all the phenomena we witness will have a reason . . . at least, not a reason that will make sense. But this time? This time won't you come? This is the ultimate battle, and the Nightmare Lord is strong. Won't you come?"

Master Gabriel stood as still as a statue. His armor dimmed. With his eyes hooded and thoughtful, he said, "No, Archer, I will not accompany you, not even this time. This is a Dreamtreader War, and you must be the one to fight it."

"But the Nightmare Lord—"

"The Nightmare Lord is not my opposite number," Master Gabriel said. "Yes, I oversee the Dreamtreaders to shepherd the Dream and keep the Nightmare Lord in check. But, Archer, he is not my task to defeat. His master is my charge."

Archer swallowed hard, the concept of something more hideous than the Nightmare Lord . . . too difficult to entertain. "The Nightmare Lord . . . has a master?"

"Yes, and he is truly a thing of horrors," Master Gabriel said. "Now, never you mind about that. You have enough to consume your thinking without bearing my burdens also. Anchor first."

Archer swallowed and replied, "Anchor deep."

DREAMTREADERS CREED, CONCEPTUS 5

F orms, Pattern, and Verse.

These are the three districts of the Dream. They are so named for the mental operation performed to gain access to each, for the Dreamscape itself is built in the architecture of the mind. The Dreamtreader will come to know them in that order, but the Creeds reveal them based on another measure.

The Verse District is the realm of creation. Of the three, Verse is the most connected to the Ethereal, the true home and blessed destination. The Dreamscape sun rises in Verse with a radiance unsurpassed, casting golden light upon its kingdoms, making poetry of meandering mountains, towering trees, rushing waters, and rolling hills. Beauty sings from every leaf, twig, and blossom. Nowhere is a breach more of a travesty than in Verse. The Dreamtreader of this realm must see to it that it is left untainted. Not even the most minute defect can be permitted. It is perfect balance, perfect peace, and perfect beauty. The Dreamtreader of Verse must be pure of heart and of motive. Beware that you do not ferry evil into Verse, for its surface will not suffer the stain for long. The land itself will rise up against the infection and cast it out.

The Patterns District is the realm of change. It lies in the heart of the Dream because it *is* the living heart of the Dream. In the Pattern District the only constant is change. It is the kaleidoscope terrain where nothing is the same from one day to the next. Its kingdoms are always in motion, changing boundaries and staking new claims each season. The Dreamtreader of Pattern must also learn to adapt, for such an ever-changing and multifaceted landscape presents special challenges. The Intrusions there are mercurial and can be devastating if not dampened by the skillful mind.

The Forms District is the realm of action, force, and peril. It claims kinship with the Waking Realm, the Dim Plane, the Temporal. The Dreamscape sun sets in Forms, leaving all in twilight, shadow, and night. Fell creatures and grim deeds await the Dreamtreader of Forms, and so this one must carry the mind of an army: its cunning, its tactics, and initiative. But the Dreamtreader of Forms must bear the weight of the deepest anchor, and learn to stem the tide of darkness.

TWENTY-SIX

DREAMSCAPE WAR

ARCHER RODE THE CRIMSON VORTEX THROUGH THE SKY, glanced at the ancient face of Old Jack, and gave careful thought to his equipment. This would not be a battle of temperance or restraint. He would have to use every ounce of his creative energies, every advantage, and every weapon he could imagine. He would spend his mental stores to do what he had to do, even if that meant spending it all.

He sighed, thinking of the strange good-night hugs he'd given his family members. His dad, Buster, and Kaylie—they hadn't really understood why Archer embraced them for so long and with such emotion. They didn't understand that it might be the last time. But Archer knew. When he agreed to be a Dreamtreader, he took a vow to hold nothing back in his service. He only hoped it wouldn't come to that.

On the ground, Archer summoned his longboard and caught a wave of Intrusions heading north. Razz appeared with a poof.

"Ready to weave up some breaches, Archer!" she said.

"We've got a much bigger task tonight, Razz," he said. Then he explained. By the time he finished answering her questions, they were halfway to Warhaven, the last civilized kingdom before entering the Nightmare Lord's domain.

"If this is to be a fight," Razz said, "then I am not properly dressed." She looked at her acorn cap beret disparagingly and then disappeared. When she popped back, she wore an acorn helm and her walnut-shell armor. Surprisingly, she had a tiny sword at her side.

"Razz," Archer said, guiding his board onto a northwesterly wave, "you look like a regular swordmaiden."

Razz zipped into the air, performed a happy somersault, and then dropped back to Archer's shoulder. "Full steam ahead, Captain!" she yelled.

Archer crossed the border into Warhaven and made for the old ruins to the far north. That was where Rigby and his Lucid Walkers were to be waiting.

Old Xander's Fortune. That was the name of the ruined fortress that sat on a hilltop surrounded by deep forest at the northernmost edge of Warhaven. Archer rode his longboard right to its doorstep. It was a shell of a building, still massive and tall, but gutted. Archer dismissed the board and heard voices as he crossed the threshold into the stone frame of the keep.

"Remember," Rigby was saying to a small group of teens, "this is not a siege. We don't have the numbers or the time. This is a surgical strike."

"Actually," Archer said, approaching, "it's more blunt force trauma than surgery."

"Dreamtreader Archer," Rigby said, his grin broad. "Please come meet the Lucid Walkers."

All eyes turned to Archer. *Very few eyes,* he thought. And though he knew the moment he'd said it that he should never have let the words leave his lips, it was too late. "Is this it? Is this all we have?"

The expressions on six faces turned sour, and Archer felt like a jerk. "I . . . I didn't mean it like that," he said. "I'm sure you all know what you're doing. It's just that—Kara?"

"Hi, Archer," Kara said quietly.

Archer turned to Rigby. "You got Kara Windchil into Lucid Walking?"

"Yeah, so?"

Archer managed to seal off his first reply before letting it be heard aloud. *Yeah, something like, "But she's the girl I like," that wouldn't go over well.* But there was something he could say.

"Look, Rigby, I don't know anything about your GIFT friends, but Kara and . . . and that's Bree Lassiter, right? They can't have been Lucid Walking for long. You're putting them in grave danger. I don't like that."

"Who died and made you king?" Bree asked.

"Sorry, Archer," Kara said, "but this isn't your choice."

Archer swallowed and hoped the rushing blood wouldn't redden his face too much.

"Now that that little tasty bit is out of the way," Rigby said, "why don't I introduce my GIFT friends."

In turn, Archer met Coop, Roach, Hyde, and Bianca. They shook hands and stared each other up and down, measuring . . . sizing.

In the end, Archer couldn't help himself. "I . . . I'm not sure we're enough."

"Enough?" Bree blurted, indignantly flipping a cable of dark hair over her shoulder. "Enough for what?"

"Enough to finish this, to defeat the Nightmare Lord." Archer glared at them. "I'm not sure we can win."

"We do have a secret weapon," Rigby said, motioning to the jagged stone archway to his left. A dark figure moved in silhouette.

Archer stepped backward, and Razz burrowed down in his duster pocket. Archer had seen that shape before. In Archaia. He still had bruised arms from the Lurker's chains.

"Come on out, Uncle Scovy!" Rigby said.

The withered old man Archer had seen lying comatose in Rigby's basement stepped out of the shadows. Only he wasn't withered and drawn. He had broad shoulders and a frame full of ropy muscle. His eyes were bright and intelligent. His white hair was as wild as ever, and his expression seemed fierce . . . on the verge of violence.

Razz whirled into a ball and disappeared in a puff of smoke.

"The Lurker?" Archer blurted. "Your uncle is the Lurker?"

"Yeah," Rigby said. "He told me that was 'is nickname here."

"That's 'cause I mainly keeps to meself," Uncle Scoville said, his upper lip curling into a snarl.

"But you work for the enemy," Archer said. "You tried to chain me up!"

"You trespassed, young man," he said. "Not only that but you stole my puzzle box, my Karakurian Chamber. Don't suppose you got it with you?"

Archer shook his head.

"Shame, that is," Uncle Scoville said. "Look, lad, I know we got off on the wrong foot, but my only enemy is the Nightmare Lord. Remember, I left you because I had to take care of the hounds? Hate Sixtolls with a passion. And it's because of that despicable resident of

Number 6, Rue de la Mort that . . . that I can't wake up. There's a chance we might could change things tonight."

Archer remembered Master Gabriel's thoughts on waking those stuck in the Dream. It wasn't in the Creeds. But Archer did not share that information openly.

"My uncle is very powerful," Rigby said. "Being committed to the Dream has given 'im unimaginable strength here."

Archer nodded. "That's obviously true," he said, staring at the Lurker. "But . . . I mean, how can we trust—"

"He's my uncle," Rigby said. "He's here to help us, right?"

Archer became very still. He readied his will for a massive onslaught attack, just in case things went south when he said, "What about my Dreamtreader friends, Uncle Scovy? You know, Duncan and Mesmeera? What have you done with them?"

"I'll tell ye what I've done with them. I fed them and sent them on their way."

"Bezeal told me that Duncan and Mesmeera came to you for the puzzle box."

"That's right," Uncle Scoville said. "They came. They asked. I said no. I liked that little box, heh, heh."

"Where are they now?" Rigby asked suddenly. "Are they in the Dream? We could use their help tonight."

"Truth is, lad," Uncle Scoville said, putting his arm on Rigby's shoulders, "I don't know what happened to them. They were talking about Shadowkeep, that's all I know."

"Well, that settles that," Rigby said. "We're all in this together. Introductions are all good. We'd best be—"

"Hey!" a squeak came from Archer's pocket. "What about me?"

Archer reached down and lifted his little friend up for all to see. "So that's where you went," he said. "This pretty little lady is Razz."

"Cute!"

"Awwwww!"

"Dude, that is awesome!"

"Can I make one?"

"Whoa!"

"I think they like you, Razz," Archer said with a wink.

Razz blinked and blushed. Then she pushed her helm forward on her head. "Okay, let's rock this joint!"

Led by Archer, the team left the ruins and made haste toward the darkness of the Drimmrwood Forest.

Some of them bounded. Some of them ran at Flash-like speeds. Some simply flew. They met in an oblong clearing in the heart of the Drimmrwood. "This is the best place I could think of to anchor," Archer said. "Secluded enough to keep unwanted eyes out, but easy enough for us to find again."

Archer heard the Old Jack toll four times. He wasn't sure what time each of the others had entered the Dream, but time was going to be a factor for all of them.

One by one, each dreamer placed his or her anchor. Archer gathered the team and said, "I don't know how much each of you know about your power here, but whatever you can do, do big. We are outnumbered a hundred to one, we are attempting to defeat an enemy on his home turf, and we've never fought together before. We need to bull our way into that fortress, so no kid gloves. Don't play it safe. Keep your head, of course. You don't want to bleed out all your energy. I'm just saying, you have to be effective."

In the distance, a violently powerful storm churned over

Shadowkeep. It was like a hurricane with six eyes, and blood-red light shown down from each eye. Archer led the team up the main rampart that led out of the Drimmrwood and up to the gate of Number 6, Rue de la Mort.

"Sure you're ready for this?" Archer whispered to Kara.

"Ready as I'll ever be," she replied. "I guess."

"I'm ready too!" Razz squeaked.

"Look, I'm not bragging here," Archer said. "But I've been doing this a long time—"

"I know that."

There it was again, that sting about Dreamtreading. Archer couldn't understand it now. Kara could do it, could Lucid Dream. But there was still bitterness. "All I'm saying is that I'm strong, and here, I know how to fight. If things get ugly and you need help, call me."

"Thanks, Archer," she said. "Same to you. I can fight here also."

Archer laughed. "That sounds like the Kara I know and, uh . . . that sounds like you."

Kara made an odd face at Archer and then fell back to speak to Rigby.

Shadowkeep's guards were already out in force, waiting. They were a sea of corpse-warriors, shambling in a great mass toward Archer and his team. These were the poor souls—Lucid Dreamers throughout history—who had consumed gort in their dreams, the black berries or even the root. Now forever locked in the Nightmare Lord's control, they mindlessly, violently served his every whim.

"Ready, Razz?" Archer asked, taking a deep breath himself.

"Ready as I'll ever be," she said, leaping from Archer's shoulder and racing toward their foes.

Archer increased his running speed, taking great loping strides, fifteen yards at a time. Their plan would involve evasion wherever possible, but the guards could not be avoided. If the group tried to fly over them, the Nightmare Lord's soldiers would surge and be there when they landed. If the team stayed in the sky, the Nightmare Lord himself would unleash a flight of dragons for the guards to ride upon. In fact, Archer thought he saw a squad of soldiers already mounted, waiting at the foot of Shadowkeep. No, there would be no avoiding this fight. They would need to push through as fast as possible.

Closing now, Archer could see the pale green in the guards' half-empty eyes. Archer glanced left and right. His team was there, Rigby and Kara running slightly ahead of the others. Old Jack chimed its fifth bell, and for once, Archer was grateful for its call. *It's time*, Archer thought.

With a kind of lunatic humor taking hold of him, Archer summoned his will and called up one of those chevron-shaped plow blades he'd seen used in construction projects. The massive steel plow head was four feet high and drove ahead like a monstrous shield. Then Archer set it on fire.

"Booyah!" he yelled as his fiery plow crashed into the guards. Their swords, battle axes, and shields did nothing against Archer's weapon. Guards were tossed aside like rag dolls. They flew through the air and were flung in great tangled heaps from the ramparts.

Archer heard their screams and felt momentary pity for them, but that was the two-edged sword of being in the Dream. You never wanted to turn away emotionally, but you couldn't become so tortured by what you saw or did that you'd become useless.

When Archer glanced to the side to check on his team, they were gone. He was so stunned by what he saw in their place that he almost stumbled off of the rampart. He'd told them to go big but . . .

Hyde had evidently decided that being a human fist wasn't nearly enough muscle. He now rode forward in an MI Abrams main battle tank. Rigby, on the other hand, now stood fifteen feet tall, and he was quite literally kicking guards out of his way.

Kara stood at the head of her own minihurricane, the winds battering guards left and right. Archer also saw a giant black panther, a bulldozer, a walking tree, and a silver 1967 Shelby Mustang with a machine gun mounted on the hood.

"I guess I did say go big," Archer said, pushing to increase speed. He was too busy staring straight ahead. The snarling guard who dove over the plow blade slammed into Archer. The Dreamtreader rolled backward, dizzy. He stood up only to find the blade of a greatsword plunged into his gut.

He knew the sword wasn't real. He knew the wound wasn't real. His mind was keen and saw the attack for what it was, but that didn't keep him from a moment of sheer panic. There was blood and pain and fear of death. He lashed out with his hand, sending ten thousand shards of white-hot metal at the guard. Archer saw its sickly pale eyes just before it disintegrated.

"I thought he had you!" Razz said, appearing suddenly at Archer's side.

"Not that easy," he said.

"Good!" Razz sped away, searching for a fight that was more her size.

It was time for a change in tactics, Archer thought, as a group of guards shambled closer. He called up a four-inch-thick cable and yelled for Kara. "Catch this!" Archer made a perfectly guided throw of the cable's end. Kara caught it in stride just as Archer surged forward. The cable went taut between them, and the pack of guards were clotheslined, tumbling away in a heap. Some tried to hold on or clamber to one end of the cable, but there were so many of them getting in each other's way that they could scarcely move.

The dreamers had made it more than halfway to Shadowkeep's gatehouse without much trouble. Archer had to give credit to Rigby. He'd trained his team well. *Amazing,* Archer thought. He didn't think that Lucid Walkers would be capable of such devastating tactics, but they were very strong and very smart.

It suddenly occurred to Archer that he had not seen the Lurker . . . or rather, Rigby's Uncle Scoville, since the clearing. The Dreamtreader looked side to side but Scovy wasn't anywhere to be seen. Archer looked over his shoulder best as he could and didn't see him there either. Then he heard something that snapped his attention forward. It sounded like an earthquake, but there was just an endless sea of Shadowkeep's guards . . . only, there wasn't.

Archer wasn't sure what he was witnessing. About a hundred yards away, a black wall materialized, cutting off the rampart for both sides. The rumbling increased its fearsome reverberation. The black wall seemed to sheer the rampart in half. As if it were made of some malleable substance rather than stone, the rampart bent sideways. Hundreds of guards toppled off its edge and into the chasm below.

The black wall disappeared, and Archer saw Rigby's Uncle Scoville at last. He stood ahead where the black wall had been and waved the team on. That was when Old Jack rang out. They all heard it.

It was Sixtolls.

TWENTY-SEVEN

NUMBER 6, RUE DE LA MORT

THE HOWLS THAT RANG OUT FROM SHADOWKEEP SHOOK the ground upon which Archer and his team now stood. Uncle Scoville walked back to the teens and said, "Are you prepared for this?"

Archer searched the team's eyes. There was indecision there . . . hesitance. "Whatever you do," he said, "do not show fear inside those gates. Wear a helmet, war paint, or turn your head into a block of iron. Do whatever you need to do to avoid showing fear. This is Sixtolls, the height of the Nightmare Lord's power. He releases his hounds to frighten us because fear increases his strength."

"Have you seen the hounds?" Kara asked.

"Yeah," Rigby said, cutting Archer off. "From a distance. But Archer's right. No fear."

"Why aren't the hounds coming out after us?" Bree asked.

"Because," Uncle Scoville said, "he wants us inside his gates. He wants to finish us off on his own terms. But we won't be letting him, will we?"

"No fear!" Archer shouted. The team answered, and with the howls echoing in the chasm far below, they pressed on toward the gate of Shadowkeep.

Everything changed inside Shadowkeep. It soon became apparent why the being who sat on its thrown was known as the Lord of Nightmares.

Archer and the others found themselves in a vast and ancient graveyard. Gnarled, misshapen trees rose up around them and lined their path. Two moons gazed out at them from the torn shreds of tattered cloud high above.

Feverish red eyes smoldered out of the gloom all around the team. They were slanted, burning with hate, much larger and much higher off the ground than they should have been.

"Remember," Archer whispered. "No fear."

A voice that did not belong to any of the team whispered back in a raspy, mocking tone, "Nooooo feeaaarrr!"

All at once, the hounds sprang. The moonlight and mist obscured their shape, their speed even more so, but what Archer saw made his heart leap into his throat. Something happened to his pulse that made him suddenly feel like he'd been thrust beneath the surface of some dark water. He gasped for breath even as the first hound was upon him.

There was a frantic tangle of tooth, claw, and mane. Archer felt rips and punctures, and the dizzying motion of being yanked back and forth. There was blood all around him and icy cold . . . and a strange, mournful cry, calling out that he should simply surrender, fall into a deep sleep, and let it be.

"Archer, fight!" a female voice commanded. Archer thought at first it was Razz, but it couldn't have been. The voice was not outside, but within his mind.

It was the Windmaiden, saving him once more.

Archer snapped awake and found himself in the crushing jaws of a monstrous thing. He forced his hand deeper into the thing's mouth and called up a twin-sided spear. The creature was skewered and released Archer, sending him cartwheeling through the air. He landed in a broken jumble and, at first, didn't think he'd ever be able to get up again. He was a bloody messy, wounds everywhere beneath his leather armor, and a blanket of eerie cold settled over him.

Dream, Archer!

He stoked his will, and he was whole again. Whole and ready to fight.

"You almost had me," Archer seethed. He turned and faced the hound, still struggling with the spear that pinned its jaws open. Archer glared at it and willed his spear to become wrapped in huge chunks of C-4 plastic explosive. He turned and ran, willing the C-4 to detonate.

He ignored the horrible sound and the brief wave of superheated air, and strode on. In this ghastly graveyard, Archer could not see any of the other team members. He suspected they were all dealing with nightmares more personal to them . . . nightmares and the hounds.

"Come to me, Archer," a voice hissed from the darkness.

The silhouette of a dark tower appeared high between the two moons. There, a presence loomed, and Archer raced toward it. The graves were everywhere and oddly shaped, and they seemed to lean toward the Dreamtreader as he ran. He'd taken a battering already when he finally realized that he needed more altitude. What he did next wasn't flight, but it wasn't running either. He willed himself to stride through the air, keeping low beneath the grasping trees but just above the tops of the gravestones.

The tower still seemed so far away, but Archer sped on. Mocking laughter surrounded him as he ran. More howls told him that he had not finished with the hounds yet either.

Suddenly, the grave nearest him exploded, vomiting a spray of gore and decay. Archer veered left to avoid the spray. The next grave vomited up its long-buried contents as well. He found himself in a desperate game of dodging and weaving, stopping and racing forward as the graves all began to erupt. The foul blasts of muck were not simply gobs of rot and filth. There were faces in the muddy water as well. Shrieking, haunted faces.

Archer stumbled, crashed into a tall gravestone, and launched into the broad side of large, ashen gray tomb. His vision fading, he slid down the stone wall and came to rest in several inches of putrid mud and water. As darkness took him, he heard the dull report of a distant bell tolling. It struck nine times before Archer knew no more.

TWENTY-EIGHT

THE TREES OF LIFE AND DEATH

"READY?" RIGBY YELLED FROM THE REAR OF THE THRONE room.

"Ready!" Kara yelled back as she hovered over the second throne.

"We've got the hounds at bay for now!" Coop bellowed. "Do that thing! Yeah boyeee!"

"Now!" Rigby commanded. Simultaneously, he and Kara used their collective dream might to power a pair of colossal stone-breaking hammers. The massive tool whirled and fell. The sound of the twin thrones shattering was five hundred cracks of thunder. On steroids.

Rue de la Mort was stunned by the sudden concussion. Even Shadowkeep fell silent. The destruction of the twin thrones was earth-shaking, a sound that could wake the dead.

A thunderous sound woke Archer with a start. He could scarcely blink away the disorientation fast enough. Someone was calling him. Shrieking to him. Begging him.

"We got the thrones, Archer!" the urgent male voice screamed. Some distant part of Archer recognized the voice. "We got the two thrones, but he caught . . . us! Get the trees . . . burn the trees!"

Rigby.

Archer blinked completely awake and found himself leaning up against a stone wall, surrounded by muck in the midst of a vast castle courtyard. The graves were gone, and a few hounds were pacing in the distance. But then Archer saw them. The Trees of Life and Death. They were separated by a hundred yards of cobbled stone, the wreckage of a throne, and a pair of the Nightmare Lord's hounds.

This was the first time the Dreamtreader had been able to actually take in the size and form of the dreambeasts. They were huge, thick-bodied animals with broad paws, barrel chests, and thick, wild manes, like a lion's but black. Most apparent, of course, were the raging red eyes, protruding muscular jaws, and livid yellow teeth.

"The trees, Archer!" Rigby screamed as if in great pain. "Please."

That did it. The pain. The searing agony in Rigby's voice, the urgency, it smacked Archer like a physical blow. He was up and running in an instant. He vaulted a hound, tossing a fistful of willed blades at the beast as he careened over its head and crash landed by the first tree. It was a tall oak or, at least, something like an oak in its form and height. But its leaves were tear-shaped and rather small.

The Tree of Life.

Archer pulled at the bounds of his imagination. This could not be a slow burn, a crackling bonfire, or an intense glowing smolder. This had to be an absolute inferno, something equivalent to a volcanic eruption or a solar flare. He eyed the tree, and great molten gobs of flame coalesced around his fists. He screamed and threw his hands up. The fire that leaped from within Archer both shocked him and knocked him backward off his feet.

From his back on the cobbled stone, Archer saw a blazing inferno rise up around the tree. It was a searing, flash-burning column like a tornado made from tongues of flame. But amidst the roar of the flame, there was also a great scream. It was sharp, agonized, tremulous . . . and brief.

The engulfed silhouette of the tree seemed to tremble. Then wither. Then crack. Pieces of raw timber flashed away into ash. Archer saw other shapes in the fire, shapes that did not belong. It was almost as if the tree had an inner skeleton, a rib cage and limbs, all completely blackened now.

A small piece of ash fell into Archer's eye, stinging him back to the task. The Dreamtreader curled and rolled to his feet, off and running for the misshapen Tree of Death before he could stop to think about his actions. As he ran, he became aware of his own tiredness. Spending his mental energy had begun to drain on his system. To consume the second tree would spend even more. He didn't know if he'd have enough left to fight the Nightmare Lord, much less prevail against him. But those thoughts were secondary. The tree had to burn.

The two hounds between the trees set against Archer, but their threat had diminished somewhat. They seemed smaller now, weaker. Maybe it was the destruction of the first tree. Archer didn't know, but before the beasts could pounce, he attacked them both. The Dreamtreader willed forth a length of chain around each of their necks. The hounds yelped and snarled and fought to get free, but Archer held them fast, constricting the chains link by link. Archer strode past the struggling hounds and said, "These are *your* tokens of doom!" He didn't look back, but he heard the fall of the beasts and the heavy clank of the chains as he leaped to the second tree. Before his feet again touched the stone, Archer unleashed streams of burning liquid from his fingertips, swallowing the trunk in front of him in a monsoon of fire.

The Tree of Death seemed swarmed by hornets of flame. Branches vanished, then limbs. The trunk split asunder and fell apart. The buring hunks twisted within the flames, and again, Archer saw those strange skeletal shapes before it all withered and was gone.

Archer had to duck his head and cover his ears at the raging howl that blasted out at that moment. Somewhere in the distance, the Nightmare Lord roared with such venom and agony that the entire keep shook, but Archer knew his job wasn't finished. He forced himself to his feet and strode in the direction from which the sound had come.

It seemed like he ran for an eternity, but then the ground fell away and he was falling, crashing madly down steps of stone. He tumbled and banged his head, his elbows, his knees—again and again. Each time he healed his wounds immediately, but he couldn't stop his momentum. He found himself sprawled midway down what looked like an old Roman theater: a bowl of stone with a central stage in the center, everything funneling down to that point in the middle.

Archer blinked stupidly. The trees were gone, withered in flame. Tiny flakes of ash rained down from the sky even now. Tired and aching, he found a way to his feet. He stood and looked down onto the stage.

There was the Nightmare Lord. He wasn't wearing his horned helm but rather a pale crown adorned with black gems. He did not look hobbled in the least. He stood like a massive statue of some mythological warrior or maybe a demon with those pale green eyes. But his face was not what Archer had expected. He was grim and fearsome but ruggedly . . . normal. A broad chin, proud cheekbones, ridged and angled brows set above the emptiness of his eyes—it was a startling contrast. Archer gaped down at his enemy and yelled, "I fear you no longer! You are mortal now!"

"No," came his hornet-infested rasp. "Young fool."

It was then that Archer realized the Nightmare Lord was not alone. There was a wide stone altar, and upon it, bound at the wrists, neck, and ankles, lay Rigby Thames. Standing at the side of the altar with a steel dagger was Kara Windchil.

The Nightmare Lord began to clap his hands in mock applause. He gazed up at Archer with those ghastly pale, greenish eyes. "Bezeal played his part well, did he not?" he said.

Archer went to speak but found his tongue knotted. He gazed at Rigby, already bruised and battered, blood leaking from a dozen wounds. But breathing. Breathing rapidly. And Kara, the look in her eyes was baffling. There was sadness, some kind of regret . . . and yet, also a steely determination that Archer couldn't quite understand.

Finally regaining his voice, Archer cried out, "Kara, what are you doing? Put down the blade!"

Kara did not move. She seemed mute, almost entranced.

"Destroy the thrones, not once but twice," the Nightmare Lord mocked. "But he who does will pay the price. Isn't that what Bezeal told you? It was a splendid exercise, or should I say expenditure of your will. And the trees, Archer? The Tree of Life and the Tree of Death, that was quite a show of strength you put on, razing them to the ground. To think that you might have used such power . . . on me? A terrible shame. I wonder whose doom you sealed."

But as Archer pondered the mysterious words of the Nightmare Lord, he studied his enemy standing over Kara and Rigby. And for a few moments, confusion overwhelmed his pain. Where were the other Lucid Walkers? They had seemed to be doing pretty well in the initial stages of the assault. What had become of them? And how had Rigby been captured? The guy was powerful in the Dream, resourceful and smart. He had the Lurker, his Uncle Scoville, watching his back. Why would the bonds on that altar even hold Rigby?

Then he knew. Fear. Archer could see it in Rigby's eyes. It was the stricken look of a man who could no longer see a way out. It was the gaze of a man who had no hope.

TWENTY-NINE

TESTED LOYALTIES

ARCHER CLENCHED HIS FISTS. HE WAS TIRED. DEAD tired.

But not dead.

He strode slowly down the stone stairs. As he walked, he cursed the day he ever bargained with Bezeal. "So it was all a trick?" Archer asked. "All a ploy to get me into Shadowkeep?"

The Nightmare Lord laughed, a sound like heavy stone grinding. "Much more than a trick," he said. "Or did you not notice the remains in the fire?"

Archer stopped walking and felt a chill.

"For so long you've wondered what became of Duncan and Mesmeera, your Dreamtreader friends. They were alive until just moments ago. They were imprisoned within the trees, the trees that you burned. You killed them, Archer. You killed Duncan and Mesmeera."

"No," he whispered. "No! But it was supposed to . . . you were supposed to die! It was supposed to be you!" He fell to his knees.

"No, Archer," the Nightmare Lord rasped. "It was supposed to be the Dreamtreaders, all of you. The Tokens of Doom were yours. And now, your greatest nightmare has come true. You betrayed them. You killed them."

Archer crumbled within himself, a thousand memories of Duncan and Mesmeera flashing through his mind. A tide of anguish and guilt threatened to drown him then. He saw, step by horrifying step, how he'd been played by the Nightmare Lord. He'd been a fool. Too inexperienced, just as Master Gabriel had warned.

Hopelessly, Archer looked up. The blade still held in Kara's hand, wavering over Rigby. For a punishing moment, Archer wondered how Rigby Thames could have been made so fearful. What could have transformed this confident warrior into a motionless captive? What could have collapsed him to such fear that he could no longer create within the Dream to help himself?

That's when the Lurker stepped out of the shadows and stood at the Nightmare Lord's side.

"One can never have too many servants," the Nightmare Lord said. "Scoville, you have done well. You have earned the right to speak if you will."

The expression on Uncle Scoville's face went from the slack, soulless glance of a zombie to something wrenched with anguish and sorry. "I . . . I'm sorry, Rigby," he said. "After being trapped here, he offered me a goblet of wine. It was brewed from gort root. I didn't know. But I am his now." Scoville's expression changed again; his eyes lost their focus and intensity. He went back to being broken and enslaved. Scoville was no more. There was only the Lurker.

"Now, my sweet Kara," the Nightmare Lord said. "Shall we have one . . . last . . . dance?"

Archer stared. Kara had the dagger in her hand. She raised it over Rigby. Her arm swung upward. Rigby's eyes were wide and riveted on to the tip of the blade.

"Kara, it is time," the Nightmare Lord said. "You see, Archer, Kara drank my wine as well."

"Rigby!" Archer yelled. "Look at the dagger. It's not real! See that it *is—not—real!*"

Rigby's head bobbed on the altar. He coughed, and blood trickled down his cheek. He still wasn't thinking clearly enough.

"This is a dream, Rigby!" Archer bellowed. "It's not real. Only a dream!"

The Nightmare Lord raised his arms high and shouted, "This is not a dream. It is a nightmare!"

"No, Kara!" Archer screamed. "Remember what I said! Remember? You would never do something like this. You are better than this!"

Her eyes were pleading and full of sorrow. "I'm sorry," she said.

"I did not give you permission to speak!" the Nightmare Lord roared at her. "Kill him, now!"

In that moment, the ash falling like snow around them, Archer readied what was left of his creative will. He was ready to throw something at Kara, either to block the blade or knock her bodily off of the platform.

But Archer froze. There was something different in her eyes. The dagger seemed to tremble in her raised fist. What was that look? There was something more than sadness there. Archer blinked.

Wait! he thought desperately. The Nightmare Lord hadn't given her permission to speak, and yet she had. That meant . . .

Archer's heartbeat seemed to slow. He saw Kara swing the dagger

down. He saw the terror in Rigby's expression. He saw the ruth-
less gleam in the Nightmare Lord livid green eyes. He saw the ash
falling . . . the dagger blade falling. Slowly. So slowly.

The ash.

Archer immediately knew. He saw the plan unfurl like a parch-
ment map. There were the steps, a kind of diabolical recipe. All he
had to do was follow. And it all began with Kara. He saw her ever-so-
slight nod. *Now!*

Time sped back up. With a shriek of rage, Kara swung the dagger
sharply down, but she halted the blade just above Rigby's throat. In a
whiplash instant, she changed the angle of the weapon and thrust it
overhand into the Nightmare Lord's left eye.

He roared in pain. At that moment, Rigby snapped awake, and
the Lurker turned and disappeared into a tunnel. Archer was already
moving. He dove into the air and ripped the silver crown off of the
Nightmare Lord's head.

"Catch me if you can!" Archer yelled. "You are lord of nothing!"

Archer raced away, bounding up onto a parapet. He glanced back
once to make sure the Nightmare Lord was following. He wasn't sure
for a moment, but then he saw a team of black horses wreathed in
crimson fire and pulling a black coach with a black rider.

Archer spared a glance to the altar and saw Kara releasing Rigby.
"Come on!" Archer yelled. "Stand with me!"

The black coach wheeled in the sky and careened toward Archer.

Rigby and Kara stood on the table where Rigby had lain. They
gazed at each other strangely and then back to Archer.

"What are you waiting for?" Archer cried out. "We can defeat
him . . . together! Come on!"

There came the sound of laughter and hornets. Archer stared at
the oncoming coach. He had little time left.

"Number 6, Rue de la Mort is ours now!" Rigby exulted. "We rule Shadowkeep now!"

Archer wanted to wake up. He wanted to wake up and never sleep again. This was impossible. This was beyond comprehension. This . . . was a nightmare.

"Kara, please!" Archer cried. "Come with me!"

"Stay with us, Archer!" Kara called. "We can rule together!"

Archer mouthed the word *no*. But there was no sound. No breath. No feeling. He wasn't sure there would be ever again. He took one last look at Rigby and Kara and then turned to face the Nightmare Lord. Alone.

THIRTY

LURE

Archer lunged away, bounding from one wall to the next. Soon he was on the top of the gatehouse. With the Nightmare Lord's dark horses right behind him, Archer leaped down to the rampart. Flying would be the fastest way, but Archer had too little mental energy left. He desperately needed to make it back to the anchor with some strength remaining.

He called up his longboard, let his Intrusion buffer lapse, and caught a raging wave south. Archer looked back. The Nightmare Lord was gaining.

"Go, Archer!" Razz shouted, appearing at his shoulder in a puff of purple mist. She raced back and buzzed in the face of the lead stallion. It shrieked and reared and, for a moment, knocked the team off course.

"Good job, Razz!" Archer yelled, taking the momentum the wave gave him into a bigger swell getting ready to curl toward the Drimmrwood. He was into the trees now, taking the wave as far as it would carry him. It took him deep into the wood, but not to the clearing. The Nightmare Lord had already redirected his team. The horses were bearing down on Archer's position.

Archer dismissed the longboard and took off at a sprint. He bounded over root, stump, and fallen trees. He tripped, rolled, scrambled back to his feet, and ran on. He held up the crown and yelled, "You'll never get this back, loser! It's mine now!"

Archer taunted the Nightmare Lord and felt a strange thrill in so doing. It was going to be a dark day if his plan didn't work, he knew. But then, it was already a very dark day. Nothing would change that, so he stuck to his plan and raced on.

He saw it: the clearing. With a yelp, he dove out of the trees and rolled toward his camouflaged anchor, the well his mother had loved so much. He was a mere yard away when he heard a crack. In that instant, he smelled sulfur. Something wrapped around his waist and began to burn.

Archer wrenched and pulled, but Vorcaust, the Nightmare Lord's flaming whip, held him fast.

"You cannot escape!" the Nightmare Lord roared.

The flames cut through his leather armor and began to sear his skin. Archer screamed. He managed an agonizing step forward. It was all he needed. "Let's take this fight to my turf!" he screamed. "See how you do!"

Archer lunged and touched the well.

THIRTY-ONE

THE WELL

When Archer awoke, he was shocked to find that he was no longer in bed. He was at his mother's well in the backyard.

The Nightmare Lord's whip was still tangled around his waist, but it no longer burned. Archer turned round to find his pale-eyed tormentor just gaining his feet. He was moving slowly, stiffly. *It's working*, Archer thought. *He's weakening.*

"How does it feel?" Archer shouted. He held up the crown for the Nightmare Lord to see. "Say good-bye to your kingdom." He tossed the crown down the well.

The Nightmare Lord gave a wrenching jerk to the whip, and Archer fell forward. Flat on his face.

"I am not finished with you," the Nightmare Lord said, his voice low and menacing.

Archer rolled up and took hold of the whipcord. It already felt brittle. The Dreamtreader gave the hardest tug he could and yanked the Nightmare Lord forward. Archer ran ahead too, but he dove to the side and dragged his leg in front of the Nightmare Lord, sweeping the bigger foe's legs.

The Nightmare Lord's momentum threw him hard. The whip-cord snapped between the two combatants. Archer ate some turf, but the Nightmare Lord slammed into the side of the well.

Archer spun back to his feet and saw the Nightmare Lord half collapsed over the edge of the well. Archer turned and raced toward him. He plowed into the enemy's back, pressing him into the old stone.

The Nightmare Lord howled, but Archer wasn't finished. The Dreamtreader wrapped his arms around the Nightmare Lord's legs and lifted with everything he had. Archer lifted and pushed, and finally, the Nightmare Lord toppled over the side. He cried out, "Dreamtreader!" Then there was silence.

Archer exhaled and spat blood.

He looked over the side of the well to see only darkness. But then, like some kind of mutated spider, the Nightmare Lord appeared in the pale moon's light. He had found a hold, maybe where the mortar was worn away, and was trying to climb back up.

"No!" Archer yelled. He looked around for some kind of weapon. He wasn't in the Dream anymore, so he couldn't just summon a sword or a grenade. There was nothing near. Just the well. He went back to the well, slamming into the loosened stone at the edge and looking down. The Nightmare Lord was ten feet away from the edge.

"No!" he yelled again. He saw those pale eyes leering up at him. But Archer grabbed the edges of the stone. He worked it with his arms, wobbling it free from the mortar. He took up the stone with both hands, held it high above his head, and then heaved it down at the Nightmare Lord.

Even as Archer fell away, he heard the sickening crunch as the thirty-pound stone slammed into the Nightmare Lord's face. Archer collapsed in a dirty, sweaty bloody heap and allowed himself the slightest of smiles.

Suddenly, a howling wind roared across the field. It blasted through the trees and flattened the tall grass. Archer crawled a few feet away from the well, got to a knee, and then stood. Just as he turned toward the well, there came a haunting groan from its depths. The well spewed up a massive blast of water and ash. Just one large spout, and it was over.

It felt to Archer like he had been holding his breath for hours and could finally exhale. He wiped the blood and sweat out of his eyes and started walking toward his house. When he saw his family again, he would hug them with all his might. But not until morning.

With whatever hours of darkness were left, Archer resolved to sleep . . . and not to Dreamtread. In fact, he was going to take a huge break from Dreamtreading . . . well, if it was okay with Master Gabriel, that is.

He wandered up the hill in his backyard and wondered at the brightness of the moon. It was a beautiful night. He glanced up at the stars. He looked at the moon's reflection in a window on the back of the house.

He stopped walking. There were two moons in the reflection.

"Watch out, Archer!" It was the Windmaiden.

Archer stood very still. "No," he whispered.

With a last bit of mental strength, Archer called up a UV light, something he should not have been able to do in the waking world. Already knowing what he'd find, Archer shone the UV light up one of his legs and down the other, and then onto his midsection. And there it was:

A tendril.

It hung loosely from his gut where it had apparently latched on as Archer had raced recklessly through the trees.

"I'm still in the Dream," Archer muttered, feeling the strength drain out of him, his will breaking, and fear seizing him. He blinked, and the world turned upside down.

Archer was there again, in the Drimmrwood clearing once more. He was wrapped bodily in the Nightmare Lord's burning whip. The fire licked at his vest and the duster. The pressure and the heat made Archer gasp.

"It was kind of you to lead me to your anchor," the Nightmare Lord hissed, ". . . to all of your anchors!"

With his bare hand, Archer ripped the tendril free and tossed it away. He still had the crown in his other hand. There wasn't much point to it, not now. After all, he'd treated the Nightmare Lord to a sneak preview of his plan. Archer had no mental energy, no physical strength. All he wanted to do was sleep. He closed his eyes and fell toward the well.

THIRTY-TWO

DANGEROUS MINDS

THIS TIME, WHEN ARCHER OPENED HIS EYES, HE WAS IN his bedroom, tangled in both the bedspread and the Nightmare Lord's whip. "I'm home," Archer whispered.

He expected to hear a gloating laugh and then to feel the deep bite of Scorghuul, the enemy's fierce axe, carving a furrow in his back. But there was nothing. Archer spun off his bed and stumbled on the rug, the whipcord tangling his feet. He found some footing and started to turn round every which way, letting the slack whipcord fall to his feet. Where was the Nightmare Lord?

A high-pitched scream. And then, "Archer, help me!" *Kaylie.*

"No," Archer screamed. "No, no, no!" He tore out of his room and turned the corner into the hall. He heard noise behind him now, a great pounding from his father's room. He couldn't stop. The hall was only twenty-some feet, but it seemed like a thousand yards. Archer slipped, lunged, and clawed forward. He tore around the doorjamb and into Kaylie's room. The first thing he saw was Patches, her scarecrow dolly, sprawled and lying on the floor in the shredded remains of her pink blanket. Kaylie screamed again. Archer looked up. His worst nightmare had become reality. He'd brought the Nightmare Lord back with him. The Dream King was weakened, yes, but he was crushing Kaylie in his hands.

"Take me to your anchor!" the Nightmare Lord commanded. "Or I will kill her."

"Archer!" she cried, whipping her blanket around. "Archer, he's hurting me!"

"Kaylie!" The shout was back up the hallway. It was Archer's father.

"Don't hurt her!" Archer yelled. "I will, I'll take you to the anchor. Just . . . don't . . . hurt . . . her!"

"Now!" the Nightmare Lord roared. He lifted one hand, and Kaylie's bedroom door slammed. In moments the doorknob jostled and there came a fierce pounding on the door.

"Kaylie, honey! I'm here! Daddy's here!"

In his rasping, hornet-stung voice, the Nightmare Lord declared, "This place . . . this house of misery . . . is my house." He brought his face near Kaylie's and said, "You never knew your mother, did you? So it must not have pained you when she gasped out her last. Perhaps, perhaps I will let your father in after all . . . so that you can watch him die!"

"Daddy!" Kaylie screamed. She kicked out, her right foot striking the Nightmare Lord in his ruined left eye.

He dropped her, and as he did, Archer lunged. The two crashed together, shattering the bedroom window behind the Nightmare Lord, Archer riding his enemy to the floor. He straddled the Nightmare Lord and started pounding his face with both fists.

Kaylie was still screaming and crying, but she had snatched up Patches and the remnants of her blanket. "Archer, get away from him!" Kaylie cried.

But Archer wasn't going to stop. His father wouldn't understand. This was not some thief or cat burglar. Archer continued to rain fists, striking with the hard bone ridge of his hand again and again. But it didn't seem enough. The Nightmare Lord's one eye was still open, still full of hate.

Archer looked for something, anything he could use for a weapon. Pillows, bedspread, desk, bookcase: there were no weapons to be found. A force struck Archer's chest. It knocked the wind out of his lungs and sent him sprawling backward. He slammed hard into something. He heard a groan behind him, and the next thing he knew, Archer was entangled in the legs of Kaylie's desk. The Nightmare Lord stood towering over Archer's sister, Scorghuul in his hands. Archer tried to get up but felt a weight upon his chest. It was as if some invisible thing sat upon him and crushed him to the ground. He fought and yanked and tried to get free.

But it was all for nothing. In the end, all Archer could do was stare. The Nightmare Lord raised his fearsome weapon, but his movement was anything but fluid. His limbs stuttered as they moved as if the axe weighed ten times what it should. *He's weakening*, Archer thought. Yet the axe was still moving.

The Nightmare Lord raised the axe higher, and then it came plunging down. Archer blinked or thought he had. There had been a blur. Something leaped out of Kaylie's arms and seemed to unfold to a much larger size.

Archer blinked again, and there was Patches, Kaylie's doll. Only this version of Patches was a foot taller than the Nightmare Lord, and it had grabbed the enemy's axe hand. He held the weapon at bay.

Archer wriggled out from the desk at last and found his legs, but his mind still staggered. "How? How is this possible?" he asked.

The Nightmare Lord began to tremble. The speed and ferocity of the convulsions increased. A fine gray powder began to radiate from every inch of his body.

Kaylie looked at Archer and said, "I hope you don't mind, but I eavesdropped on you and Rigby in his basement. Then I read your Dreamtreader book."

"But you cannot have the will!" the Nightmare Lord howled. "You are just a child . . . a weak-minded child."

Kaylie turned back to the enemy and said, "I might be a child, but I am anything but weak-minded!" She closed her hand into a fist. There came a swift crackling, like a dozen branches breaking at once. Patches collapsed, crushing the the Nightmare Lord in its embrace. Arms, legs, neck, and head cracked and crumbled. Then he exploded.

Ash rained down in Kaylie's room. The Nightmare Lord was gone.

THIRTY-THREE

RECKONING

A WEEK LATER, ARCHER SAT WITH KAYLIE IN RIGBY'S
basement. It had been Kaylie's idea, of course. Archer and Rigby had
become bitter enemies since that fateful night and had barely spoken to
each other. At first, Archer planned to keep as far away from Rigby as
he could, but Kaylie's nonstop whining about the "zoo" pushed Archer
to reconsider. That's when he remembered something Master Gabriel
had once said. "Keep your friends close, and keep your enemies closer."

With Rigby's reluctant permission, they'd taken on the animals'
care three days a week and loved every minute of it. Almost every
minute.

Archer still didn't like dealing with "poop duty." But he was happy
to have Doctor Who perched on his shoulder again. He was happy to
be there with his little sister.

The Nightmare Lord had turned completely to ash, leaving
Archer's father at a loss for what he'd heard that night. But Archer
knew that Kaylie knew what happened. She'd been wide-awake, and
she'd understood.

"One thing I want to know, Archer," she said.

"Okay," he replied. "But it'll have to be a trade. Something you want to know for something I want to know."

"Sure," she said. "But me first."

"Okay."

"I want to know if you can still go into dreams . . . and make things real?"

"Yes," he said. "I can."

"I thought so," she said.

"Ah," Archer said. "Now, my turn, but I think I already know the answer. I want to know if you can still make things real here?"

Kaylie closed the meerkat pen and blushed almost as red as her pigtails. "Well . . ." She held up a hand, and a double-scoop ice cream cone materialized. "Cotton candy flavored," she said. "My favorite."

"I think . . . ," Archer said. "I'm going to need to tell Master Gabriel about you."

It was the seventh of June, the first day of Archer's summer break from school. It was no surprise when Master Gabriel appeared. He always came on the seventh of the month.

"The time has come for reckoning," Master Gabriel said.

Archer stared at the floor. He pictured Duncan laughing, always laughing . . . and Mesmeera faithfully pruning her rose bushes. And it all consumed by hungry flames.

"I killed them," Archer whispered. "I didn't mean to, but . . . I killed them."

Master Gabriel placed a hand on Archer's shoulder. "Duncan and Mesmeera knew the risks involved in Dreamtreading," he said. "Just as you do. They made choices, wrong choices, just as you did. But none of you acted in a vacuum. There was an enemy at every turn, an enemy who lived to cause nightmares. He is the root, and he is no more."

"I'm sorry," Archer said. "I should have listened from the beginning."

"That wisdom was hard won," Master Gabriel said gently. But then his tone snapped back to his usual abrupt command. "In any case, there are still consequences."

Archer pulled away, went to his closet, and came back with *The Dreamtreader's Creed*. "Here," he said.

"What's this, then?" Master Gabriel asked.

"I'm turning it in," he said. "I failed. I revoked my Dreamtreading privileges. You're going to make me go back to being . . . just a regular person."

"My dear Archer," the master Dreamtreader said, "you really have gone quite mad, haven't you?"

"What?"

"I'm going to make you go back, all right," he said. "But back to Dreamtreading. There is only you for the time being. Your consequence is to patrol, not just Forms, but Patterns and Verse as well. At least until we can find two more to bear those Dreamtreader stations."

"I'm not fired?"

"No, you misguided boy, you are not 'fired.' You will recompense your actions by shepherding the Dream alone, for now. Begin with a close scrutiny of Shadowkeep."

"But the Nightmare Lord is dead," Archer said. "You just said—"

"Yes, but his master is not," Master Gabriel replied. "And as you know, I am afraid that Number 6, Rue de la Mort is occupied again. Not only that, but something is making the Dream more unstable. If nothing changes, it could reach rift-level in less than a month."

"Breaches?"

"That is what I suspected," Master Gabriel explained. "But I have had no reports from any of the kingdoms. I have inquired, but no one has seen a breach anywhere."

"And yet, the Dream is unstable," Archer said. "I don't like it."

"Neither do I," Master Gabriel said. "You will have to look into it."

"I will," Archer said. "But, before you leave, we need to talk about my sister."

EPILOGUE

"HE SHOULD BE HERE ANY MINUTE," RIGBY SAID, LEADING Kara into the kitchen.

"Will he go for it, do you think?" Kara asked as they sat at the table.

"My father said he would," Rigby said, scratching at his sideburns. "And my father usually knows if there's money to be made."

"What are we going to do about your uncle?" she asked.

Rigby stared at the tabletop. "I don't know what to think," he said. "When the Nightmare Lord died, Uncle Scovy was free from enslavement."

"He didn't try to fight us," Kara said.

"I know that. But Scovy really was quite mad to begin with. I don't know that he can be trusted."

"What are you going to do?"

"Well, I'm not going to pull the plug, if that's what you're suggesting."

"Of course not," she said, biting her lower lip. "But what if he comes back to Shadowkeep? What if he gives us trouble?"

"We'll burn that bridge later."

That phrase gave Kara pause. She thought of Archer. *I really have burned my bridges with him, haven't I?* He'd never trust her again, that was certain. And that meant he wouldn't text her during storms any-more. He wouldn't make her laugh on the bus. He wouldn't walk to Main Street with her. She blinked out of reflection and asked, "What about the other Lucid Walkers? They really can't go back?"

"No," he said. "Never. They died in the Dream. Their brains will reject Lucid Dreaming for the rest of their lives."

The doorbell rang.

"Bet that's him," Rigby said, standing. He went to the front door with Kara trailing just behind.

When he opened the door, a man in a dark suit stood there. "Are you Rigby Thames?" he asked. "Nephew of Dr. Ebenezer Scoville?"

"That's me," Rigby said. "And this is my . . . uh, associate, Kara Windchil. Why don't you come in and sit down."

"Thank you," he said.

Rigby and Kara led the man to the table. They sat.

"I've come because I understand you've taken up your uncle's mantle."

"That's right," Rigby said. "I've made several . . . breakthroughs."

"I have questions," the man said. "Is Lucid Dreaming possible? And . . . can anyone do it?"

"Yes, it's real," Rigby said. "And most anyone can do it . . . with the training I provide, that is."

The man nodded. "Only one more question." He leaned forward. "Can you bring things back?"

"Why don't you come with us?" Rigby said. He stood and looked at Kara.

"Now?" she asked.

"I think we have to," Rigby replied.

"If you say so," Kara said. She stood.

Rigby led Kara and their visitor down the basement stairs. They ignored the zoo, turned left, and Rigby went to work on the keypad. A hiss of air, and the door opened. Rigby and Kara led the man inside.

"Great Scott!" the visitor exclaimed. "Is this . . . ?"

"My Uncle Scoville," Rigby said.

"Is he . . . ?"

"In the Dream, yes," Rigby said. "He stayed too long."

"This is what happens," the man said, his voice a bit higher now. "This is what happens to people who stay too long? I don't know if my investors will be too keen—"

"We didn't bring you down here for Uncle Scovy," Rigby said. He turned to a bank of monitors, leaned over the highest unit, and said, "He wants to know if we can bring things back. Bezeal, do you want to show 'im?"

The man took three steps backward and eyed the doorway as a hooded figure stepped out from behind the computers.

"Who . . . what is that?" the man stammered.

"A friend," Rigby said. "Someone who knows how to get things done."

"Go on, Bezeal," Kara said. "Show the man what we can bring back."

Bezeal reached into the bottom pockets of his robe and pulled out two handfuls of slimy, wriggling creatures. Scurions. He dropped them to the floor to feed. Slowly, a softball-sized breach opened across the dimensions. Bezeal swatted the scurions away and reached a hand into the small breach.

One at a time, Bezeal took three objects out of the breach. He showed them to the man.

The man took off his dark sunglasses, pocketed them, and set a black briefcase on the table.

"I have a Lucid Walking club started at school," Rigby said. "But school's out. And I have bigger plans. But to go any bigger with this . . . will require funding."

The man, still blinking from what Bezeal had showed him, asked, "Will this do for starters?" He popped the lid on the case. Kara gasped as they looked inside. She had never seen a thousand-dollar bill, much less bundles of thousand-dollar bills. Rigby simply nodded.

"That's four million," the man said, "for start-up costs."

Rigby smiled his sly, sideways grin and said, "I think that will do nicely."

There is an unseen world of good and evil where nightmares are fought and hope is reborn.

Enter The Door Within.

Aidan's life is completely uprooted when his parents move the family across the country to care for his ailing grandfather. But when he begins having nightmares and eerie events occur around his neighborhood, Aidan finds himself drawn to his grandfather's basement—where he discovers three ancient scrolls and a mysterious invitation to another world.

By Wayne Thomas Batson

www.tommynelson.com

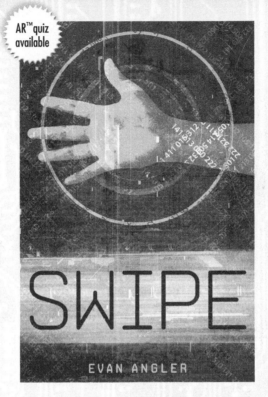